THOMAS MERTON

NML NEW MONASTIC LIBRARY
Resources for Radical Discipleship

For over a millennium, if Christians wanted to read theology, practice Christian spirituality, or study the Bible, they went to the monastery to do so. There, people who inhabited the tradition and prayed the prayers of the church also copied manuscripts and offered fresh reflections about living the gospel in a new era. Two thousand years after the birth of the church, a new monastic movement is stirring in North America. In keeping with ancient tradition, new monastics study the classics of Christian reflection and are beginning to offer some reflections for a new era. The New Monastic Library includes reflections from new monastics as well as classic monastic resources unavailable elsewhere.

Thomas
MERTON

Twentieth-Century Wisdom for
Twenty-First-Century Living

PAUL R. DEKAR

Foreword by
PAUL M. PEARSON

 CASCADE *Books* • Eugene, Oregon

THOMAS MERTON
Twentieth-Century Wisdom for Twenty-First-Century Living

New Monastic Library: Resources for Radical Discipleship 9

Cascade Books
An Imprint of Wipf and Stock Publishers
199 W. 8th Ave., Suite 3
Eugene, OR 97401

www.wipfandstock.com

ISBN 13: 978-1-60608-970-5

Cataloging-in-Publication data:

Dekar, Paul R.

Thomas Merton: twentieth-century wisdom for twenty-first-century living / Paul R. Dekar; foreword by Paul M. Pearson.

xviii + 242 p. ; 23 cm. — Includes bibliographical references.

New Monastic Library: Resources for Radical Discipleship 9

ISBN 13: 978-1-60608-970-5

1. Merton, Thomas, 1915–1968. I. Pearson, Paul M. II. Title. III. Series.

BX4705.M542 D45 2011

Manufactured in the U.S.A.

To my sisters and brothers of the Memphis School of Servant Leadership. Being renewed toward the image of Christ through the journeys inward and outward, members of the Memphis School of Servant Leadership have formed a community of love that models for me God's realm of love, justice, and peace on earth as it is in heaven.

CONTENTS

FOREWORD

In the final years of his life, Thomas Merton had a brief but intense exchange of correspondence with the theologian Rosemary Radford Ruether, who had recently joined the faculty of Howard University in Washington, having completed her graduate work at Claremont Graduate School. Over the course of their correspondence, as Ruether writes, they were like "two ships that happened to pass each other on our respective journeys. For a brief moment we turned our search lights on each other with blazing intensity" and dialogued with an "existential urgency."[1] Central to their exchange was Ruether's probing of Thomas Merton concerning his position in the monastery at Gethsemani, and even within the Catholic Church, using, as she writes, Merton as "my 'test case' for whether integrity was possible for Catholics" or, to put it another way, "Could Catholics speak the truth and be Catholics?"[2] As any reader at all familiar with Merton's journals or correspondence would expect, Thomas Merton took her questions deeply seriously. Her questions really challenged some of the central aspects of Merton's own perceptions of himself, what he would describe in an introduction to a Japanese edition of *The Seven Storey Mountain* written in 1963 as: "the definitive decisions taken in the course of my life: to be a Christian, to be a monk, to be a priest."[3]

Thomas Merton was never afraid to ask difficult questions, such questions would lead to his silencing by the church in 1962 from writing on issues relating to war and the nuclear arms race. Merton did not just ask those questions of other people, or institutions, but of himself and

1. *At Home in the World*, xiv.
2. Ibid., xvii.
3. Merton, *Reflections on My Work*, 71.

his own community, including the Abbot, at Gethsemani. This relentless and intensive questioning, combined with one of the finest intellects of his generation, enabled Merton to become a prophetic figure in so many of the areas that were, remain, and will remain, central to the genuine spiritual search—writing about the human quest for God and opening up the contemplative way in an accessible manner for twentieth- and twenty-first-century seekers; the need for this contemplative life to overflow in love to other people, especially those suffering, and seeking to change the sources of oppression through non-violent means; the relationship between Christians of different denominations and, ultimately, relations with people of other faiths or of no faith at all; and lastly, questioning the institution of the church, in particular the Catholic Church and, closer to home, questioning the monastic life he himself was living and the place of the monastery in, and its relationship to, the post-Christian world.

Ruether's questions, her challenges to Merton, were not new to him. But rarely had he been challenged so directly and by a young woman on the cutting edge of theology in the first years after the Second Vatican Council. Put in the starkest of terms, her challenge to Merton was to get out of the monastery and to get involved with the real world, challenging him as the saying goes, to put his money where his mouth was. However, Thomas Merton, frequently acknowledged as the greatest Catholic writer of the twentieth century, chose to stay in the monastery.

Merton's choice begs the question for his readers of whether it is possible for a voice from the monastic enclosure to speak to us here in the new millennium? Can Merton's voice still speak to us? Can he still be heard over the ever-growing technological babble, the degradation of human language, and the breakdown of communication and communion between people that seems to mark our current age? Does monasticism have a message in our time, a time described by Morris Berman as *The Twilight of American Culture* and as *Dark Ages America*?

Thomas Merton was certainly not afraid to challenge the darkness of his time. He saw its pervasiveness, and in his book *The Inner Experience*, Merton went as far as to suggest that the dark night, so long associated with the apophatic mystical tradition, was no longer limited to a spiritual minority.

> The contemplative life in our time is . . . necessarily modified by the sins of our age. They bring down upon us a cloud of darkness

far more terrible than the innocent night of unknowing. It is the dark night of the soul which has descended on the whole world . . . In our contemplation, God must often seem to be absent, as though dead. But the truth of our contemplation is in this: that never more than today has [God] made [the divine] presence felt by "being absent."[4]

Merton could certainly see the darkness in our world, but he was also fully aware of our possibilities, of our potential to allow Christ to "Easter in us" and to, in the words of the Jesuit poet Gerard Manley Hopkins, "be a day-spring to the dimness of us, be a crimson-cresseted east."[5] Nonetheless, Merton could see that the horrors of the twentieth century, the cruelty of human life, was making manifest the darkness within each and every one of us, and Merton through his writings on war and violence, his prose, poetry, and art work of this period, was trying to stand and face the darkness and encouraging others to do the same. As he wrote in his introduction to *Raids on the Unspeakable*:

Christian hope begins where every other hope stands frozen stiff before the face of the Unspeakable . . . The goodness of the world, stricken or not, is incontestable and definitive. If it is stricken, it is also healed in Christ. But nevertheless one of the awful facts of our age is the evidence that it is stricken indeed, stricken to the very core of its being by the presence of the Unspeakable.

Against this background Merton can speak words of hope to us: "Be human in this most inhuman of ages; guard the human image for it is the image of God."[6]

In *Thomas Merton: Twentieth-Century Wisdom for Twenty-First-Century Living*, Paul Dekar demonstrates in numerous practical examples the myriad ways that Merton's vision of monasticism is also a vision of hope that is being lived out in our world today, guarding the human image and kindling the spark of God in the human spirit. Dekar explores all the major themes that Merton was addressing and suggests that Merton was overall working to lay the foundations for a new monastic vision, one that would enable the building of communities of love.

4. Merton, *Inner Experience*, 121–22.
5. Hopkins, "Wreck of the Deutschland."
6. Merton, *Raids on the Unspeakable*, 5–6.

In facing the darkness of the bomb, our ecological degradation of the planet, our unbridled, rampant technology, the breakdown of community and ultimately of communion between people, Merton continually stresses that the Christian vision is greater than the darkness which all too frequently seems ready to overwhelm us. As the great Benedictine and Cistercian monasteries of earlier centuries served as a remnant and a preserving glimmer of light through the period of the dark ages, so perhaps the new monastics will serve a similar function in our own era.

It is most timely to be reminded of the power of love, of the share we have been given in God's creation, the task to which we are continually called anew, to build, in Paul Dekar's words, communities of love. This vision is at the core of Merton's writing, as he himself suggests, "Whatever I may have written, I think it all can be reduced in the end to this one root truth: that God calls human persons to union with Himself and with one another in Christ,"[7] and it is both the message of hope and the challenge that Dekar presents to each and every one of us in this book.

Paul M. Pearson
Director, Thomas Merton Center
The Feast of St. Benedict, July 2010

---

7. Merton, "Concerning the Collection," in *Thomas Merton Studies Center*, 15.

ACKNOWLEDGMENTS

The comments of several readers of draft materials have been of enormous benefit. I am grateful to Nancy Rose Dekar, Donald Grayston, Geoff Hearn, Stacy Li, Gordon Oyer, and Michael Webb. They have read this manuscript at early stages of the writing of this book.

Paul M. Pearson, past president of the International Thomas Merton Society and director of the Thomas Merton Center at Bellarmine University in Louisville, Kentucky (ITMS), has been an excellent guide to archives that house over fifty thousand Merton-related materials, including books, journals, letters, recordings, over thirteen hundred photographs, and nine hundred Merton sketches, and also to crucial secondary literature. For this project, Dr. Pearson has forwarded copies of needed material, commented on drafts, and written a gracious Foreword. Mark C. Meade, Assistant Director of the Thomas Merton Center, has also provided crucial assistance.

In his journals, Thomas Merton mentioned that the Abbey of Our Lady of Gethsemani in Trappist, Kentucky, received groups of students. On several occasions, E. Glenn Hinson brought church history students from Louisville for visits. Onetime colleague A. H. Mathias Zahniser drew my attention to a course offered at Asbury Theological Seminary during which students did a retreat at the monastery.

These models led me to introduce a retreat-based course on Thomas Merton and contemporary monasticism in the curriculum at Memphis Theological Seminary where colleagues, students, and an excellent library staff supported my writing and teaching about Merton. I served as a member of the faculty from January 1995 until May 2008 and have been pleased to maintain this association as Professor Emeritus of Evangelism and Mission.

The Abbey of Our Lady of Gethsemani has received me several times in the spirit of a sign at the entrance, "Let all guests that come be received like Christ." I first visited there in 1996 and returned in 1997 and 1999. I hoped to meet Patrick Hart OCSO, mentor to many scholars. I was disappointed each time as he and other monks were away at ITMS gatherings.

Local ITMS affiliates and chapters are active in Australia, Canada, Holland, the United Kingdom (UK), the United States (US), and elsewhere. ITMS has hosted conferences every other year since the late 1980s. ITMS also organizes pilgrimages to sites associated with Merton's life and supports publication of two journals, *The Merton Seasonal* and the *Merton Annual: Studies in Culture, Spirituality and Social Concerns.*

In 2001, an upcoming sabbatical prompted me to adjust the timing of my Merton course and retreat at Gethsemani. Was Brother Hart available or not? I sent a note through the guest master. Later that day, a monk tapped me on the shoulder while I was eating in the retreatants' dining area. Brother Hart whispered to me, "I know a place where we can talk."

Brother Hart encouraged me to do some research about Merton. He suggested that the theme of technology might be productive. Brother Hart also mentioned that, since 1997, the Shannon Fellowship Committee of ITMS has provided funding to facilitate research at the official repository of Merton's estate, the Thomas Merton Center at Bellarmine University in Louisville, Kentucky. Brother Hart graciously offered to write a letter of reference and encouraged me to apply for a Shannon Fellowship.

I did. Brother Hart and Donald Grayston, longtime friend and future ITMS president, wrote letters on my behalf. In 2002, the committee provided funds that enabled me to do the preliminary research for this book.

In November 2002, I presented the initial fruit of this research at Whitley College, Melbourne, Victoria, Australia. Subsequently, on visits to the Abbey of Our Lady of Gethsemani, James Conner OCSO, Patrick Hart OCSO, Matthew Kelty OCSO (d. February 2011), and Paul Quenon OCSO have graced me with conversation and spiritual direction. Sisters of Loretto have also welcomed me at their motherhouse in Nerinx, Kentucky. Elaine Prevallet, SL, the late Mary Luke Tobin SL, and other members of the community exemplify the Benedictine values—hospitality, humility, love, simplicity, and care of God's creation—needed if we are to free ourselves from the iron grip of militarism and the allure of materialism that so dominate the world.

During the 2003 winter term, Nancy and I resided at the Institute for Ecumenical and Cultural Research at Collegeville, Minnesota. Patrick Henry, Killian McDonnell OSB, Dolores Schuh CHM, and Wilfred R. Theisen OSB encouraged me as I read and studied Merton.

Quoting Merton can be a challenge. In journals or correspondence, Merton mentions drafts of books that have sometimes appeared under different titles. Merton also re-wrote material. *What Is Contemplation?*, a pamphlet that appeared in 1948, became *The Inner Experience* (2003). *Seeds of Contemplation*, published in 1949, grew into *New Seeds of Contemplation* (1961).

I write with attention to gender. Generally, "monk" refers to male monastics, "nun" to female monastics. If a citation is not inclusive, I follow the text, using Merton's own words. Writing in English during the nineteen forties, fifties, and sixties, Merton generally adopted the literary conventions of his day with respect to pronouns. If Merton were writing today, I trust that he would use gender-free language.

One decision concerned our subject's names. Some were given to him. Merton assumed some. Friends invented some. Michael Mott, appointed by the Thomas Merton Legacy Trust to write an official biography, mentioned nearly fifty names. I have limited myself to just Thomas Merton.

I am grateful to members of the Thomas Merton Legacy Trust. They gave permission to include in this book previously unpublished talks by Merton.

I am grateful to New Directions Publishing for permission to publish excerpts as follows: Thomas Merton, from *New Seeds of Contemplaction*, copyright ©1961 by The Abbey of Gethsemani, Inc . Reprinted by permission of New Directions Publishing Corp.

New Directions Publishing also granted permission to publish excerpts from poems in *The Collected Poems of Thomas Merton*, as follows:

"The Trappist Cemetery–Gethsemani" and "The Victory" by Thomas Merton from *The Collected Poems of Thomas Merton*, copyright ©1946 by New Directions Publishing Corporation. Reprinted by permission of New Directions Publishing Corp. "Aubade-Harlem," "For My Brother: Reported Missing In Action, 1943," "Song: Contemplation," and "The Tower of Babel" by Thomas Merton from *The Collected Poems of Thomas*

Merton, copyright ©1948 by New Directions Publishing Corporation, 1977 by The Trustees of the Merton Legacy Trust. Reprinted by permission of New Directions Publishing Corp. "I Have Called You" by Thomas Merton, from *The Collected Poems of Thomas Merton,* copyright ©1966 by The Trustees of the Merton Legacy Trust. Reprinted by permission of New Directions Publishing Corp. "Song: If You Seek . . ." by Thomas Merton, original in *Emblems of a Season of Fury,* from *The Collected Poems of Thomas Merton,* copyright ©1963 by The Abbey of Gesthemani, Inc. Reprinted by permission of New Directions Publishing Corp. Credit line: Sales territory: U.S. and its territories rights.

I use the New Revised Standard Version of *The Holy Bible,* copyright 1989, Division of Christian Education of the National Council of Churches of Christ in the United States of America. Used by permission. All rights reserved.

ABBREVIATIONS

BCE	Before the Common Era
CD	Compact Disk
CE	Common Era
CGB	*Conjectures of a Guilty Bystander*
CP	*Collected Poems*
CPF	Catholic Peace Fellowship
CWA	*Contemplation in a World of Action*
CHM	Congregation of the Humility of Mary
DC	District of Columbia
DWL	*Dancing in the Water of Life*
FOR	Fellowship of Reconciliation
GI	Government Issue (term used for soldiers in the United States Army)
HGL	*Hidden Ground of Love*
ITMS	International Thomas Merton Society
LE	*Literary Essays*
MSSL	Memphis School of Servant Leadership
MTS	Memphis Theological Seminary
OblSB	Oblate of Saint Benedict
OCSO	Order of Cistercians of the Strict Observance
OSB	Order of Saint Benedict
MA	Master of Arts
MTS	Memphis Theological Seminary
NSC	*New Seeds of Contemplation*
RJ	*Road to Joy*
RM	*Run to the Mountain*
Rule	*The Rule of Saint Benedict*
SC	*School of Charity*
SJ	*Sign of Jonas*

SL	Sisters of Loretto
SS	*Search for Solitude*
SSM	*The Seven Storey Mountain*
TTW	*Turning Toward the World*
WF	*Witness to Freedom*
UK	United Kingdom
U.S.	United States

ONE

Stirrings of a New Monasticism

The whole purpose of the monastic life is to teach men to live by love.
—Thomas Merton, talk at Bangkok on December 10, 1968, *Asian Journal*

From December 10, 1941, until his death near Bangkok on December 10, 1968, Thomas Merton lived as a monk of the Abbey of Our Lady of Gethsemani, located about an hour's drive south of Louisville in central Kentucky. The monastic life provided Merton a context in which he produced some of the great spiritual literature of the twentieth century. Merton's writings have continued to inspire members of contemplative communities that have formed in recent times.

In September 1968, Merton visited the Monastery of the Precious Blood, in Eagle River, Alaska, and led a retreat for the small community of nuns on the theme of building community on God's love. Merton said that Jesus came "to overcome death by love, and this work of love . . . is our job." Merton highlighted the victory of love over death on the cross, which reality "seeks to be manifested in a very concrete form on earth in the creation of community." Merton affirmed that the only real community is one "which is concerned with the problems of underprivileged people." Merton argued that when people experience the life of love and collaborate with God in transforming the world, they confirm the presence of the Spirit of God.[1]

---

1. Merton in Arnold, *Why We Live in Community*, 34, 53, 60–62.

Merton's talks in Alaska opened a window into his prophetic role in two processes. One was to make contemplative practices accessible to every person. The other was to nurture individuals and groups seeking to build communities shaped by and sharing God's love among all people, especially the poor and underprivileged.

Merton called for a new monasticism. His exploration of monasticism and its relevance for the modern world has transformed the institution and challenged innumerable people around the world to claim their truest selfhood, to deepen their lives of prayer, and to work for a world congruent with a Biblical vision of the dream of God.

Philosopher Alasdair MacIntyre contends that contemporary people must emulate medieval monasteries by forming local communities within which they adopt similar practices and may similarly prolong life through a coming time of decline. In an incisive analysis of contemporary Western culture, he writes,

> If my account of our moral condition is correct, we ought also to conclude that for some time now we too have reached that turning point. What matters at this stage is the construction of local forms of community within which civility and the intellectual and moral life can be sustained through the new dark ages that are already upon us. And if the tradition of the virtues was able to survive the horrors of the last dark ages, we are not entirely without grounds of hope. This time however the barbarians are not waiting beyond the frontiers; they have already been governing us for quite some time. And it is our lack of consciousness of this that constitutes part of our predicament. We are waiting not for a Godot, but for another—doubtless very different—St. Benedict.[2]

In this passage, MacIntyre referred to the "last dark ages." The dark ages were a time of cultural and economic disruption that took place in Europe after the decay of the Roman Empire. During this time of social collapse in the West, around 540 CE, Saint Benedict of Nursia completed what we now call *The Rule of Saint Benedict*, a text of 73 chapters giving instructions for forming and administering a monastery. For several centuries, Benedictine monasteries provided Western European society stability. Communities grew up around them. Many leaders were Benedictine monks or patrons of the Benedictine monasteries.

2. MacIntyre, *After Virtue*, 244–45.

MacIntyre's suggestion that the "new dark ages" are already upon us offers a commentary about a deep cultural malaise. Early in the twenty-first century, many people whose roots are secular as well as those who have a religious background are rebelling against racing through meals, work, social encounters, and the physical landscape. They have discovered that they have been in too much of a hurry to appreciate or notice fulfillment in living. They wonder what they have been missing. They want to incorporate into their busy schedules more time with God, with family members, with friends, or with themselves alone. They associate their lack of time for God, self, and others with an experienced need to explore new dimensions of freedom, illumination, love, self-realization, wholeness, and calm.

In response, many single and married people, both lay and clerical, are becoming companions of traditional monasteries. The Benedictine order offers opportunities for those who are not monks or nuns formally to associate with a particular monastery and to follow *The Rule of Saint Benedict*. Members of the Order of Cistercians of the Strict Observance (OCSO) also follow this *Rule*, including lay contemplatives. Another stream of Western monasticism, the Franciscan order, provides for celibate male and female communities along with a third order of lay Franciscans who follow many of the practices of their religious brothers and sisters but in a less formal, institutional way.

Many contemporary Christians are also engendering an explosive expansion of new experiments in monastic and communal living. These offer countless seekers a spiritual home in which to ground their lives and address the challenges of living in the modern world.

Nevertheless, negative and stereotypic views abound of monks and nuns, of monasteries and convents, and of the monastic life. One Sunday morning in June 2009, as I entered Canada from the U.S., I stopped at a border crossing. The immigration officer asked, "Where have you been?" I replied, "Rochester, New York." He continued, "Why were you there?" I answered, "Attending a conference." Then he said, "What was the conference about?" I simply said, "A monk." His incredulous response was, "A monk?" followed by silence.

Were my wife Nancy with me, she would have said, "Don't say anything. . . ." I followed her implicit wisdom and did not.

Waved on, I reflected on this brief exchange as I drove home. Did the official really believe I had attended a conference about some unnamed monk? Did he share any of the negative notions of monks that appear in popular culture?

Around the time of the conference, Canada's national weekly current affairs magazine *Maclean's* published an interview with Gaston Deschamps, age eighty-six, a member of a Cistercian monastery relocating from Oka, Quebec, to a smaller, quieter place seventy-five miles northeast of Montreal. Brother Deschamps joined in 1941, a time when the order was growing. Once two-hundred strong, there are now only twenty-six monks in the community. The interviewer, Martin Patriquin, asked about the long-term viability of the monastery. Brother Deschamps responded, "It brings me a lot of pain to think about this . . . we pray a lot for our survival. . . . You need religious people in the world, to pray for everyone."[3]

The interview prompted two readers to comment about "monk bunk." David Magrel of Winnipeg, Manitoba, observed that there are many interesting people in Canada; reading about this "archaic way of life was a waste of time." Adrian Peetoom of Edmonton, Alberta, wrote, "Monastic life is not a virtue when all it amounts to is 'to live inside ourselves.'"[4]

In a recent book of "nonreligious thoughts on Christian spirituality," Donald Miller mentioned monks with a negative image. Miller was living in the Rockies with some friends. They had adopted a militant Christianity and were "manning up to Jesus, bumping Him chest to chest as it were, like Bible salesmen on steroids . . . necklace on my neck . . . cross in the center, a reminder . . . that we were going to be monks for a year . . . after a while that necklace started to choke me."[5]

Are Christian monastics bound by restrictions and controls? In some sense, of course, but any community has checks and protocols. Is monasticism archaic? By no means. Monasticism offers a way to engage God, self, and others deeply. Is monasticism a waste of time? It is a waste of time only if you believe that living by love is a waste of time. Do monks or nuns live inside themselves? This has been neither my experience, nor that of many others.

James Orbinski, who is not a monk, implicitly offers another perspective. Orbinski is a Canadian physician, human rights activist, and past international president of Doctors without Borders (*Médecins sans*

3. *Maclean's*, April 6, 2009, 17.

4. *Maclean's*, April 20, 2009, 4.

5. Miller, *Blue Like Jazz*, 80.

Frontières). In his autobiography, Orbinski records his struggles with questions about humanitarian service, politics, and the relationship between the two. On several occasions as a young person, Orbinski visits a monk at Oka, Brother Benedict. With his counsel, Orbinski finds direction in his life and life-long friendship with his spiritual mentor.[6]

Reading Orbinski's story resonated with my own experience. In the mid-1970s, I began a teaching career at McMaster University in Hamilton, Ontario, Canada. I sometimes found work deadening and my ever-accelerating pace of life a problem. I felt a great need to recover a sense of God's presence in my life. I was especially aware of a lack of connect between my *ME? TOO!* work and the whispers of my heart.

To address this need, I sometimes attended retreats organized for pastors and other leaders of my congregation's denomination, at the time the Baptist Convention of Ontario and Quebec. I discovered that the focus was on the speakers who gave talks or led seminars and workshops. The gatherings felt like they were just conferences filled with words rather than opportunities for spiritual renewal.

Once, I slipped away. With a beautiful hilltop view, I sat beneath a cross and read in the Bible, prayed the Lord's Prayer, and meditated. Refreshed, I was returning to the main meeting place. A pastor, notorious for his disregard for theological educators like me, saw me coming down the hill, approached me, and asked incredulously, "Did you finish your sermon or class?"

At the time, I said nothing. The question may have been innocent. However, the apparent supposition bothered me that I was at the retreat preparing a homily or lecture.

As I reflected on this brief exchange with the pastor, I considered a possible difference in reasons for which we were attending the retreat. I realized that prayer was a major need in my life. I also pondered whether this pastor had any time to experience the presence of God in his life. He was perhaps too busy with the presence of others in his life. He had possibly received little training in the historical practices of Christian spirituality. Maybe no one encouraged him to do continuing education around this aspect of professional ministry.

This musing led me to seek to fill a real lacuna in my personal life. I became part of a prayer group with other people active in social

6. Orbinski, *Imperfect Offering*, 29, 127.

ministry. We were intentional in bringing together people from diverse economic situations and several traditions: Anglican, Baptist, Catholic, Mennonite, Quaker, United Church of Canada, Presbyterian, and seekers. We met weekly for an hour of silence and reflection at the Welcome Inn Community Center, which served (and serves) the underprivileged in the poorest neighborhood in Hamilton. Occasionally, family members and friends joined us for a meal or a day of reflection, renewal, recreation, or participation in public witness for peace and justice. Upon moving to Memphis, I sought out a similar group of soul friends. Notably, this led to participation in the Memphis School of Servant Leadership.

Another resolution was to take an annual spiritual retreat. Thanks to this decision, I have visited many monasteries. Monks and nuns have helped me to develop my spiritual life. They have helped me to experience God's power in my life and thereby to live in a more humane manner.

A third consideration had to do with my professional work in pastoral formation at McMaster University and, later, Memphis Theological Seminary (MTS) in Tennessee. I introduced regular courses on prayer and contemporary monasticism in the curriculum of each institution. Over the years, these classes attracted over two hundred students. The syllabi included books by Joan Chittister, Laurence Freeman, Thomas Keating, Thomas Merton, Kathleen Norris, Basil Pennington, Elaine Prevallet, Buddhist nun Chân Không, and Buddhist monk Thich Nhat Hanh. Students had to carve from their busy schedules a regular time and to set aside a fixed place for prayer, reading, and journaling.

In such courses, I discouraged participants from reading slavishly, as if preparing for an exam or as providing a wellspring of knowledge. I also encouraged focusing less on the theology of the writers and more on the authors' journeys. I cited a passage by Thomas Merton in which he advises readers to approach a book of meditations with a sense of openness to God's leading in one's life.

> The purpose of a book of meditations is to teach you how to think and not to do your thinking for you. Consequently if you pick up such a book and simply read it through, you are wasting your time. As soon as any thought stimulates your mind or your heart you can put the book down because your meditation has begun. To think that you are somehow obliged to follow the author of the book to his [or her] own particular conclusion would be a great mistake. It may happen that his [or her] conclusion does not ap-

ply to you. God may want you to end up somewhere else. [God]
may have planned to give you quite a different grace than the one
the author suggests you might be needing.[7]

Students explored varied ways to express themselves, for example,
through journaling, writing poetry, photography, or other visual arts.
As Merton put it, "Learn to meditate on paper. Drawing and writing are
forms of meditation. Learn how to contemplate works of art. Learn how
to pray in the streets or in the country. Know how to meditate not only
when you have a book in your hand but when you are waiting for a bus or
riding in a train."[8]

On eight occasions, MTS students have had the opportunity to take
a course on Merton and monasticism. They have undertaken five days
on retreat at Merton's home, the Abbey of Our Lady of Gethsemani in
Trappist, Kentucky. Some have opted to stay nearby at the Motherhouse
of the Sisters of Loretto.

Many MTS students have expressed a sense of empowerment and
grace in having an opportunity simply to dwell with God. Others have
found freedom to address a previously unrecognized spiritual hunger, a
desire to extend the love of Jesus to a hurting and suffering world, and a
need to listen more with the heart, especially to those from whom they felt
distant. Some have continued to read Merton's writings, to incorporate his
insights into the practice of ministry, as well as their personal lives, or to
do graduate-level work in spiritual direction and Christian spirituality.

In these and other ways, the course has enabled many persons to
grow, to find meaning in life, and to flourish in their professional contributions. Since my retirement, Dr. Gray Matthews, Assistant Professor
in the Department of Communication at the University of Memphis, has
continued to offer the course.

For several years in Memphis, Tennessee, I shared with members of
two groups in building communities rooted and grounded in God's love.
One was a local ITMS chapter. About ten times a year, Gray and Lynne
Matthews graciously offered hospitality for the group. Each year, we
choose a book by Merton to read and discuss. Insights of group members
not only enhanced my understanding of Merton, but also encouraged
all of us to pray regularly, to nurture our artistic gifts, and to respond to

7. *New Seeds of Contemplation*, 215, hereafter *NSC*.
8. Ibid., 216.

Merton's social witness. In addition, the group provided crucial logistical support for the tenth general ITMS meeting, June 7–10, 2007, at Christian Brothers University in Memphis, Tennessee.

Our Merton group did not limit membership exclusively to academic specialists or pastoral professionals but attracted a much broader segment of society. Group members have courageously opposed the proliferation and potential use of nuclear weapons. They have also worked to overcome society's excesses by seeking to eliminate unjust conditions that engender unparalleled destitution such as hunger, poverty, and climate change. They have encouraged me as I have explored new forms of contemplative living.

Another group was the Memphis School of Servant Leadership (MSSL), one of many independent schools of servant leadership around the United States. The first opened in 1986 in Washington, DC, as part of the Church of the Saviour. Its goal was to begin "a seminary for all people."

MSSL began in 1997 when an ecumenical group of lay and clergy leaders in and around Memphis, Tennessee, undertook a formation program. Participants were open to growth, change, risk, stepping from the known to the unknown, including responding to new callings.

The Reverend Sharon Lewis-Karamoko and I facilitated one of the first classes in the MSSL. With a particular focus on race, racism, and reconciliation, we explored taking steps to work specifically for the health and well-being of children. We emphasized the importance of making personal connections with people living in the immediate area, especially those less privileged in terms of economic security.

Growing out of this emphasis, several MSSL participants formed a ministry of presence in Binghamton, one of the least-served and most impoverished inner-city neighborhoods in Memphis. The Caritas Community, an intentional Christian community, formed in 2000. One of its ministries, Caritas House, has hosted weekly community meals and Bible studies as well as various spiritual formation groups, MSSL classes, and other gatherings.

The Caritas Community also helped to create Caritas Village in Binghamton. Opened in late 2006 with support from neighborhood residents and the MSSL, Caritas Village is a place of hospitality offering food, worship, speakers, arts events, a community garden, and other activity.

In 2008, the Reverend Phyllis Faulkner and I facilitated a MSSL class on Thomas Merton and Peacemaking. Participants read two Merton titles, *Peace in the Post-Christian Era* (2004) and *A Book of Hours* (2007). We met weekly at Caritas House to discuss Merton's relevance for our lives and the life of the world. We ate meals together at Caritas Village. We concluded our class with a three-day retreat at the Abbey of Our Lady of Gethsemani.

In 1998, my wife and I briefly visited Holy Transfiguration Monastery. At the time, the community was located in Breakwater, a suburb of Geelong fifty miles from Melbourne in the state of Victoria in southeastern Australia. The welcome by members of this new monastic community, their powerful worship, and the beauty of the grounds utterly overwhelmed us. We were at Breakwater but a few hours and regretted the brevity of this visit. At the time, we were unaware that God had opened up a new path on our journeys of faith, a road that still leads into the future.

I went to Australia again in 2000 for an international human rights gathering. The brothers and sisters of Holy Transfiguration Monastery invited me to spend a few days at the monastery and to give a talk on Merton, a key influence for members. A three-day retreat followed in 2002. My wife and I have subsequently returned several times and become Greater Community members.

Having experienced Merton's writings as a source of growth for my-self and for many others, I now write for all persons seeking to enrich their lives, to find their place in the world, and to experience community. I trust that this book will encourage readers to explore writings by Merton and other monastic authors and to grow in faith, hope, and love (1 Cor 13:13).

After this introduction, the next chapter introduces Thomas Merton without any intent to interpret or to guide readers through his literary output. Readers familiar with the broad outline of Merton's life and writings may want to skip to the rest of the book. Chapters 3 through 9 explore monastic renewal and prayer; radical simplicity; technology; earth care; war, peace, interfaith dialogue; and monastic experiments of his day. Drawing on Merton's insights on the new monasticism, I close with reflections on building community grounded in God's love for an interdependence urgently needed in our twenty-first-century world.

TWO

Introducing Thomas Merton

My Lord God, I have no idea where I am going. I do not see the road ahead of me. I cannot know for certain where it will end. Nor do I really know myself, and the fact that I think I am following your will does not mean that I am actually doing so. But I believe that the desire to please you does in fact please you. And I hope I have that desire in all that I am doing. I hope that I will never do anything apart from that desire. And I know that if I do this you will lead me by the right road, though I may know nothing about it. Therefore I will trust you always though I may seem to be lost and in the shadow of death. I will not fear, for you are ever with me, and you will never leave me to face my perils alone.

—Thomas Merton, *Thoughts in Solitude*

Thomas Merton was the first son of Owen Heathcote Grierson Merton (1887–1931) and Ruth Calvert Jenkins Merton (1887–1921). Of Welsh background, Owen was born in New Zealand. Also of Welsh ancestry, Ruth was born in the U.S. Aspiring artists, Owen and Ruth lived in Paris when they met. Shortly after their marriage, they settled in Prades, a village in the south of France where Thomas Merton was born on January 31, 1915. In accord with French law, Owen and Ruth registered their newborn baby as a French national.

It was wartime. Holding pacifist convictions, Ruth feared Owen would be conscripted. She suggested relocating to the U.S., which had not yet entered the war. They moved in August 1916. New Zealand did not yet have its own system of citizenship, so young Thomas traveled on his father's British passport.

These were difficult economic times for the family. The family lived with Ruth's parents Samuel and Martha Jenkins in Douglaston, Long Island, New York. To establish his independence and to earn a living, Owen turned to landscape gardening. He also played the piano at a small movie theater and the organ for a local Episcopal congregation.

On November 2, 1918, just days before the end of the war, Merton's brother John Paul was born. Three years later, on October 3, 1921, Ruth Merton died from stomach cancer. Thomas Merton suffered when as a child of six he learned of this in a note that Ruth wrote to him about her impending death.

Immediately afterwards, Thomas lived in Bermuda with his father and the novelist Evelyn Scott, Owen's lover. John Paul remained in the U.S. with his grandparents. Thomas' non-acceptance of this arrangement contributed to the decision of Owen to return to France in 1925. Owen and Thomas settled in Saint-Antonin-Noble-Val in the Midi-Pyrénées region in southern France. Thomas attended Lycée Ingres, a Protestant boarding school in Montauban a short distance to the west.

In 1928, with John Paul still in the U.S., Owen took his older son with him to England. Merton continued his schooling initially at Ripley Court south of London and then at Oakham east of Leicester. Compared with other private boarding schools, the fees of these schools were modest. Nonetheless, Sam Jenkins set up trusts to provide for the education of his two grandsons. Owen had limited resources and was under treatment for a brain tumor that would prove to be fatal. Owen Merton died on January 18, 1931.

In his autobiography, *The Seven Storey Mountain*, Thomas Merton used an expression from Dante to describe these teen-aged years as the harrowing of hell. This Old English term referred to the triumphant descent of Christ into hell between the time of His crucifixion and His resurrection. Merton had in mind his lack of secure roots or direction in life. In the following passage he speaks of this to the Virgin Mary.

> I was not sure where I was going, and I could not see what I would do. . . . [W]hen I thought there was no God and no love and no mercy, you were leading me all the while into the midst of His love and His mercy, and taking me, without my knowing anything about it, to the house that would hide me in the secret of

His Face . . . Glorious Mother of God, shall I ever again distrust you, or your God. . . ?

As you have dealt with me, Lady, deal also with all my millions of brothers who live in the same misery that I knew then: lead them in spite of themselves and guide them by your tremendous influence, O Holy Queen of souls and refuge of sinners, and bring them to your Christ the way you brought me. . . . Show us your Christ, Lady, after this our exile, yes: but show Him to us also now, show Him to us here, while we are still wanderers.[1]

Thomas Merton's sense of being lost and wandering in exile arose in part from a need for a place to call home. Owen's peripatetic lifestyle had had the effect of disconnecting young Thomas from relatives in New Zealand, England, and the U.S. Among his closest relatives were a great uncle and aunt. Ben Pearce and Maud Grierson Pearce lived in England, where Merton was in school from 1928–1934. When Maud died in November 1933, Thomas recalled, "She it was who had presided in a certain sense over my most innocent days. And now I saw those days buried with her in the ground."[2] Thomas Merton's maternal grandparents died in 1936 and 1937 followed in 1943 by his brother John Paul and in 1946 by his guardian T. Izod Bennett, MD.

During school breaks, Merton vacationed in Strasbourg (1930); Florence and Rome (1931); Germany (1932); and the U.S. and Rome (1933). During this second visit to Rome, the architecture and mosaics of Byzantine churches caught Merton's attention. However, he kept to himself any stirrings of a religious awakening.

Perhaps because of Thomas Merton's enjoyment of travel, his guardian in Britain, Dr. Bennett, along with his wife Iris Weiss Bennett, encouraged Merton to pursue a career in the British diplomatic service. His Oakham teachers groomed him for an elite university. In the fall of 1933, Merton received a scholarship to Cambridge University and enrolled at Clare College.

Merton's time at Cambridge proved scholastically unremarkable. He partied and womanized. He once confided to a friend that a girlfriend was pregnant and that she was sure Thomas Merton was the father. He also mentioned that lawyers had worked out some legal settlement.

This may have been nothing more than youthful bragging, but there is corroborating evidence. On February 17, 1944, a month before he for-

1. *Seven Storey Mountain* 129–30; hereafter, *SSM*.

2. Ibid., 121.

mally took his monastic vows, Merton provided in his will that most of his assets should go to the monastery. He bequeathed equal shares of one savings account to Dr. Bennett and his widowed sister-in-law. Dr. Bennett's share was "to be paid by him to the person mentioned to him in my letters, if that person can be found."[3] According to Edward Rice, whose friendship with Merton began when both were students at Columbia University in New York City, the woman and her son died in World War II during the London blitz.[4]

In January 1935, Merton moved to the U.S. where he would reside the rest of his life. He enrolled at Columbia University. He joined but quickly abandoned a student organization connected with the Communist Party in the U.S. In 1938, Merton received his Bachelor of Arts degree in English literature and began graduate work in this area. He wrote a Master's thesis, "Nature and Art in William Blake: An Essay in Interpretation." On February 22, 1939, he received the Master of Arts degree.

After a vacation trip to Bermuda, Merton plunged into a doctoral program in English at Columbia University. He intended to write a dissertation on Gerard Manly Hopkins. He taught English composition in Columbia University's extension program. He published book reviews in New York City newspapers and drafted several novels.

In a collection of essays of people who had studied and taught at Columbia University, Merton recalled his experience as a student and teacher there. Merton stressed that the purpose of education is to help students to discover themselves, to recognize themselves, to move beyond their superficial selves, and to claim selfhood in freedom.

> The purpose of education is to show a person how to define himself authentically and spontaneously in relation to his world—not to impose a prefabricated definition of the world, still less an arbitrary definition of the individual himself. The world is made up of people who are fully alive in it: that is, people who can be themselves in it and can enter into a living and fruitful relationship with each other in it. The world is, therefore, more real in proportion as people are able to be more fully and more humanly alive; that is to say, better able to make a lucid and conscious use of their freedom. Basically, this freedom must consist first of all in

3. Mott, *Seven Mountains of Thomas Merton*, 83–84, 90; *School of Charity*, 8, hereafter SC.

4. Rice, *Man in the Sycamore Tree*, 22–23.

the capacity to choose their own lives, to find themselves on the deepest possible level.[5]

Merton likened the university to a monastery. Both could be in conflict, but Merton saw each as a microcosm of paradise. For Merton, each had its own sphere, the university intellectual knowledge and the monastery mystical knowledge. Through each, one arrived at a consciousness and a wholeness that transcend all division and all separation.

Merton grounded his teaching in the experience of students rather than in abstractions or rules. In 1939, he told his friend Robert Lax that he enjoyed his class. "It is interesting and instructive to teach a class: it is not true that any of them are crazy at all, but nor is it true that many of them can write English. Also it is true that they are beginning to write better than before once they can write about their families and their summer vacations . . ." Later, he reported, "I lost my section of English composition, and they were going to give me a class teaching spelling to old ladies instead, and I declined, saying no thanks for the offer of that stupid spelling class."[6]

Merton's lack of geographic roots in his life paralleled the absence of a secure spiritual home. In *The Seven Storey Mountain*, Merton mentioned his baptism as an infant. He did not think there was any power in the waters of the baptism that he received in Prades "to untwist the warping of my essential freedom, or loose me from the devils that hung like vampires on my soul."[7] If Merton received the sacrament of baptism, it would have been in the Anglican tradition of his father.

Thomas Merton's mother Ruth related to the Religious Society of Friends, or Quakers. On occasion, Thomas accompanied her to Meetings for Worship. Merton recalled the experience as having been "about as supernatural as a Montgomery Ward catalogue,"[8] he had no enduring interest in the denomination. Yet through the silent worship, antiwar convictions, and body of spiritual teaching of the Quakers, Ruth's religious influence on him was considerable.

5. Merton, "Learning to Live," as published in *Love and Living*, 3.

6. Del Prete, "Teaching Is Candy," 158.

7. *SSM*, 5. In an email dated April 12, 2010, Paul M. Pearson of the Thomas Merton Center at Bellarmine University writes that he has never seen proof of Thomas Merton's baptism. The registers of baptism of the Anglican bishop of London at that time should have a record of a baptism on the continent. I have not confirmed if this is the case.

8. Ibid., 116.

During his early years, Thomas Merton observed few formal religious practices. In 1920, his paternal grandmother Gertrude Merton accompanied by Agnes Gertrude Stonehewer Merton, or Aunt Kit, his father's younger sister, arrived from New Zealand for a visit. When asked if he prayed, Merton acknowledged he did not know the "Our Father."[9] His grandmother taught Merton the prayer. He rarely recited it. On August 6, 1955, Merton wrote his friend Thérèse Lentfoehr, a Salvatorian sister. He asked her to "say a good big prayer for my old New Zealand grandmother who is really OLD. She is going to be a hundred . . . I hope it doesn't run in the family."[10] Gertrude Merton died the next year at the age of a hundred and one.

Among relatives, Merton felt closest to Aunt Kit. He corresponded with her more or less regularly. She died just before Easter 1968 in a shipwreck.

At Columbia University, Merton sought God's call on his life. A Hindu friend, Mahanambrata Brahmachari, seeded Merton's journey into Catholicism. He encouraged Merton, "There are many beautiful mystical books written by the Christians. You should read St. Augustine's *Confessions*, and *The Imitation of Christ*."[11] Merton did. Pursuing this path, Merton was baptized as a Roman Catholic on November 16, 1938.

Starting the fall of 1940, Merton taught English literature in Olean, New York, at St. Bonaventure College, a Franciscan institution. Merton had previously explored joining the order. In his application, he revealed his past and possibly continuing sexual escapades. Moreover, he was a recent convert. Following Canon Law, an applicant should have been a practicing Catholic for two years before being accepted into an order. When Merton applied to the Franciscans in New York City, he had been a Catholic for only a few months. Accordingly, the Franciscans rejected his application.

Merton led a comfortable life at Olean. Despite the insularity of campus life, he wrestled with the idea of remaining there. During this period, the Russian-born Baroness Catherine de Hueck (1896–1985) had come to the conviction that she must witness to Jesus through her life. As she implemented a radical way of living in New York City, young men and women came to join her. In 1938, she opened a Friendship House in

9. Ibid., 9; some call the prayer "The Lord's Prayer."

10. *Road to Joy*, 220. Hereafter, *RJ*.

11. *SSM*, 198.

Harlem. Residents concentrated on racial justice and on living the spirituality of St. Francis of Assisi. Informally, Catherine became Merton's spiritual advisor. She invited him to join her in serving the poor in Harlem. Hoping Merton would join her work, she advised, "St. Bonaventure is a respectable golf club where quite a few saints have lost themselves on its greens. Some day it is going to change all the golfers into saints."[12]

Catherine's ministry and her closeness to people who loved Christ appealed to Merton. He spent the summer of 1941 in Harlem. In the fall, as Merton struggled with God's call on his life, he considered a career at the Friendship House, which provided him a "close and immediate and visible association with any group of those who had banded themselves together to form a small, secret colony of the Kingdom of Heaven in this earth of exile."[13] In his journal, Merton mentioned the values that flowed from his experience of Catherine's ministry.

> There is no question I can't stay at Saint Bonaventure any more: I must go and find Christ where He really is—in real poverty and sacrifice.
>
> But then, what about Friendship House: it has this one great thing: it is real poverty, it is real sacrifice; it is real love of Christ in the poor. It is holy. The work is holy. The Baroness is a saint. Harlem is full of saints. And in Harlem there is no doubt of possibility even of martyrdom, in which my sins would all vanish at once. . . .[14]

Merton wrote poetry for the *Harlem Friendship House News* and acknowledged he owed much to Catherine. He dedicated "Aubade-Harlem" to Catherine. The poem reads in part,

> Daylight has driven iron spikes,
> Into the flesh of Jesus' hands and feet:
> Four flowers of blood have nailed Him to the walls of Harlem.
>
> Along the white halls of the clinics and the hospitals
> Pilate evaporates with a cry:
> They have cut down two hundred Judases,

12. Baroness to Merton, October 14, 1941, in Wild, *Compassionate Fire: Letters of Merton and Doherty*, 12.

13. *SSM*, 349.

14. *Run to the Mountain*, 464, entry for November 29, 1941; hereafter *RM*.

Hanged by the neck in the opera houses and the museum.

Across the cages of the keyless aviaries,

The lines and wires, the gallows of the broken kites,

Crucify, against the fearful light,

The ragged dresses of the little children.[15]

In the spring of 1941, Merton's spiritual wrestling led him to spend a few days on retreat at the Abbey of Our Lady of Gethsemani. Asked if he had come to stay, Merton replied, "Oh no!" The question sounded too much like the voice of conscience. It terrified Merton.[16]

Merton had a tremendous experience at Gethsemani. In his journal, he observed, "This is the center of America. I had wondered what was holding this country together, what has been keeping the universe from cracking in pieces and falling apart. It is this monastery if only this one. (There must be two or three others.)"[17]

In September, Merton made a retreat at another Trappist monastery in Cumberland, Rhode Island. Merton described the Abbey of Our Lady of the Valley (now Saint Joseph's Abbey in Spencer, Massachusetts) in his journal. He wrote that he had a sense God was leading him elsewhere. "To love this place, just as a pretty place, is harder than to love the pleasantness of Gethsamani, with the hills and fields all around it."[18] In *The Seven Storey Mountain,* Merton observed, "Here at the Valley I was filled with the same unutterable respect for the Cistercian life, but there was no special desire to enter that particular monastery."[19]

Committing to the monastic life at Gethsemani, Merton explained to Catherine that the routines at Friendship House seemed no different from those teaching at St. Bonaventure. In response, Catherine affirmed his decision. "Dear Tom, Your letter was awaiting me upon my return. It would be foolish for me to say that I wasn't disappointed, and yet . . . probably it is the will of God. . . . How wonderful, how perfect! A Trappist and a priest! High is your calling, dear friend, and wonderful to behold the Face of God in silence. It is awesome and ever so consoling. . . . God be with

---

15. *Collected Poems,* 82–83, hereafter *CP; In the Dark before Dawn,* 5–6.

16. *SSM,* 321.

17. *RM,* 333, entry for April 7, 1941, cf. *SSM,* 325.

18. Ibid., 393, entry for September 2, 1941.

19. *SSM,* 352.

you as well as my poor and humble prayers. Write to me. Affectionately, Catherine de Hueck."[20]

Others were less excited. Learning of his decision, Columbia University advisor Mark Van Doren said, "We'll never hear from him again. He's taken a vow of silence, he can't write to us nor we to him—he's leaving the world. I think he's an extraordinary young man, and I don't believe we'll ever hear another word from him." Naomi Burton, Merton's literary agent, reacted, "Oh God! He'll never write again!"[21]

In late 1941, as Merton prepared to set off for the Abbey of Our Lady of Gethsemani, he packed all that he would take in one suitcase. He gave most of his clothes for Catherine to distribute at Friendship House in Harlem, New York City. Merton also sent her a manuscript with the understanding she would arrange to publish his Cuban journal and use the royalties in support of her ministry. In 1959, the book appeared as *The Secular Journal*. Merton wrote, "I owe much to Catherine, and I am glad that this book can help Madonna House in some way."[22]

Merton gave notes and books to the library of St. Bonaventure College. He threw a great deal of other material into an incinerator with the exception of the draft of one novel and several poems that Merton sent to Mark Van Doren, his faculty advisor at Columbia. These poems were published as Merton's first book, *Thirty Poems*, in 1944. Van Doren arranged for the publication with New Directions.

Van Doren also arranged for publication of *Selected Poems of Thomas Merton*, which appeared in two editions. The first, in 1959, included an introduction by Van Doren, seventy-two poems (all but four of which had appeared in Merton's earlier books), and an essay by Merton entitled "Poetry and Contemplation: A Reappraisal." An enlarged edition appeared in 1967.

20. Merton to de Hueck, December 6, 1941; de Hueck to Merton, December 13, 1941, both in Wild, 21–25.

21. Robert Giroux cites Van Doren in Wilkes, *Merton, by Those Who Knew Him Best*, 18; Van Doren, *Autobiography*, 268. Mott, *Seven Mountains*, 202, cites Naomi Burton. She was an agent for several aspiring writers, including Merton. Unsuccessful in selling Merton's novels to a publisher, she sent the manuscript of *The Seven Storey Mountain* to Robert Giroux, an editor at Harcourt Brace, which published the book in 1948. In 1951, she married Melville E. (Ned) Stone. When Merton set up the Merton Legacy Trust to administer his estate on behalf of the monastery, she was one of the original three trustees. When she resigned, Robert Giroux replaced her.

22. *Secular Journal*, xiv, as reprinted in Wild, *Compassionate Fire*, 104.

Before his entrance into the Abbey of Our Lady of Gethsemani, Merton worked on a number of novels. One, *My Argument with the Gestapo*, eventually appeared in print in 1969 with the subtitle, *A Macaronic Journal*. This referred to Merton's frequent introduction of dialogue in a mixture of various European languages as well as to the book's original title, *Journal of My Escape from the Nazis*. In the preface that he wrote in January 1968, Merton recalled, "The novel is a kind of sardonic meditation on the world in which I then found myself: an attempt to define its predicament and my own place in it."[23]

On December 10, 1941, Merton arrived at the Abbey of Our Lady of Gethsemani. Merton recognized Brother Matthew, who had received him earlier in the year. Merton greeted the monk, "Hullo, Brother." Brother Matthew glanced at Merton's suitcase. He asked, "This time have you come to stay?" Merton replied, "Yes, Brother, if you'll pray for me." Brother Matthew responded, "That's what I've been doing, praying for you."[24]

God called Merton to become a Trappist monk at the Abbey of Our Lady of Gethsemani. The abbey enfolded and sheltered Merton from storms about and within. For Merton, Gethsemani offered more than a place to call home. It was paradise on earth, a place of "ceaseless adoration of God: this is the monastic ideal."[25]

Merton received a new name, Louis, after the French saint. In contrast with his libertine student days, Merton immersed himself in a schedule that was "arduous, confined, raw."[26] He described the rhythm of work and study as "recreation."[27] On March 19, 1947, he made his final vows and, on May 26, 1949, he was ordained as a priest. Work assignments included those of forester, master of students (1951–1955), and master of novices (1955–1965).

The heart of Merton's monastic practice revolved around prayer in the monastery chapel where the monks gathered eight times daily to pray together. Monks also sometimes went alone to the chapel, or to a small oratory, which comes from the Latin *orare*, reserved to the monks for private prayer.

23. *My Argument with the Gestapo*, 6.
24. *SSM*, 371.
25. *Gethsemani Magnificat*, 38.
26. Mott, *Seven Mountains*, 208.
27. *RM*, 340–41, entry for April 9, 1941.

The monks of Gethsemani followed Benedictine practice. Over a two-week period, they chanted the psalms antiphonally, the alternate singing of verses by one side of the choir, then the other. During the night prayers, called *Compline*, the monks chanted Psalms 4, 91, 134, and, in honor of the Virgin Mary, the *Salve Regina* or another hymn appropriate to the season of the Christian calendar, Advent, Lent, or Eastertide. Silent prayer and the examination of conscience generally preceded confession. The following was the daily schedule in winter:

2 a.m.	Rise (Sunday, 1:30). Little Office of the Blessed Virgin Mary until 2:30.
2:30	Mental Prayer for half an hour.
3:00	Night Office (*Matins* and *Lauds*), Angelus, Private Masses.
5:30	*Prime* (Mass), Chapter, Work, Breakfast.
7:45	*Terce*, High Mass on Sundays, *Sext*, Work.
10:45	End of work.
11:07	*None*, examination of conscience. Angelus.
11:30	Dinner followed by time for reading and private prayer.
1:30 p.m.	Work.
3:30	Reading or private prayer.
4:30	*Vespers* followed by time for meditation.
5:30	Light refreshment.
6:10	*Compline*.
7:00	Retire to Dormitory for sleep.[28]

At the time that Merton chose the monastic life, he probably was not aware that his first abbot, Frederick Dunne, had grown up loving books; that Dunne's father had been a bookbinder and publisher in the town in Ohio where Merton's grandfather had once owned and operated a bookstore; or that Dunne had supported one other writer, Father Raymond Flanagan.

Judging from the maudlin quality of some of Merton's early writings, one might ask if Abbot Dunne had any inkling about the direction Merton's literary efforts might take. When he encouraged Merton to ex-

28. Merton, *Waters of Siloe*, x–xi; Merton also provides a summer schedule; Mott, *Seven Mountains*, 595.

ercise his gift as a writer, Dunne doubtless felt that Merton, like Flanagan, might bring needed revenue or recruits to Gethsemani.

Among his earliest books, Merton wrote monastic history, his autobiography, and four volumes of poetry: *Thirty Poems* (1944); *A Man in the Divided Sea* (1946); *Figures for an Apocalypse* (1948); and *Tears of the Blind Lion* (1949). Merton's publisher James Laughlin observed, "I was immediately taken with Tom's work even if it wasn't the sort of thing we usually published at New Directions. They were religious poems but not pietistic; and they weren't homilies. They were verbally colorful, full of rich imagery and inventive fantasy."[29]

A directness of language, spirituality, and sensitivity to nature marked these collections. Subjects that dominated Merton's later writing emerged in these early books. One was the natural world as setting and source for prayer. In "Song: Contemplation," Merton wrote:

> O land alive with miracles!
> O clad in streams,
> Countering the silver summer's pleasant arrows
> And beating them with the kind armor
> Of your enkindled water-vesture,
>
> Lift your blue trees into the early sun![30]

Another theme was Merton's desire for more time alone to spend in meditation. Merton linked love of nature with silence in an early poem "The Trappist Cemetery-Gethsemani" first published in *A Man in the Divided Sea*:

> Brothers, the curving grasses and their daughters
> Will never print your praises:
> The trees our sisters, in their summer dresses,
> Guard your fame in these green cradles:
> The simple crosses are content to hide your characters. . . .
>
> Teach us, Cistercian Fathers, how to wear
> Silence, our humble armor.[31]

29. Laughlin, "Thomas Merton and His Poetry," in *Random Essays*, 3.

30. *CP*, 157; *In the Dark before Dawn*, 100.

31. *CP*, 117; *In the Dark before Dawn*, 32–34.

"Song: If You Seek. . . " was published in a later collection, *Emblems of a Season of Fury* (1963). The poem captured the richness of Merton's thinking about solitude.

> If you seek a heavenly light
> I, Solitude, am your professor!
>
> I go before you into emptiness,
> Raise strange suns for your new mornings,
> Opening the windows
> Of your innermost apartment.
>
> When I, loneliness, give my special signal
> Follow my silence, follow where I beckon!
> Fear not, little beast, little spirit
> (Thou word and animal)
> I, Solitude, am angel
> And have prayed in your name.
>
> Look at the empty, wealthy night
> The pilgrim moon!
> I am the appointed hour,
> The "now" that cuts
> Time like a blade.
>
> I am the unexpected flash
> Beyond "yes," beyond "no,"
> The forerunner of the Word of God.
>
> Follow my ways and I will lead you
> To golden-haired suns,
> Logos and music, blameless joys,
> Innocent of questions
> And beyond answers:
> For I, Solitude, am thine own self:
> I, Nothingness, am thy All.
> I, Silence, am thy Amen![32]

32. *CP*, 340–41; *In the Dark before Dawn*, 95–96.

Another topic was Merton's distrust of technology. In "Tower of Babel," Merton dealt with misuse of language to conceal or distort, in ways that shape reality and manipulate people.

> Now the function of the word is:
> To designate first the machine,
> Then what the machine produces
> Then what the machine destroys.[33]

A final theme in Merton's early poems was his Christ-centered spirituality. In "The Victory," Merton identified Christ at the heart of his search for roots.

> This is the word You utter
> To search our being to its roots:
> This is the judgement and the question
> And the joy we suffer:
> This is our trial, this the weight of gladness that we cannot bear,
> But turn to water and to blood. . . .
>
> Make ready for the Christ, Whose smile, like lightening,
> Sets free the song of everlasting glory
> That now sleeps, in your paper flesh, like dynamite.[34]

In "For My Brother Reported Missing in Action, 1943," Merton responded to news of the death of his brother John Paul with a strong sense of Christ's presence. The final stanza read,

> For in the wreckage of your April Christ lies slain,
> And Christ weeps in the ruins of my spring:
> The money of Whose tears shall fall
> Into your weak and friendless hand,
> And buy you back to your own land:
> The silence of Whose tears shall fall
> Like bells upon your alien tomb.
> Hear them and come: they call you home.[35]

33. *CP*, 21 and 256; *In the Dark before Dawn*, 146. The poem appeared in *Early Poems: 1940–42*, published in 1971. It also appeared as part of a speech by the Professor in part 1, scene 2 of a longer verse drama of the same title published in *The Strange Islands* (1957).

34. *CP*, 114–15.

35. *CP*, 36; *SSM*, 404; *In the Dark before Dawn*, 181.

Merton wrote in genres other than poetry. Books, essays, letters, pamphlets, and drawings flowed from his pen. He used his given name rather than his monastic name, Louis. New Directions published most of Merton's titles, including *The Asian Journal of Thomas Merton*, which Laughlin co-edited with Naomi Stone and Brother Patrick Hart after Merton's death.

Thomas Merton's published autobiography was *The Seven Storey Mountain*. On June 20, 1948, Merton received a letter from Robert Giroux of Harcourt Brace saying the book was to appear on the feast day of St. Clare, August 12. In his journal, Merton commented on the book's limitations, ". . . the thing isn't finished. There are parts badly written, but on the whole, it is the book in which I have tried to put something." He continued,

> . . . now it is about to be launched.
>
> It has been growing so long that I can no longer be diffident or scared.
>
> Since I belong to God and my life belongs to Him and my book is His, and He is managing them all for His glory, I only have to take what comes and do the small part that will be allotted to me: reading the letters of people who will hate me for having been converted and for having written about it, and those of people who will perhaps be pleased. It seems to me there can be great possibilities in all this and that God has woven my crazy existence and even my mistakes and my sins into His plan for a new society . . . [all things work together for good (Rom 8:28)].[36]

The Seven Storey Mountain appeared on October 4, 1948. At once, Merton began to receive letters from people who had read the book and responded in great simplicity. Merton found most of the letters beautiful, spiritual, and filled with the love of God. Though he felt as if he had known the people who wrote to him for a long time, Merton was unable to do more than respond with a printed card. In his journal, he observed that his correspondents were genuine,

> It is beautiful to see God working in souls . . . . The most beautiful thing about it is to see how the desires of the soul inspired by God so fit in and harmonize with grace that holy things seem natural to the soul, seem to be part of its very self. That is what God wants to create in us—that marvelously simple spontaneity in which His life becomes perfectly ours and our life His, and it

36. *Entering the Silence*, 213.

seems absolutely inborn in us to act as His children, and to have
His light shining in our eyes.[37]

The writer Evelyn Waugh, who prepared a shorter version for readers in the UK with the title *Elected Silence*, thought that *The Seven Storey
Mountain* "may well prove to be of permanent interest in the history of
religious experience." Another writer, Graham Greene, called it "an autobiography with a pattern and meaning valid for all of us." The publisher
Clare Boothe Luce predicted, "It is to a book like this that men will turn a
hundred years from now to find out what went on in the heart of man in
this cruel century."[38]

Merton presented the story of his spiritual journey in an accessible
way. Merton had something to say that people—not specifically Catholics
or Christians—needed or wanted to hear. Best-seller lists, church bul-
letins, reviews in various publications, and word-of-mouth helped the
book attain a wide readership around the world. For over sixty years, it
has proved to be one of the most readable and approachable presentations
of one person's search for God.

On May 26, 1949, the day of Merton's ordination as a priest, his
editor Robert Giroux visited Gethsemani and presented Merton the
200,000th issue off the press, done in special morocco binding as a presentation copy. Translations appeared in Argentina, Belgium, Brazil, China,
Czechoslovakia, Denmark, France, Germany, Hungary, Italy, Japan, the
Netherlands, Poland, Portugal, South Korea, in Spain in both Castilian
and Catalan, and Sweden. The various editions and translations have sold
millions of copies.

Publication of *The Seven Storey Mountain* did not necessarily mean
that Merton fully resolved his struggle to find an intellectual, spiritual,
professional, familial, and geographic center. Merton desired to spend
more time in solitude and, gradually, came to chafe at the busy-ness and
business aspects of monastic life as generally practiced at Gethsemani.
Excessive activity undermined his desire to spend time in silence and listening. Merton once observed,

> For it seems to me that our monasteries produce very few pure
> contemplatives. The life is too active. There is too much move-
> ment, too much to do. That is especially true of Gethsemani. It

37. Ibid., 243. Entry for November 9, 1948.
38. Mott, *Seven Mountains*, 243; Bamberger, *Thomas Merton, Prophet of Renewal*, 15.

is a powerhouse, and not merely a powerhouse of prayer. In fact, there is an almost exaggerated reverence for work . . . [d]oing things, suffering things, thinking things, making tangible and concrete sacrifices for the love of God . . . goes by the name of "active contemplation." The word active is well chosen. About the second half of the compound, I am not so sure. It is not without a touch of poetic license.[39]

James Fox was Merton's abbot from 1948 until he retired from that role in 1967. At the time of his election, Abbot Fox inherited a monastery deep in debt and with many buildings in need of essential repairs. Fox initiated many new projects including mechanizing Gethsemani Farms with the goal of increasing income from it. In his role as spiritual leader, Fox also sought to meet the needs of individual members of the community. Fox granted Merton use of an abandoned tool shed in the woods where he could spend some hours each day alone in silence and stillness. In a February 9, 1953, entry in his journal, Merton wrote,

It is a tremendous thing no longer to have to debate in my mind about "being a hermit," even though I am not one. At least now solitude is something concrete—it is "St. Anne's"—the long view of hills, the empty cornfields in the bottoms, the crows in the trees, and the cedars bunched together on the hillside. And when I am here there is always lots of sky and lots of peace and I don't have distractions and everything is serene.[40]

The hut offered Merton a partial solution to his need for solitude. It also provided Merton a place to write. In a letter to Benedictine scholar Jean Leclercq, Merton observed, "Writing is deep in my nature, and I cannot deceive myself that it will be very easy for me to do without it. At least I can get along without the public and without my reputation . . . we must be poor and live by God alone . . . The time has come for me to enter more deeply into that poverty."[41]

In 1955, Merton had a new assignment, that of master of novices, one of the most important positions in a monastery. He wrote Jean Leclercq,

My new life as master of novices progresses from day to day. It is an unfamiliar existence to which I often have difficulty in

39. *SSM*, 389.
40. *Search for Solitude*, 29, hereafter *SS*.
41. *SC*, 90, letter of August 11, 1955.

adapting myself. I sometimes feel overcome with sheer horror at
having to talk so much and appear before others as an example.
I believe God is testing the quality of my desire for solitude, in
which perhaps there was an element of escape from responsibility.
But nevertheless the desire remains the same, the conflict is there,
but there is nothing I can do but ignore it and press forward to
accomplish what is evidently the will of God.[42]

Merton was restless. Especially in his journals and letters, he complained that he was making little or no progress in his life of prayer and
contemplation. He wanted more time for solitude and silence. He proposed becoming a hermit. Merton thought of founding a new monastery,
perhaps in South America.

On November 10, 1958, Merton wrote to John XXIII. His purpose
was to congratulate him on his elevation to the papacy. He also hoped the
pope would sanction a move.

> It seems to me that, as a contemplative, I do not need to lock my-
> self into solitude and lose all contact with the rest of the world;
> rather this poor world has a right to a place in my solitude. It is
> not enough for me to think of the apostolic value of prayer and
> penance; I also have to think in terms of a contemplative grasp
> of the political, intellectual, artistic and social movements in this
> world—by which I mean a sympathy for the honest aspirations
> of so many intellectuals everywhere in the world and the terrible
> problems they have to face. I have had the experience of seeing
> that this kind of understanding and friendly sympathy, on the
> part of a monk who really understands them, has produced strik-
> ing effects among artists, writers, publishers, poets, and . . . intel-
> lectuals from other parts of the world.

Merton continued by characterizing his literary activity as an "apostolate of friendship" that also enhanced the reputation of the monastery.
Gethsemani was receiving many new recruits.[43]

John XXIII responded generously. He sent Merton a gift. However,
he did not sanction Merton moving.

In 1959, still early in his pontificate, John XXIII proposed convening an ecumenical council. To describe its purpose, the pope used the
Italian word *aggiornamento*, which means bringing up to date. Bishops,

42. *SC*, 95, letter of February 6, 1956.
43. *Hidden Ground of Love*, 481–83, hereafter, *HGL*.

clergy, media, and others used the word during the sessions of the Second Vatican Council (1962–1965) to describe the spirit of change and open-mindedness that marked the gathering.

Merton corresponded with John XXIII on this and other subjects. Monsignor Capovilla, private secretary to the pope, acknowledged that the Holy Father was "impressed" by a letter dated November 11, 1961. In this communication, Merton lamented an "unsettling mood in the United States . . . it is practically impossible to reverse the war machine and to disarm." Merton observed, "Sad to say, American Catholics are among the most war-like, intransigent and violent; indeed, they believe that in acting this way they are being loyal to the Church." The letter may have been a source of inspiration for John XXIII's encyclical *Pacem in Terris,* "Peace on Earth."[44]

In the early 1960s, Abbot Fox permitted Merton to move in stages to a hermitage a short walk away from the main monastic complex. There, Merton read, wrote, and received visitors, including literary friends. He still went to the main house to give conferences and for mass, meals, and mail. On August 20, 1965, Merton became a full-time hermit. He expected eventually to end his days there.[45] Merton described his life in the hermitage in the following passage:

> There is a mental ecology, too, a living balance of spirits in this corner of the woods. There is room here for many other songs besides those of birds. Of Vallejo, for instance. Or Rilke, or René Char, Montale, Zukofsky, Ungaretti, Edwin Muir, Quasimodo, or some Greeks. Or the dry, disconcerting voice of Nicanor Parra, the poet of the sneeze. Here is also Chuang Tzu whose climate is perhaps most the climate of this silent corner of woods. A climate in which there is no need for explanations. Here is the reassuring companionship of many silent Tzu's and Fu's; Kung Tzu, Lao Tzu, Meng Tzu, Tu Fu. And Jui Neng. And Chao-Chu. And the drawings of Sengai. And a big graceful scroll from Suzuki. Here also is a Syrian hermit called Philoxenus. An Algerian Cenobite called Camus. Here is heard the clanging prose of Tertullian, with the dry catarrh of Sartre. Here the voluble dissonances of Auden, with the golden sounds of John of Salisbury. Here is the deep vegetation of that more ancient forest in which the angry birds, Isaias and Jeremias, sing. Here should be, and are, feminine voices from

44. Ibid., 486.
45. *Other Side of the Mountain,* 282.

> Angela of Foligno to Flannery O'Connor, Theresa of Avila, Juliana
> of Norwich, and, more personally . . . Raïssa Maritain. It is good
> to choose the voices that will be heard in these woods, but they
> also choose themselves, and send themselves here to be present
> in this silence.[46]

Life in the hermitage enabled Merton to experience the silence and solitude he had sought for years. He felt he was getting somewhere at last. On April 26, 1965, Merton wrote André Louf, abbot of the Cistercian abbey of Sainte-Marie-du-Mont in the French-speaking area of Flanders. Merton explained that the hermitage enabled him to live more fully into his calling as a monk.

> . . . for me the experience has been wonderful, and it has dissipat-
> ed any doubts I may have had about my own need for and happi-
> ness in solitude. I have at last the complete sense of having found
> my monastic vocation. At least in my own mind, I am convinced
> that I have now found the place which God had destined for me
> when He called me to the monastic life, and that if before this I
> was always to some extent unsatisfied and looking for "more," it
> was simply because this was needed to complete what God had
> given me before.[47]

By "vocation," from the Latin *vocare* (to call), Merton understood his specific calling as priest or monk. He was also expressing his sense of a wider calling to wholeness and salvation.

Twelve months after he had written this letter, Merton underwent a surgical procedure in a Louisville hospital. A relationship developed with a nurse, introduced as "M" in a collection of poetry dedicated to her. Merton was in love! Upon discovery of Merton's liaison with M, Abbot Fox ordered that any association with the young woman end. It did.

Merton did not regard this as just an episode but as a profound event in his life. It moved him deeply, as it did M. She has chosen not to make public her own reflections on their romance. Publication of Merton's once restricted journals and of Michael Mott's biography have brought their friendship to light.

---

46. "Day of a Stranger," *Dancing in the Water of Life*, 239–42; hereafter, *DWL*. Reprinted in *Hudson Review* 20 (1967) and McDonnell, *Thomas Merton Reader*, 432–33.

47. *SC*, 276.

Given the powerful emotions unleashed by the relationship between Merton and James Fox, it is remarkable that the abbot turned to Merton as his personal confessor. That Merton served in this role for fifteen years attests to the abbot's respect for Merton, as did his appointment of Merton to key roles in the formation of the monks who would be the future of the community.

In the fall of 1967, Fox announced his wish to resign as abbot. Fox followed Merton by withdrawing to a hermitage where he lived his final years. His life took a tragic turn. In 1977, two men broke into his hermitage and severely beat him. Fox moved to the abbey's infirmary, where he lived another ten years. He died on Good Friday, April 17, 1987. Fox's grave next to Merton's in the abbey's cemetery offers a poignant symbol of their complex relationship.

In early 1968, the monks of Gethsemani chose Flavian Burns to succeed Fox as abbot. The election of a new abbot portended change in the community, including relaxation of restrictions on travel by the abbey's illustrious monk.

Benedictine practice had placed Thomas Merton under a vow of stability. Merton rarely left the monastery except to travel to Louisville on monastery business or for medical reasons. Beyond this, his only trips away were these: in July 1952, he was part of a delegation that looked at land for a new foundation in Ohio; in July 1956, he attended a workshop at St. John's Abbey in Collegeville, Minnesota; in June 1964, Merton met Japanese Zen master Daisetz T. Suzuki in New York City.

In a letter of April 28, 1968, Merton responded to a letter of invitation to conduct a seminar on non-violence at the University of Kentucky in Lexington. Merton explained that, with new developments in the Catholic Church, he had given a lot of thought to the question of whether or not he would eventually go out and talk in various places. Merton explained,

> The rules of the Order have not yet been changed, but I guess it is quite likely that I could slip out to someplace like Lexington. On the other hand my new Abbot [Flavian Burns] though not being like the old one, would not be very much in favor. And I agree with him. Because if I once started to say "yes" it would be impossible to say "no"—or to do so consistently. And I am afraid that not all invitations would turn out to be worthwhile. In fact, I'd end up just going around talking perhaps rather irresponsibly, and not doing the thing I am really meant to do.

Merton closed by offering to send some sort of statement and recommended people who could read the paper in his absence.[48]

Abbot Burns did permit Merton to look for sites for hermitages. During his travels, Merton led retreats for communities in California and New Mexico in May 1968 and in Alaska in September 1968. Abbot Burns also allowed Merton to accept an invitation to address a gathering sponsored by an international Benedictine organization, *Aide à l'Implantation Monastique*, of Buddhist and Christian superiors at Samutprakarn, a few miles from the center of Bangkok, Thailand.

On October 15, 1968, Merton departed from California on a pilgrimage that promised to be his first extended time away from Gethsemani in twenty-seven years. Rumors abounded and have persisted that Merton had left Gethsemani permanently, or had abandoned Christianity. From his letters of this time, it was clear that Merton looked forward to returning to his monastery, the only home he had ever really known. He felt homesick for Gethsemani and insisted, "I'll always be a monk of Gethsemani."[49]

On the morning of December 10, 1968, Merton addressed the Bangkok gathering. After lunch, he retired to his room. A few hours later, another conferee found Merton's body with a fan lying on top of his body. Merton had probably tried to move the fan. Perhaps he stepped on its faulty wiring. While it was impossible to be certain of the circumstances, the cause of Merton's death was electrocution. Shock and tributes followed. Mark Van Doren, Merton's mentor at Columbia, observed that Merton was one of the great persons of his time or of any time.

---

48. Merton to George Lewis Fields, April 28, 1968, *RJ*, 368.

49. Merton to Hart, December 8, 1968, *SC*, 417. *Other Side of the Mountain*, 166, entry for September 9, 1968.

THREE

Thomas Merton on Monastic Renewal

Abbot John said: A monk must be like a man who, sitting under a tree, looks up and perceives all kinds of snakes and wild beasts running at him. Since he cannot fight them all, he climbs the tree and gets away from them. The monk, at all times, should do the same. When evil thoughts are aroused by the enemy, he should fly, by prayer, to the Lord, and he will be saved.

—Thomas Merton, *The Wisdom of the Desert*

From 1941 until 1968, Thomas Merton was a Benedictine monk of the Cistercian reform. To appreciate Merton's contribution to monastic renewal, we begin by introducing his monastic order. Benedict was the son of a Roman noble in Nursia, the modern Norcia in Umbria, a hundred miles northeast of Rome. He founded twelve communities for monks at Subiaco, about forty miles to the east of Rome. He then moved to the mountains of southern Italy and founded a monastery at Monte Cassino. While earlier Christian monasticism had often stressed individual asceticism and rigorous self-denial, Monte Cassino attracted ordinary human persons.

Benedict wrote a *Rule* that offered his community direction for their way of life. His twin sister Scholastica led a community for women at Plombariola, about five miles from Monte Cassino. The nuns also followed *The Rule of Saint Benedict.*[1]

---

1. References to the *Rule of St. Benedict* will be given parenthetically in the text.

In addition to its importance in the history of monasticism, the *Rule* has influenced wider society. Over the centuries, many laypeople have adopted spiritual practices set forth in the *Rule*.

An important charge of the *Rule* was that monks are to clothe themselves "with faith and the performance of good works" (Prologue, 23). To this end, the *Rule* establishes a daily rhythm of prayer, work, and sacred reading. Insisting that "the presence is everywhere" (*Rule*, 19.1), Benedict encouraged being reverent in every aspect of life. He encouraged monks and nuns, when reciting the daily offices, to stop, to reflect for a moment on the demands of all prior activity, and to stand to sing the psalms in such a way that their minds are in harmony with their voices (*Rule*, 19.7).

The cycle of prayer begins before sunrise and ends at sunset. Times for personal reading and for prayer follow the morning office or *Matins*. Community mass and breakfast follow prayers known as *Lauds*. After the office known as *Terce*, monks work until noon. After the noontime prayers, known as *Sext*, the monks eat a main meal followed by time for personal reading, prayer, and, perhaps, a siesta. Mid afternoon prayers, or *None*, follow. Members of each Benedictine monastery have time in the afternoon for chores, personal reading, and private prayer. After *Vespers*, supper, and *Compline*, monks and nuns retire for the night.

For Benedict, physical labor enabled monks and nuns not only to provide for their livelihood, but also to participate in God's ongoing work of creating and renewing earth. "When they live by the labor of their hands, as our [monastic mothers and fathers] and the apostles did, then they are really monks" (*Rule*, 48.8).

Benedict intended his *Rule* for beginners. The Bible was the basis for its guidance to disciples (*Rule*, Prologue 21; 73.8). Benedict mandated that monks should be conversant with Scripture as a spiritual practice for growing into Christ-likeness. The *Rule* provided for silent, private reading of the Bible. Monks and nuns should follow the pattern of Jesus who periodically withdrew for prayer. In solitude, Jesus waited on and listened to God. "O that today you would listen to his [God's] voice! Do not harden your hearts . . ." (*Rule*, Prologue citing Ps 95:7b–8a). Benedict also designated times for corporate reading of Scripture. He stipulated that community members should undertake such reading quietly, slowly, and meditatively.

Benedict called poverty, community, humility, and other monastic practices "instruments of good works." By observing them, Benedictine sisters and brothers could attain to "the perfect love [that] casts out all fear" (*Rule*, 7.67, quoting 1 John 4:18).

.   Early Benedictine monasticism arose in Western Europe during a period of cultural, economic, and social upheaval. Amidst the fragmentation and turmoil of the times, Benedictine monasteries provided stability. Benedictine monks and nuns performed crucial roles. They had a virtual monopoly in matters of liturgy and prayer, learning and the interpretation of the Bible, aesthetics and architecture, music, and other art forms. They arbitrated political and ecclesiastical matters. They were producers, consumers, and missionaries. They endowed Western civilization with a positive body of religious teaching concerning holiness and salvation.

By the late eleventh century and early twelfth century, Western monastic life needed revitalization. In 1098, several monks sought to return to and renew the purity of observances set forth in the *Rule* such as simplicity, humility, poverty, and silence. They created a new monastery at Cîteaux in the south of France. They wanted principally to establish a community of prayer that would nurture an all-consuming desire for and an experience of union with God.

The Cistercian movement initially flourished but gradually declined. By the sixteenth century, a number of movements sought to recover the spiritual ideals of the founders of the Benedictine and Cistercian movements. One architect of reform was Armand de Rancé (1626–1670). So significant were the changes he enacted as abbot of the Abbey of La Trappe in Normandy, France, that reformed Cistercian monks have been called Trappists.

In the mid-twentieth century, a spirit of openness to the world again stirred in the church. A careful interpreter of monastic traditions, Thomas Merton thought deeply about aspects of monastic life in need of renewal. He saw monastic practices as a means to this essential end: restoring awareness of, or mindfulness of, our essential human nature as daughters and sons of God. Merton encouraged changes taking place within his monastery and his order, notably in monastic formation, prayer, contemplation, and engagement with people in the world.

Merton wrote with honesty and transparency about his calling to the monastic life, with its rhythm of liturgy and prayer, work and study. Merton opened a window into a way of living by which all readers—not just monks, nuns, or religious specialists but all persons—might embrace God and allow God to guide them in life-giving ways. Merton's insights, coupled with his inherent gifts as a writer, have contributed to the durability of his writings for people seeking God and wholeness.

MONASTIC FORMATION

Thomas Merton accepted that much of what society offered was good and essential for human life. He acknowledged his attraction to temptations, recreations, and preoccupations "... mercifully provided by society, which enable a man to avoid his own company for twenty-four hours a day." He called such diversions, or *divertissements*, as having one goal,

> ... simply to anesthetize the individual as individual, and to plunge him in the warm, apathetic stupor of a collectivity which, like himself, wishes to remain amused. The bread and circuses ... may be blatant and absurd, or they may assume a hypocritical air of intense seriousness, for instance in a mass movement. Our own society prefers the absurd. But our absurdity is blended with a certain hard-headed, fully determined seriousness with which we devote ourselves to the acquisition of money, to the satisfaction of our appetite for status, and our justification of ourselves as contrasted with the totalitarian iniquity of our opposite number.[2]

Deciding in 1941 to become a Trappist monk at Gethsemani, Merton sought to withdraw from the most widely followed paths of progress and success offered by the modern world. He abandoned a life of independence and self-indulgence for one of growth in inter-dependence and community. In his journal, Merton prayed, "Help me to get away from myself."[3]

Frederick Dunne was abbot of the Abbey of Our Lady of Gethsemani from 1935 until 1948. During Merton's novitiate, Vital Klinski (d. 1966) was master of novices. He had been shaped by the writings of Vital Lehodey and Jean-Baptiste Chautard and by the spirituality of Abbot Dunne. These teachers had a body of doctrine that was consistent, coherent, harmonious, and simple. At the heart of it was the idea that everything that God does or permits is for your good. God cannot will anything that is not for the best.[4]

2. "Notes on a Philosophy of Solitude," *Disputed Questions*, 178–79.

3. *Entering the Silence*, 45, entry for March 12, 1947.

4. Gethsemani tape 161, Track 3, talk "Dom Vital. Technological society," June 5,

Describing his experience at Gethsemani as the "Gospel pure and simple," Merton felt liberation from preoccupation with self and freedom to give himself entirely to God.[5] Merton progressed through the formation process. In early 1947, as he prepared to make solemn profession, Merton acknowledged that life at Gethsemani was not all he wanted it to be. He had dry times in his prayer life. He had difficulty ridding himself of attachments and temptations. He struggled to quiet his active mind and to do everything—reading, study, writing, work—in such a way that it was prayer or preparation for prayer.

Merton was committed to the "pure love of [God] growing in my heart. That is the thing that will make me a Cistercian."[6] Merton called Gethsemani a school of charity in which monks are to prefer nothing to the love of Jesus Christ. Monks learned love in living, not from books.

For twenty of Merton's twenty-seven years as a monk of Gethsemani, James Fox was abbot of the monastery. Shortly after the election of Fox in 1948, Merton began to correspond with him. He wrote one letter on September 10, 1949. At the time, Abbot Fox was in Cîteaux, France, for the annual meeting of representatives of Cistercian houses from around the world. In his letter, Merton made three proposals regarding monastic life that he hoped Gethsemani would adopt.

First, Merton highlighted the need to strengthen theological training at the monastery. He wanted to make Gethsemani a sort of "West Point or Annapolis for Cistercians." Merton explained, "We should really organize our little seminary and make the house a center of really first-class studies in spiritual theology, especially Cistercian Fathers and mystical theology, with stress also on the canon law and other points so necessary for future superiors." Merton proposed erecting a separate building with room for classes and study. In terms of curriculum, Merton wanted to expand the range of studies "*without putting an inhuman burden* on the students."[7]

Second, Merton wanted to create a place for monks (or nuns) to get away for retreats, solitude, and silence. Gethsemani's many acres of woodlands and fields afforded extensive space for prayer and contemplation. Merton proposed building a small chapel near a pond about a twenty

---

1966. Dom is a title originally given to the pope and later to church leaders such as an abbot. It is now a general term of respect.

5. *Entering the Silence*, 145, entry for December 14, 1947.

6. Ibid., 152, entry for December 28, 1947.

7. *SC*, 15–16, Merton's emphasis.

minutes' walk from the monastery buildings. He suggested that it would be especially valuable for those with heavy jobs, guest masters, cellarers, cooks, priors, and even abbots.

Finally, Merton recommended the appointment of a retreat master. According to Merton's plan, groups of five or six monks would recite the offices together. At other times, each monk would have time alone to read and pray. Generally, novices would not go out there, at least at first. Only mature members of the community would have access to the place and would always observe strictest silence. Meals would be frugal and simple.

Abbot Fox was sympathetic to Merton's ideas. He relaxed several restrictions that confined monks to the monastery's enclosed space. As an example, on one occasion he permitted Merton to walk with his publisher James Laughlin outside the enclosure.[8]

Merton welcomed these changes. In his journal, he wrote of a shift in emphasis away from the old, narrow, and rather cold insistence on ascetic exercises to more time in prayer.[9]

During the 1950s, as he continued to do research and to write about monastic history, Merton articulated his ideas on monastic formation and monastic renewal for a wider audience. Discussing words that adorn the gate that opens into the monastic quarters, Merton observed, "written, most appropriately, over the doors of Cistercian monasteries: GOD ALONE. Not contemplation, not action, not works, not rest, not this or that particular thing, but God in everything, God in anything, God in His will, God in other men, God present in his own soul."[10] Elsewhere, Merton differentiated means and the one reason for the monk's existence, as follows:

> not farming, not chanting the psalms, not building beautiful
> monasteries, not wearing a certain kind of costume, not fasting,
> not manual labor, not reading, not meditation, not vigils in the
> night, but only GOD.[11]

8. *Sign of Jonas*, 135, entry for October 31, 1948; hereafter *SJ*. References are from the Image paperback edition.

9. Ibid., 42, entry for March 30, 1947.

10. Merton, introduction to Chautard's *Soul of the Apostolate*, 19; Aprile, *Abbey of Gethsemani*, 207 for a photo.

11. Merton, *Waters of Siloe*, 335.

Years later, when Merton was master of students, Dom Gabriel Sortais, Abbot General of the order, visited the Abbey of Our Lady of Gethsemani from France. Merton served as translator and pleaded that an area be set aside for them in the woods. To everyone's surprise, the Abbot General agreed. On Sundays and feast days, students and novices could withdraw for several hours to relax in a beautiful setting, read Scripture, and pray.

On April 22, 1950, Merton wrote Jean Leclercq, Benedictine monk and scholar of Clervaux in Luxembourg. Merton spelled out his ideas for training monks at Gethsemani. He explained he had helped remodel the vault containing rare books to serve as a library. Books on the Bible, liturgy, and early Christian writings constituted the nucleus of the collection. Merton hoped to use the space to form brothers with competence in spiritual theology. He thought monks should use their time and talents to develop the seed of the word of God in their lives.

When in 1951 Merton became master of students, he could implement changes he had long advocated. He disparaged university-level instruction as conducted in the nineteen forties and fifties in the U.S. He feared such an education would choke monks with an overgrowth of useless research. Believing reading and writing about traditional monastic sources could strengthen their contemplative life, Merton emphasized that by such study, monks "should be able to find expression in channels laid open for it and deepened by familiarity with the Fathers of the church. This is an age that calls for St. Augustines and Leos, Gregorys and Cyrils!"[12]

From 1955 until 1965, Merton was master of novices. In this role, Merton was primarily a teacher. His approach was experiential and participatory. He sought to make each individual aware of his human experience so that it might be a channel for self-knowledge and a way of opening to the life of the Spirit. He taught in a way whereby students and teacher explored what is meaningful, real, and true for oneself and in life.

According to Merton, the role of a teacher was to help students define self authentically and spontaneously in relation to their world and not to impose a prefabricated definition of the world, still less an arbitrary definition of self. Truth-telling was crucial. "If I insist on giving you my

12. *SC*, 20.

truth, and never stop to receive your truth in return, then there can be no truth between us."[13]

To study with Merton must have been like being present with an artist whose thinking and creativity brought clarity and insight through the very process of teaching. In the course of Merton's presentations, questions or flashes of insight could divert him. He explored ideas for the sheer delight of doing so and found the real joy in reading. For Merton, it was not the reading itself that mattered, but the thinking that reading stimulated and that might take the reader far beyond the written word.

As master of novices, Merton introduced a new educational approach that was experiential and participatory rather than catechetical. He covered a staggering breadth of subjects including the rich heritage of monasticism, literature, music, philosophy, science, and the world's religions. "The monastery should by no means be merely an enclave of eccentric and apparently archaic human beings who have rebelled against the world of science . . . We need to form monks of the twentieth century who are capable of embracing in their contemplative awareness not only theology . . . [but also] the modern world of science and revolution."[14]

For one of Merton's novices, Father Michael Casagram OCSO, Merton could threaten and/or cajole. Father Michael understood Merton's goal as one of making the novice aware of one's own human experience so that it might be a channel for self-knowledge and a way of opening to the life of the Spirit.[15]

Tapes and transcripts of Merton's conferences and weekly talks are available at Bellarmine University in Louisville, Kentucky. Patrick F. O'Connell, who teaches in the departments of English and Theology at Gannon University, in Erie, Pennsylvania, has edited and provided extensive notes for some of this material. Four volumes have so far appeared in print. *Cassian and the Fathers* (2005) were talks given immediately after Merton became master of novices. *Pre-Benedictine Monasticism* (2006) were conferences given on Sunday afternoons beginning in February 1963. *An Introduction to Christian Mysticism* (2008) were talks given in

13. "A Letter to Pablo Antonio Cuadra Concerning Giants," *CP*, 383.

14. Merton, *Love and Living*, 217.

15. Lewis, "Merton's Students Remember His Teaching," 99. In 1961, Father Michael entered Holy Cross Trappist Monastery in Berryville, Virginia. In 1963, he transferred to Gethsemani, where he attended Merton's conferences. At the monastery, he has served as printer, tailor, cook, guest master, and vocation director.

early 1961 as part of a new curriculum for young priests. *The Rule of Saint Benedict* (2009) introduced novices to a document that guides the lives of many monks and nuns around the world. A fifth volume, *Monastic Observances*, appeared in 2010.

The Second Vatican Council would encourage religious orders to return to their sources, but Merton was already doing this many years earlier. Reviewing his lecture notes, one discerns his commitment to return to the sources of monastic life and to explore them with intellectual rigor and honesty. Merton's aim was not to create specialists in monastic theology but rather to encourage monks to be in dialogue with their monastic forbears. To this end, he published a compilation of fourth-century monastic wisdom.

> What the [early Christian monks who went to wilderness hermitages] sought most of all was their own true self, in Christ. And in order to do this, they had to reject completely the false, formal self, fabricated under social compulsion in "the world." They sought a way to God that was uncharted and freely chosen, not inherited from others who had mapped it out beforehand. They sought a God whom they alone could find, not one who was "given" in a set, stereotyped form by somebody else. Not that they rejected any of the dogmatic formulas of the Christian faith: they accepted and clung to them in their simplest and most elementary shape. But they were slow . . . to get involved in theological controversy. Their flight to the arid horizons of the desert meant also a refusal to be content with arguments, concepts and technical verbiage.[16]

Merton made an effort to relate the material in a topical manner. He was not interested in the institution of monasticism as such, or in the particularities of various monastic families. Merton focused more on the vision expressed in classic monastic sources and on insights for contemporary monks seeking to apply the material in a manner relevant to their lives.

> If for some reason it were necessary for you to drink a pint of water taken out of the Mississippi River and you could choose where it was to be drawn out of the river—would you take a pint from the source of the river in Minnesota or from the estuary at New Orleans? . . . tradition and spirituality are all the more pure

16. Merton, *Wisdom of the Desert*, 5–6.

and genuine in proportion as they are in contact with the original sources and retain the same content.[17]

Merton highlighted John Cassian (ca. 360–435) as a bridge between the early Christian monks of the wilderness places of Egypt and Palestine and organized community life. Cassian was also a link between Western and Eastern Christian monasticism.

Cassian taught that monks should cling to a spirit of simple faith and avoid a worldly spirit and worldly vices such as anger. Merton stressed the importance in Cassian's writings of the *Pax* (exchange of signs of peace) before Holy Communion as something important for *all* Christians, not just monks. Speaking about the psychological dynamics of those who seek to escape into solitude, Merton cautioned against projecting one's own weaknesses upon others in the community. One should differentiate between "true and false love of solitude." He wondered if "those who want to change their Order or go into solitude . . . are weak in virtue."[18]

Merton insisted that only the perfect can rest assured that they have based their desire for solitude on a true love of contemplation rather than on pusillanimity. Those who go into solitude without seeking holiness or freedom from sin not only fail to get away from their own vices but also become more deeply enmeshed in them. For Merton, it was illusory to think of oneself as being patient and meek when one is not put to the test by adversity. If one has offended someone, one should not go to prayer without forgiveness in one's heart and without attempting to be reconciled with one's sister or brother.

Another key source for Merton was *The Rule of St. Benedict*. Merton explained,

> The important thing is for monks to love the *Rule*, not as a document printed on paper but as a life that should take possession of their inmost hearts. St. Benedict did not call us to the monastery to serve him, but to serve God. We are not here to carry out the prescriptions of men, but to love God. The purpose of the *Rule* is to furnish a framework within which to build the structure of a simple and pure spiritual life, pleasing to God by its perfection of faith, humility, and love. The *Rule* is not an end in itself, but a means to an end, and it is always to be seen in relation to its end. This end is union with God in love, and every line of the *Rule* in-

17. Merton, *Cassian and the Fathers*, 5.
18. Ibid., 177.

dicates that its various prescriptions are given us to show us how
to get rid of self-love and replace it by love of God.[19]

As Merton made clear, monasticism was not an end in itself. He saw
the whole purpose of monastic practices as enabling monks and nuns to
live by love. In his account of the history and practices of Cistercian life,
Merton described love as "the beatitude of heaven."[20] He explained that
formation prescribed by *The Rule of Saint Benedict* has as its goal becoming what we love. "If we love God, in Whose image we were created, we
discover ourselves in Him and we cannot help being happy. . . . If we love
anything else but God, we contradict the image born in our very essence,
and we cannot help being unhappy."[21]

In *Love and Living*, Merton explored what is special about unselfish
love.

> Love is the revelation of our deepest personal meaning, value and
> identity. . . .
> Love, then, is a transforming power of almost mystical in-
> tensity that endows the lovers with qualities and capacities they
> never dreamed they could possess. Where do these qualities come
> from? From the enhancement of life itself, deepened, intensified,
> elevated, strengthened, and spiritualized by love. Love is not only
> a special way of being alive, it is the perfection of life. He who
> loves is more alive and more real than he was when he did not
> love. . . . love seems dangerous: the lover finds in himself too many
> new powers, too many new insights. Life looks completely differ-
> ent to him and all his values change.[22]

Merton corresponded with Father Ronald Roloff, a monk of St.
John's Abbey in Collegeville, Minnesota. In a letter dated September 26,
1962, Merton observed, "as Novice Master of Benedictine monks of the
Cistercian reform, I feel myself obligated to instruct the novices not in a
fanciful 'Cistercian spirituality' but to try as best I can . . . to give them a
monastic formation in elements which are *common* to us all. I have never
found it relevant to stress the fact that we don't have parishes and that you

19. Merton, *Rule of Saint Benedict*, 6.
20. Merton, *Waters of Siloe*, xviii.
21. Ibid., 349.
22. Merton, *Love and Living*, 35–36.

do. . . . You are monks, we are monks. The big thing is, do we really seek God?"

In this letter, Merton addressed a problem with which he had considerable personal experience. He desired to recover the depths of silence, solitude, prayer, and contemplation. Failure at Gethsemani to achieve fully these marks of early Cistercian life led to times when Merton was not quite at peace with his monastic home. He felt that such a problem "could be obviated to some extent if our monastic families allowed more latitude for different kinds of solution within their own framework."[23]

In another letter to Roloff, dated October 21, 1962, Merton dealt with changes taking place in his own monastery as well as with circumstances of nuns at St. Benedict's Monastery, near Collegeville in St Joseph, Minnesota. He believed they had too heavy a load of work and other duties. Merton expressed concern that the Cistercian lifestyle, "even with its claims to contemplation is basically an active life . . . in the sense that a great deal goes on in the monastery, including a great deal of work, profitable work, highly organized and pushed hard. . . ." He concluded, "There is overwork here [at Gethsemani] as well as anywhere else. We lose people who go into work too deeply. . . . A very top-heavy schedule full of extra offices and community exercises has been considerably alleviated . . . [yet] a lot of people have taken advantage of this leeway to waste time diddling around . . . spending hours shaving, shining their shoes, standing around and watching the clouds go by."[24]

Monks and nuns must support themselves. In the case of Gethsemani, the Abbey now sells products for which it is justly renowned, notably cheese and fruitcake.

Merton was concerned about the effects of the business side of monastic life. At Gethsemani, sales boomed. Monks worked overtime. Merton felt keenly the hypocrisy of the situation. It was a fantasy to hold that in the world was "power, pleasure, and popularity" while in the monastery was "the cross." For Merton, all the monks were doing was "vegetate and dream and sell cheese and get involved in petty projects."[25]

In part because he received an inordinate number of teaching and writing assignments, Merton often complained that he was making little

23. *SC*, 147–48, Merton's emphasis.
24. *SC*, 150–51.
25. *SS*, 351, entry for December 5, 1959.

or no progress in his practice of prayer and contemplation. He once mused, "Sick of writing, sick of letters, sick of self-expression. . . . Even if everything else is noise, I can be silent within my own house. Every time I go to Chapter such ties as still bind me to Gethsemani are weakened still more."[26]

Merton wanted more time for solitude and silence. He proposed becoming a hermit. He explored transferring to another monastery. Among options were the Camoldolese, who offer a hermit tradition within the Benedictine family of monastic communities. Merton explored the Carthusians. Rather than *The Rule of Saint Benedict*, the Carthusians follow the *Statutes*, compiled in the twelfth century by Saint Guigo, the fifth prior of la Grande Chartreuse, the Great Charterhouse.

Merton considered transferring to another Benedictine monastery. He also explored joining *Our Lady of the Resurrection,* an experimental community led by Gregory Lemercier in Cuernavaca, Mexico, or a religious group associated with liberation theology located on an island in Lake Nicaragua. Ernesto Cardenal (Brother Lawrence), poet and leader at Solentiname, developed his vision for the community when he was a novice under Merton's tutelage at Gethsemani.

During the Second Vatican Council, Merton thought the task of bringing the church into the twentieth century, or *aggiornamento,* should not be restricted to bishops, cardinals, or the papacy. He welcomed new experiments as "signs of genuine life and apostolic renewal, in vital contact with the world and in sympathy for the secular spirit of the time." As "familiar monastic structures tend in fact to frustrate some of the deep aims of the monastic vocation," Merton encouraged a general movement in favor of more contemplative practices such as praying scripture and thoughtful study of monastic texts. In fact, he tended to think that "a more simple and authentic form of monastic life" might be found in "new monastic communities" where monks and nuns pray not only for themselves, but also for the life of the world.[27]

Merton believed the social aspect of the monastic life was important. Notably, concern for the world should grow out of a deep personal awareness of God's love for humanity in Christ, and a response of praise and adoration. Monks and nuns had all too often forgotten this area. Merton

26. SS, 338–39, entry for November 2, 1959.

27. *Monastic Journey,* 213–17.

did not overemphasize its importance to the detriment of the spirit of prayer and solitude. If, for example, Cistercians overdo active work, they merely imitate what can be done better by members of other orders, the secular clergy, or laity.

In another letter to Roloff, dated November 13, 1962, Merton elaborated his thinking about monastic formation. Novices, both those who become choir monks and those who eventually go on to the priesthood, should have at least six years of training, three years in the novitiate followed by three years of courses. According to Merton's "pet plan," during the first two years of their novitiate, monks would study the Bible, monastic history, early Christian thought, and one of the Biblical languages, Hebrew or Greek. In a third year of training, before taking final vows, monks would study philosophy and a sort of *lectio divina* of texts from St. Anselm, St. Augustine, Boethius, and other writers.

Sacred reading, in Latin *lectio divina*, is a key Benedictine practice. There is no single method for it. Rather, one makes time each day in personal interaction with sacred Scripture and a variety of other readings. "A word or passage may speak to the praying person, moving from image to image, flowing from thought to feeling. It may set a mood for the day or bring the calming that takes one into the night. It is the transforming presence of God. . . ."[28]

Merton believed novices needed more time for meditation on the Bible than for an overloaded schedule of formal classes. These would take only a little time away from manual labor but allow about two hours after the night office and before Prime for *lectio divina*. "Three years of that (after the novitiate) will really create a taste for the contemplative life in its simple monastic form."[29]

In 1967, at the request of Dom John Morson, English Definitor or counselor in Rome, Merton returned to the matter of formation of monks in monastic theology. Merton detailed guiding principles regarding the formation of modern Cistercian monks. Merton's wish list included areas in which Merton believed candidates were poorly prepared, such as appreciation of the arts and their relevance to the spiritual life of a monk. Merton called for the following,

28. Sutera, *Work of God*, 99.

29. *SC*, 156.

1. instruction in the disciplines of an ascetic life and in the means provided by the Cistercian order to respond fully and intelligently and generously to the calling of a monk;

2. formation that does not merely transmit factual information but rather instills wisdom;

3. introduction to the humanities;

4. training in contemplative theology that included Christian and non-Christian traditions;

5. study of comparative religion with an opening to psychiatry;

6. theological education that is deeply and thoroughly Biblical and informed by early Christian writers;

7. understanding of contemporary problems and their background or history; among the great problems of our time, Merton highlighted peace and war, civil rights, and the responsibilities of rich nations towards the poor; and

8. study of science and technology.

In his lectures to novices and priests in formation, Merton covered a staggering breadth of subjects, including the rich heritage of monasticism, literature, music, philosophy, science, and world religions. Convinced the monastery should not be an enclave of eccentric or archaic human beings who have rebelled against the world, Merton sought to form monks for the twentieth century. In their practice, they should embrace not only the Mystery of Christ, but also the modern world of science, technology, and revolution.

As mentor of novices and priests, Merton formed monks in the traditions of Christian monasticism. He encouraged those in his charge and others to embrace not only the classical understandings of the Mystery of Christ, but also the possibilities of new wisdom offered by non-Christian traditions and by the modern world of science and revolution. Merton insisted that a monastery should not be a ghetto. Having discovered their true selves, monks could use their spiritual liberty to forge new pathways to God and "to build, on earth, the Kingdom of God."[30]

In September 1968, Merton gave talks to the nuns at the Monastery of the Precious Blood in Eagle River, Alaska. He spoke of the education of

30. Ibid., 24.

a monastic person as "the education of the heart." He stated that novitiate formation should be "the formation of the heart to know God." Merton saw this idea in Judaism and Sufism as well as in Christianity. "It is your living self that is an act of constant love for God and this inmost secret of man is that by which he contemplates God, it is the secret of man in God himself."[31]

Merton argued that the goal of monastic formation is to acquire a heart that knows God, not just a heart that loves God or communes with God but one that knows God. Merton's basic understanding was that monastic living should enable people to ground themselves in God's love. He saw his own destiny in life as living towards a final integration. This would be a total, complete, and unconditional yes to God. For Merton, the most important means to enter into the full mystery of life in God was prayer.

Through his formation of monks at Gethsemani and his wider contributions, Merton was able to come to the heart of traditional monastic literature. He made accessible this body of teaching for the monks and nuns of his day, and for an ever-widening audience.

MERTON ON PRAYER

Prayer, contemplation, and meditation dominated Merton's twenty-seven years as a monk of the Abbey of Our Lady of Gethsemani. Merton chanted in the choir. He recited liturgical prayers. He prayed Scripture. He practiced vocal prayer. He meditated. We have come to call this practice by a more popular word, contemplation.

Merton understood prayer as something best done in silence. Listening prayer, which he called meditation, was Merton's preferred practice at Gethsemani. In early 1949, on a "day of recollection" before his ordination as a priest, Merton described his ideal in the priesthood. "I ask Jesus to make me a purely contemplative priest. He has plenty of active workers, missionaries, preachers, spiritual directors, masters of novices, etc. But He has so few who are concerned with Him alone, in simplicity, silence, recollection and constant prayer."[32]

Merton explained his life of prayer through correspondence and other writings. In a letter to Abbot Fox, Merton offered a picture of a

31. "The Life that Unifies," in Bochen, *Thomas Merton, Essential Writings*, 163.

32. *SC*, 11, letter dated Spring, 1949.

week-long, private retreat that he had undertaken. Merton set aside his mornings for quiet work. He organized things in the vault and typed lecture notes. After the noonday meal, Merton spent three and a half hours of solid prayer in solitude. He took a book along but read very little. Most of the time Merton simply entered into the presence of God and stayed quiet, letting the silence sink in. Sometimes, the only noise was the sound of a tractor on the farm.

Solitary times of silence and meditation empowered Merton to detach himself from things going on in the community. The rhythm of choral prayer sometimes had had an effect opposite to the intent of his order's founders. Merton explained, "When I try to make my faculties act in order to intensify my union with God a sense of anxiety, frustration and discomfort overpowers me and if I keep on trying I feel spiritually . . . nauseated." However, on silent retreat, Merton seemed able simply to rest and let God act. "When I was out there praying alone it came to me that surely in this solitary prayer above all else I was *giving myself to God*. I have never come so close to the conviction that for once I really belonged completely to Him."

After several days without any distractions, Merton felt he was able to return to the community with renewed confidence and trust in God. From this experience, Merton drew three conclusions. He needed regular periods away from the community. At the same time, he expressed deeper appreciation for community life. Finally, he recognized that solitude was essential for his self-giving to God.[33]

Merton provided a window into his life of prayer and meditation in his correspondence. In a letter dated August 28, 1949, Merton wrote Sister Thérèse Lentfoehr. He stressed taking time daily for meditation and prayer. He cautioned against thinking about anything in particular, but relaxing in the presence of God.[34]

In a book published in 1949, *Seeds of Contemplation*, Merton offered readers a collection of unconnected and rather compressed reflections about things he believed people most needed to know: the interior life and contemplation. From his own experience, Merton wrote of contemplation as springing from the love of God. He stressed that every moment and every event of every person's life on earth has spiritual meaning. The chief

---

33. Ibid., 27, letter of October 7, 1951 to Abbot Fox, Merton's emphasis.

34. *RJ*, 195.

concern of everyone should not be to find pleasure, success, health, life, money, rest, or even things like virtue and wisdom. In all that happens, one's chief desire and one's joy should be to know this: "Here is the thing that God has willed for me. In this His love is found, and in accepting this I can give back His love to Him and give myself with it to Him, and grow up in His will to contemplation, which is life everlasting."[35]

Merton was convinced that human life achieves fulfillment when a person discovers herself or himself as coming from God, belonging to God, and bearing God's image and likeness in the world. Merton observed, "to be a saint means to be myself. Therefore the problem of sanctity and salvation is in fact the problem of finding out who I am and of discovering my true self."[36]

When the first copy of *Seeds of Contemplation* arrived at the monastery, Merton expressed disappointment in his journal. "It lacks warmth and human affection. . . . The book is cold and cerebral."[37] Merton felt it did little good trying to teach people about the love of God without emphasizing Christ more. A slightly revised edition appeared a few months later. Twelve years later, Merton published major revisions with new material. This book, *New Seeds of Contemplation*, became Merton's most popular work on the theme of contemplation.

In this later work, Merton claimed that contemplation is the highest expression of a person's intellectual and spiritual life. "It is that life itself, fully awake, fully active, fully aware that it is alive. It is spiritual wonder. . . . It is gratitude for life, for awareness and for being. It is a vivid realization of the fact that life and being in us proceed from an invisible, transcendent and infinitely abundant Source. Contemplation is, above all, awareness of the reality of that Source."[38]

In "A Body of Broken Bones," a chapter in both *Seeds of Contemplation* and *New Seeds of Contemplation*, Merton cautioned against praying or meditating simply because one likes to be alone. One prays to find one's identity in the Mystical Christ. As one meditates, one discovers that Christianity is not merely a doctrine or a system of beliefs but Christ living in us and uniting us to God and to others. To seek God and to come

35. *Seeds of Contemplation*, 9.

36. Ibid., 16.

37. *Entering the Silence*, 287, entry for March 6, 1949; *SJ*, 166.

38. *NSC*, 1.

into consciousness that God is already there, one experiences God's love. Hence, willing to love is not central to prayer, or meditation. Rather, one is to know, in faith, that he or she is beloved of God. By faith, a person believes that God loves all of us, however unworthy we may think we are. God not only loves Thomas Merton, but also all other persons. For Merton, claiming these truths was the outcome of the journey or struggle against self-hatred, triumphalism, and fanaticism.

> If you regard contemplation principally as a means to escape from the miseries of human life, as a withdrawal from the anguish and the suffering of this struggle for reunion with other men in the charity of Christ, you do not know what contemplation is and you will never find God in your contemplation. For it is precisely in the recovery of our union with our brothers in Christ that we discover God and know Him, for then His life begins to penetrate our souls and His love possesses our faculties and we are able to find out Who He is from the experience of His mercy, liberating us from the prison of self-concern.[39]

Merton entitled the final chapter, new to *New Seeds of Contemplation*, "The General Dance." He described moving beyond the external self, which seems to be real, to one's true self. "It is this inner self that is taken up into the mystery of Christ, by His love, by the Holy Spirit, so that in secret we live 'in Christ' . . . if we could let go of our own obsession with what we think is the meaning of it all, we might be able to hear His call and follow Him in His mysterious, cosmic dance."[40]

One of Merton's correspondents was Abdul Aziz, a Sufi Muslim who lived in Karachi, Pakistan. He worked in government service and was a Sufi, a stream of Islam that seeks to find divine love and knowledge through direct personal experience of the Holy. Sufi Muslims also have a strong devotion to the person of Jesus.

Aziz studied Christian sources. He read Merton's *Ascent to Truth*, a study of the mystical theology of St. John of the Cross. Aziz was favorably impressed.

In 1959, Aziz met Louis Massignon (1883–1962), a French specialist in Islamic studies. Aziz asked him for the name and address of a genuine

39. Ibid., 78.
40. Ibid., 295–96.

Christian saint and contemplative mystic. Massignon provided Merton's contact information.

Encouraged by Massignon, Aziz wrote to Merton in 1960. A lively correspondence developed through the 1960s. Aziz and Merton exchanged books and ideas. Aziz characterized his correspondence with Merton as based on "'poverty of spirit,' being humble to learn from each other, without display of any scholarship or erudition."[41] In a letter dated January 2, 1966, Merton explained that he had a very simple way of prayer centered entirely on attention to the presence of God, God's will, and God's love. He explained that his way of prayer grew from faith by which alone people can know the presence of God. Merton drew comparisons with meditative practices of Muslims, as follows:

> One might say this gives my meditation the character described by the Prophet as "being before God as if you saw Him." Yet it does not mean imagining anything or conceiving a precise image of God, for to my mind this would be a kind of idolatry. On the contrary, it is a matter of adoring Him as invisible and infinitely beyond our comprehension, and realizing Him as all. My prayer tends very much toward what you call *fana*. There is in my heart this great thirst to recognize totally the nothingness of all that is not God. My prayer is then a kind of praise rising up out of the center of Nothing and Silence. If I am still present "myself" this I recognize as an obstacle about which I can do nothing unless He Himself removes the obstacle. If He wills He can then make the Nothingness into a total clarity. If He does not will, then the Nothingness seems to itself to be an object and remains an obstacle. Such is my ordinary way of prayer, or meditation. It is not "thinking about" anything, but a direct seeking of the Face of the Invisible, which cannot be found unless we become lost in Him who is Invisible. I do not ordinarily write about such things and I ask you therefore to be discreet about it. But I write this as a testimony of confidence and friendship.

Merton closed by affirming his appreciation of Sufism and his offer of a prayer relation with Aziz during Ramadan, a month of fasting and prayer in the Islamic calendar. Merton invited Aziz to join him in adoration of God and prayer for the world, which Merton characterized as in great

41. Apel, *Signs of Peace*, 14.

trouble and confusion. He stated that he appreciated Aziz's prayers for him and asked God to bless Aziz and give him peace.[42]

Merton described his practice as something more than a way to reach out to God. His ultimate goal was to offer "a kind of praise" that could lead to direct, authentic union of the simple light of God with the humility of his own movement towards the Holy One. For that reason, he chafed at formal prayers that sometimes made it impossible for him to experience God. In an entry for April 16, 1963, Merton wrote,

> It is Easter Tuesday. The less said about the Easter celebration the better. Pomposity, phoniness, display, ultra-serious, stupid. Interminable pontifical mummering, purple zucchetto, long train, Mexican novice as train bearer . . . all of course for the "glory of God." The Church was morally, spiritually stifling with solemn, unbreathable unrealities.[43]

In 1963, Merton responded to questions put to him by high school students who, he noted to his Louisville friend Mrs. Tommie O'Callaghan, "want me to write essays for them." For Merton, the contemplative life meant "the search for truth and for God. It means finding the true significance of my life and my right place in God's creation."

Merton explained that there are many ways to God. He chose and accepted, as God's will for himself, his Catholic faith, his monastic calling, and his calling as a writer. Merton acknowledged that others who really seek the truth might come to understand reality elsewhere and by some other way of life. As for himself, after he made his decision to become a monk, he never had the slightest desire to be anything else, though this would be seriously tested in his relationship with a student nurse and in his search for an even more solitary life than was generally possible at Gethsemani.

Merton addressed a question about poetry that the students may have asked. Why did he write poetry? He explained that at one time he thought he ought to give up writing poetry because it might not be compatible with the life of a monk. Merton continued: "I don't think this any

---

42. *HGL*, 63–64, Merton's emphasis. Merton wrote the letter during the month of Ramadan.

43. *Turning toward the World*, 313, hereafter, *TTW*.

more. . . . A poem is for me the expression of an inner poetic experience, and what matters is the experience, more than the poem itself."[44]

In his writing about prayer, contemplation, and the true self, Merton eloquently expressed what contemplation meant for him and what contemplation can mean for others. In a statement made on November 10, 1963, concerning the establishment of the Thomas Merton Studies Center at Bellarmine University, Merton summarized, "whatever I may have written, I think it all can be reduced in the end to this one root truth: that God calls human persons to union with Himself and with one another in Christ . . ." Merton noted that he had written about interracial justice or nuclear weapons because these issues were terribly relevant to this one great truth: "man is called to live as a son of God. Man must respond to this call to live in peace with all his brothers in the One Christ."[45]

Through solitude and silence, Merton discovered God. Sharing his path, Merton has shown us a way to reach the end for which God has created all persons. Merton was aware that many people do not know that they are beloved of God. He believed that life can be richer and fuller by virtue of knowing God's light, truth, and love, and that it is possible to attain union with God in Christ. He offered people pathways to live well on earth, not simply as a way to get credits for life at some future time in heaven, but with integrity in the here and now. He saw the paths of solitude and meditation as important elements of life, under-appreciated by some monastics and neglected by many people in the world at large.

OPENNESS TO WIDER SOCIETY

Merton initially experienced Gethsemani as a place of escape or flight from the world. Over time, Merton deepened his engagement with the world. Certain of God's creative and dynamic intervention in his life, Merton understood that this was true not simply for monks and nuns, but for everyone. He came to understand the contemplative life as available to every person. Every person who is fully active, alive, awake, and aware can know God as God really is. Knowing God, one discovers God at the core of one's being. Such knowledge is to enjoy unity with God in perfect love and freedom.

44. *RJ*, 89–90, circular letter to friends, 1963.
45. Cited by Higgins, *Thomas Merton on Prayer*, 14.

In 1948, Merton published a pamphlet entitled *What Is Contemplation?* He wrote, "The seeds of this perfect life [contemplation] are planted in *every* Christian soul at Baptism. But seeds must grow and develop before you reap the harvest." Merton expressed concern about a Christian philosophy known as Quietism, a form of mysticism that insists on passivity as a condition of perfection. Proscribed as heretical during the seventeenth century, quietists, as described by Merton, were people who are "empty . . . of all love and all knowledge and remain inert in a kind of spiritual vacuum." In contrast with such selfishness, pure contemplatives let go of everything and, trusting God, allow the brightness of Jesus to shine in their lives.[46]

In *Seeds of Contemplation*, published the following year, Merton counseled that anyone could lead a contemplative life in pursuit of the love of God because God is active every moment and in every event of every person. One claims this reality not by flight to a monastic setting. Rather, virtually any space in one's home setting will do. Anyone can claim this reality by finding time to unfetter self from the world.

Merton urged that a contemplative must be clear about her or his motivation. One should not try to escape from this world merely by leaving the city or hiding oneself in solitude. Nor should one withdraw to the quiet places of our lives to escape others. Nor should a monk, nun, or retreatant go to the monastery because it is there that one can be "holier than thou."

Anywhere and anytime, one can turn to God in prayer. Anywhere and anytime, one can find time and place to be alone with God. One should never go withdraw to quiet places of retreat to escape people but rather to find them. But this is only a secondary end. "[I]t is dangerous to go into solitude merely because you happen to like to be alone. . . . [W]e have to remember that we look for solitude in order to grow there in love for God and in love for other men. The one end that includes all others is the love of God. The truest solitude is not something outside you, not an absence of men or of sound around you: it is an abyss opening up in the centre of your own soul. And this abyss of interior solitude is created by a hunger that will never be satisfied with any created thing."[47]

46. *What Is Contemplation?* 17, 71–77, my emphasis.
47. *Seeds of Contemplation*, 48–49; "Learn To Be Alone," NSC, 80–81.

In 1948, Merton served as translator for Gabriel Sortais OCSO. Sortais was at the time Abbot of Bellefontaine in France and had come to Gethsemani to preside over the election of the new abbot James Fox. Sortais later became Abbot General of the Cistercian order. Merton accompanied Sortais to Louisville along with Charles I. Dawson, onetime Kentucky Attorney General and an unsuccessful candidate for the U.S. Senate in 1950. A sense of compassion stirred within Merton. Meeting the "wicked world" face to face, Merton found that it was not so evil after all. Though he did react negatively to the advertising he witnessed, Merton realized "for the first time in my life how good are all the people in the world and how much value they have in the sight of God."[48]

In *Sign of Jonas*, published in 1953, Merton wrote about looking explicitly for God. He sounded a cautionary note that later became a loud refrain, especially in his journals and letters. He experienced monastic life as too busy. This made it difficult for him to maintain a healthy balance between contemplation and the active life. "Those who love God should attempt to preserve or create an atmosphere in which He can be found. Christians should have quiet homes. Throw out television. . . . Radios useless. . . . Maybe even form small agrarian communities. . . ."[49]

In *Monastic Peace* (1958), Merton identified as a true mark of being a monk or nun, "really to know Christ living in us. . . . The true contemplative life is simply a deep penetration and understanding of the ordinary Christian life . . . . God living in us!" Merton highlighted major signs of aptitude for the monastic life. Indicators included openness to *metanoia*, a complete change of heart and conversion of life, a twofold act of turning from sin and towards Christ; seeking and finding God in inchoate and mysterious ways; self renunciation; willingness to be guided and governed by the common will; public and private meditative prayer; spiritual poverty; normal physical and mental health.[50]

In 1958, on monastery business in Louisville, Kentucky, Merton stood at the corner of Fourth and Walnut (now Fourth and Muhammad Ali) and awakened to his love of people. Describing this moment of revelation, Merton wrote,

48. *SJ*, 97–98.

49. *SJ*, 60, 301–2.

50. "Monastic Peace," reprinted in *Monastic Journey*, 73, 109, 114–17.

I have the immense joy of being *man*, a member of a race in which God Himself became incarnate. As if the sorrows and stupidities of the human condition could overwhelm me, now I realize what we all are. And if only everybody could realize this! But it cannot be explained. There is no way of telling people that they are all walking around shining like the sun.[51]

Merton had come to believe that many monastic practices interfered with what he saw as most essential, namely union with God and neighbor on a deeply spiritual basis. However, the Louisville experience did not lead Merton to disparage or reject the monastic institution as such. It did strengthen his commitment to the renewal of monasticism and to the role monastic practices could play in the lives of lay solitaries "of the sort most remote from cloistered life, like Thoreau or Emily Dickinson," who are called not to leave society, but to renounce many of its diversions.[52]

Subsequently, Merton's writings on monastic renewal reflected an increasing openness to the world. Writing in 1963 for the Japanese translation of *The Seven Storey Mountain*, Merton insisted, "The monastery is not an 'escape' from the world. On the contrary, by being in the monastery I take my true part in all the struggles and sufferings of the world."[53]

Sister Elaine M. Bane wrote to the Novice Master at Gethsemani on behalf of a small band of Franciscan Sisters of Allegany, New York, asking for suggestions on orienting the sisters from an active to a contemplative life. Merton responded as follows,

Remember that in the enclosed and solitary life, your solitude itself will do an immense amount for you. The sisters need not strain and struggle and worry too much about "degrees" of prayer. The great thing is to be emptied out, to taste and see that the Lord is sweet, and to learn the way of abandonment and peace. Littleness is the chief characteristic of the solitary. . . . Silence is a rare luxury in the modern world, and not everyone can stand it: but it has inestimable value, that cannot be purchased with any amount of money or power or intelligence. The gift to be silent and simple with the Lord is a treasure . . .[54]

51. *Conjectures of a Guilty Bystander* 140 (157), Merton's emphasis. Hereafter *CGB*. Paperback in parentheses.

52. "Notes on a Philosophy of Solitude," *Disputed Questions*, 177, 182.

53. "*Honorable Reader*," 65.

54. *SC*, 145, letter dated July 4, 1962; *Cold War Letters*, 163.

Merton wanted not only monks, but also every Christian to develop a rhythm of action and contemplation. Whether engaged in prayer, everyday work life, or dialogue with others, Merton had one goal in view, namely *agape*, or Godly love. In one passage, he wrote, "*agonia* (and peace!) . . . I see one central option for me: to let go of all that seems to suggest getting somewhere, being someone, having a name and a voice, following a policy and directing people in 'my' ways. What matters is to *love*, to be in one place in silence . . . not try to have a public identity." Merton concluded, "Life is very funny!"[55]

Given that a loving relationship with a woman was about to erupt in his life, Merton's description of life as funny is remarkably ironic. At the same time, Merton's comment reflects his continued struggle to find balance in life. Benedictine scholar Jean Leclercq characterizes Merton as a coincidence of opposites, reconciling the active and contemplative, the ordinary and the sacred, a literary career with a monastic life centered on silence, stillness, and solitude.[56]

While few Christians are inclined to join a traditional monastic order, many ordinary people have adapted and adopted monastic practices in their daily living. In a succession of publications, Merton expressed his growing understanding that the majority of people can participate in a contemplative way of living while serving as a good street sweeper, bartender, or other call.[57]

Initially, Merton worried that life outside the monastery was not entirely conducive for people to enter into the experience of meditation and prayer. However, he gradually modified his perspective on lay contemplatives. Two titles grew out of pamphlets, articles, and manuscripts written over a number of years on the theme: *Contemplation in a World of Action* (1973) and *The Inner Experience* (2003). Both appeared after Merton's death, and in both, Merton overcame reservations he may have held concerning possibilities for lay people to adapt monastic practices and form new kinds of monastic communities.

In *The Inner Experience*, which appeared in installments in *Cistercian Studies Quarterly* in 1983 and 1984, Merton celebrated the growth of communities and individual men and women who live in every way

---

55. *Learning to Love*, 13–15, entry for January 29, 1966.

56. Leclercq, "A Coincidence of Opposites," in Hart, *Legacy of Thomas Merton*, 157–70.

57. Merton, *No Man Is an Island*, 67.

as ordinary people in the world. Merton called such lay people quasi-contemplatives, solitaries, or hidden contemplatives. Dedicated to God, they have focused all their lives upon a contemplative center. Merton considered it "strange that contemplative monasteries are content simply to receive individuals as retreatants, encourage them to receive frequent Communion and make the Way of the Cross, but do not do more to form groups . . . [to] help and support one another. One thinks . . . of a kind of contemplative Third Order."[58]

Merton highlighted the disciples of Charles de Foucauld (1858–1916), whose writings and martyrdom in Algeria inspired the founding of the Little Brothers of Jesus and Little Sisters of Jesus, and Jules Monchanin (1895–1957) a French priest who took the name of Parana Anandan Aruba. With Henri le Saux (1910–1973), or Abhishiktananda, Monchanin founded the Shantivanam ashram near Tiruchirapali, South India.

With these models in mind, Merton urged that lay contemplatives should not withdraw and meditate while others struggle to make a living. Lay contemplatives must not forget the world, with its political or cultural upheavals, and sit absorbed in prayer while bombers swarm in the air above. "Most of the trouble with the contemplative life today comes from this purely negative approach." While turning within to an extent, lay contemplatives fuse their creative love with God's love to fulfill their true vocation to divinity as sons and daughters of God.[59]

Merton encouraged small contemplative communities to explore opportunities to dialogue with members of the surrounding society while preserving their life of prayer.[60] For Merton, such openness to the world entailed a willingness to speak out on issues like war and the threat of nuclear annihilation, and to relate to adherents of other religions.

In a Catholic publication called *America*, Merton had reviewed favorably Aelred Graham's book *Zen Catholicism*. In a letter to Graham, Merton acknowledged that Zen had become something of a fad in the United States. However, Merton saw Zen as "actually a life-saver for many people, here at the exhausted end of an era in which thinking has been

58. *Inner Experience*, 136–37. See 64 for "hidden contemplatives," a phrase that replaced "quasi contemplatives" in the earlier version, *What Is Contemplation?* Shannon, *Thomas Merton's Dark Path*, 221–22.

59. Ibid., 147, 149.

60. *SC*, 165, letter of April 5, 1963 to Archbishop Paul Philippe, then Secretary of the Vatican's Sacred Congregation for Religious.

dominated by Cartesianism, Kant and so on ... We have to *be* real, not just mean to be. And the paradox is of course that we *are*: and we try to make our being real ... through useless mental gyrations."[61]

Merton corresponded with members of a circle who frequented the home of his friends Jacques and Raissa Maritain. Pieter Van der Meer de Walcheren and his wife were members of this group. They had wanted to become Benedictines and got permission to join Dutch monasteries. After a while of living as a nun, Pieter Van der Meer's wife wanted to return to married life and opted to leave. Church law required Pieter's departure from his monastery as well. After his wife died, Pieter returned to the Benedictines in Oosterhout, Netherlands. In a letter to him, Merton wrote on July 28, 1961,

> The world has changed much since my entry into the monastery. It is no longer the society which I lately know, the world of my youth, of my parents. I think of myself as an exile two times, three times over. The way toward the Homeland becomes more and more obscure. As I look back over the stages which were once more clear, I see that we are all on the right road, and though it be night, it is a saving one.[62]

Pieter became quite the focal point of gatherings similar to those envisioned by Merton. Some of his journals have appeared in French translation. Pieter and his wife produced two monastics: one son became a Benedictine monk, and their daughter a Benedictine nun. The daughter eventually was part of a monastic "experiment" of living monastic life in "the heart of the city" rather than in some quiet remote and undisturbed place in the countryside. By then an elderly monk, Pieter heartily endorsed this endeavor.[63]

For Merton, a monk's primary responsibility was to allow himself or herself to deepen his or her own self-understanding in freedom, integrity, and love. Without this foundation, one who tries to act and do things for others or for the world will not have anything to give others.

Merton understood prayer and action as interrelated. He saw both as essential in enabling people to explore new life ways. He thought that

61. Ibid., 167, letter dated April 24, 1963, Merton's emphasis. For the review, "Zen: Sense and Sensibility," *America* 108 (May 25, 1963) 752–54.

62. *SC*, 139–40.

63. Sister Helen Rolfson, email dated August 13, 2008. Sister Rolfson teaches monastic spirituality at the College of Saint Benedict and Saint John's University in Minnesota.

prayer should be an expression of a deep and grace-inspired desire for newness of life and an orientation toward a future rather than a blind attachment to what is familiar or safe. While one's ultimate hopes for a decent new world in which there will not be injustice, poverty, or war may never be realized fully on earth, Merton encouraged people to strive to achieve these ideals in compassion and love.

REFLECTIONS

Merton's understanding of monastic practice was never static. In some of his early writings, Merton to some extent idealized Gethsemani as a fortress of silence. This was, of course, an objective of the Cistercian founders. They wanted to create communities of prayer and, ideally, to nurture an all-consuming desire for God and union with God. Merton experienced the peace of union with God at Gethsemani and claimed "the sweet savor of liberty."[64]

Whatever the circumstances that led Merton to Gethsemani—his wild youth, his sexual adventures as a young person, his concern about war, his horror at a world marked by genocide and other evils—withdrawal from society freed him to be open to a new world of possibility for embracing and serving others. By the time of his Louisville experience in 1958, Merton had resolved his own personal identity struggles and was at peace with his sense of calling in the church and the world.

In November 1960, E. Glenn Hinson brought church history students to the monastery as part of a course on medieval Christianity. In an interview, Hinson recalled that Merton, looking like any farmer, greeted the group wearing his customary monastery denim work clothes. Someone asked what value there is in the monastic life. Merton explained, "It is my vocation to pray," a perspective that I too have heard on monastic retreats.[65]

On another occasion, Merton characterized his particular calling in the church and in the world as that of a "solitary explorer who, instead of jumping on all the latest bandwagons at once, is bound to search the existential depths of faith in its silences, its ambiguities, and in those

64. Title of the final chapter of *SSM*.

65. Interview with Hinson, August 20, 2002; *TTW*, 109, 175 entries for April 18, 1961 and October 30, 1961.

certainties which lie deeper than the bottom of anxiety." He thought of himself as "a very strange kind of person, a marginal person, because the monk in the modern world is no longer an established person with an established place in society." From his vantage point, on the fringe of society, Merton believed he could contribute to a deepened, fundamental human experience.[66]

Merton had come to understand his calling in an entirely new way. God had called him to the monastic journey not to escape from the world but to engage the world at the deepest level, in suffering and transformation. Prayer, contemplation, and other monastic practices enabled him to deepen his sense of participation in the Divine Nature, to become one with the God of infinite love and with others, and thereby to fulfill a role of nurturing others.

Many of Merton's students went on to positions of responsibility within and beyond the order. As an example, John Eudes Bamberger, a psychiatrist, was a student of Merton from 1952–1955. After his ordination in 1956, he worked with Merton in screening applicants to the abbey. He served as abbot of the Abbey of the Genesee in upstate New York from 1971 until 2001. Since returning from a term as superior in the Philippines, he has served as editor of *Cistercian Studies Quarterly*. He lives in a hermitage at the Abbey of the Genesee.

Bamberger characterized Merton as "a prophet to his Order and to his time."[67] In this role, Merton was not a utopian dreamer. He did not just want people to claim their true selves. Through his monastic calling, especially through his teaching, his publications, his correspondence, and his friendship with countless people, Merton helped make monastic innovation possible.

Merton inspired many of his brothers at Gethsemani and throughout the Cistercian order, as well as people around the world, to live with a more contemplative and spiritual grounding. As an example, for Natalie Smith, the start of her "love affair with Trappist monasticism" began when, spiritually starved, she went to a library and perused the pages of the *Catholic Encyclopedia*. She saw the face of a man that struck her as the embodiment of everything that she ever wanted to become in Christ. In this photograph, she saw someone who embodied many virtues at once: extreme sweetness, kindness, strength, love, manliness, courage, sensitiv-

66. Merton, *Faith and Violence*, 213; *Asian Journal*, 305.

67. Bamberger, *Thomas Merton, Prophet of Renewal*, 15.

ity, deep love, serenity, and understanding. "I had never seen Christ in anyone in my life who had even come close to the Christ-like beauty of this man in the picture. I guess you could say that in him I truly saw Christ incarnate. In his face I saw elements of everything that I ever hoped to become on my journey toward Christ."[68]

Thus began Smith's journey. The picture turned out to be that of Thomas Merton. At the time, Smith had never read any of his writings. She began to read Merton's books, as well as writings by some of Merton's former students, including Basil Pennington OCSO. He became her spiritual director. Trappist monks came to represent the arms that Christ has used to embrace her and to give her life.

Smith tries to live monastic spirituality as best as she can as an ordinary person. She encourages others to follow this path as cofounder of the Lay Cistercians of South Florida. Smith characterizes herself as an "anonymous monk." These are ordinary persons of all ages, religions, and economic or social backgrounds who desire to live a prayerful life in the modern world. Some who experience the beginning of this calling may not even be aware they have it. However, God is working in their lives. As a farmer plants a seed and nurtures its growth, God has opened a way by which she has committed herself to a semi-cloistered life, as have many others, especially those in her network who are oppressed by chronic illness or other conditions.[69]

We may read Merton's writings on social issues and inter-religious dialogue, discussed later in this book, as the fruit of Merton's dual affirmation of his true self and of his monastic identity. Without delineating a detailed plan for a transformed world, Merton anticipated that a renewed monasticism would become a sign of God's presence in the world and a source of compassion, grace, and love. Merton's writings have proved to be as controversial now in the early twenty-first century as they were in the 1960s, yet they continue to inspire countless readers to share in the creative process by which God is bringing a new world into being. This world is free of bombs, racism, the worst effects of technology, media, big business, and everything that prevents people from claiming our truest selfhood.

68. Smith, *Stand on Your Own Feet*, 160.
69. Ibid., 17–18.

Christian living is stunted and frustrated if it is limited to the bare externals of worship. Living out of a monastic rhythm involves more than saying prayers, performing rituals, being obedient to one's superiors, or fulfilling one's duty. For people searching for the kind of life revealed in Biblical accounts of those first touched by the experience of the risen Christ, the monastic life offers monks, nuns, and lay people a way to live a sanctified life and to embrace the world.

Merton and other monastic mentors invite contemporary religious seekers to drink from the life-giving waters of monastic spirituality. Many new monastic communities are coming into being. The new monastic communities point to God's dream of a new world, in which people may attain full maturity as daughters and sons of God. Members of new monastic communities are making real the light and love of God through acts of kindness, generosity, and sacrifice; by practices of prayer and meditation; and by words of peace and gentleness.

FOUR

Thomas Merton on Simplification of Life

We must liberate ourselves, in our own way, from involvement in a world that is plunging to disaster. But our world is different from [that of the men and women who filled the deserts of Egypt and Palestine]. Our involvement in it is more complete. Our danger is far more desperate. Our time, perhaps, is shorter than we think.

—Thomas Merton, *The Wisdom of the Desert*

There is widespread confusion between what is needed for living and what extravagances are. We need stuff. We need the basics of living, but we do not need excess, debt, anxiety, and waste. These conditions arise from the dogged acquisition of material things.

In short, we do not need affluenza. This malady values stuff over people, the external over the internal, competition over cooperation, and individualism over interdependence.[1]

The disordered use of material goods is a pervasive aspect of modern society. It takes a special consciousness and firm resolve to resist the stream of messages telling us that we are a nobody unless we buy this or that. Whatever one's condition, every person is a somebody. Period. Paragraph.

In her animated film "The Story of Stuff," Annie Leonard explores the problem North Americans have with "stuff." With just 5 percent of the world's population, the United States consumes 30 percent of the world's

---

1. Neufeld and Neufeld, *Affluenza Interrupted*, 16, 59.

resources and creates 30 percent of the world's waste. She argues that if everyone consumed at U.S. rates, we would need three to five planets! This fact alarmed Leonard and led her to follow her film with a book of the same title in which she tracks the production, distribution, and consumption of the stuff we use daily and where it goes when we throw it out.

Like *Silent Spring* by Rachel Carson, *The Story of Stuff* may prove a landmark that will change the way people think and the way they live. Annie Leonard's message is clear. We have too much stuff, and too much of it has repercussions.

Putting stuff in right perspective concerned Thomas Merton. He believed that one could not serve equally both God and wealth (Matt 6:24). In part, when he entered the monastery, Merton was saying "no" to the Western socio-economic system. He was intent on rejecting economic tyrannies that seemed geared for global destruction.

Had Merton simply denounced excesses of modern society, he might not have struck so responsive a chord among his contemporaries or among countless readers ever since. Merton was also saying "yes" to all that is "good in the world . . . to all that is beautiful in the world . . . to all the men and women who are my brothers and sisters in the world, but for this yes to be an assent of freedom and not of subjection."[2]

Merton described the monastery as but one context in which to live with moderation, compassion, and concern for the common good. He shared his own wrestling as but one person's struggle. Committed to his vows, he wanted to contain the natural desires of his being. He lived well, simplified his life, and wrote with transparency and honesty concerning his monastic journey.

For years at the Abbey of Our Lady of Gethsemani, many retreatants have gathered informally after *Compline*. The setting has been in a small chapel next to the main oratory. Father Matthew Kelty OSCO has shared readings and reflections on why monastic life matters.

I often attended these brief sessions. On one of my retreats, Father Kelty observed that the monastery is in some sense an anomaly. In a fast-paced world, the monks pray. In a world that devalues the ordinary, the monks make cheese and fruitcake. In a world that has proved all too destructive, the monks take responsibility for making life less random and cruel. Most important, we—monks and retreatants—are here. Daily, cars go up and down Highway 247. People notice the monastery, hear the bells,

2. Merton, introduction to the Japanese translation of *SSM, Honorable Reader*, 65–66.

and see people moving about. For those who pass by, our very existence offers a garden of grace amidst the knob hills of Kentucky.

En route home, I discussed this perspective with students who had accompanied me to the monastery. Several of them shared that their time there had greatly encouraged them. They were returning home with a resolve to nurture several monastic practices in their daily living. They wanted to clear out some of the clutter of their lives and simplify their life ways. These soul friends have lived faithfully into this resolution.

Perhaps the lives of the monks and nuns led the retreatants to reflect on God and on the state of their own lives. Possibly the occasion of being with men or women given to God in prayer and service made a difference.

From experience, I know how difficult it is to sustain good intentions. Each year, I record resolutions in my journal. I review the list mid-year. All-too-frequently, I reiterate my resolve yet end up recording the same New Year Resolutions the next first of January.

Conversion of the will is but a starting point. One also needs support from a loving spouse, friend, or faith community like a monastery. Nuns and monks offer hospitality and spiritual direction to multitudes of people. This has enabled many retreatants to find God and to live with greater serenity and sense of abundance. The new monastic communities also offer participants a radical way to experience the spiritual dimensions of life. From this can grow self-criticism and freedom from the purported imperatives of our consumer culture.

The Spirit of Simplicity: Merton's First Book of Monastic Theology

Early on at Gethsemani, Merton wrote full-length books about two early Cistercian sisters, the Spanish Carmelite Saint John of the Cross, and the twelfth-century Cistercian Abbot of Clairvaux, Saint Bernard. Merton also published in 1948 an essay about Saint Bernard's thinking on interior simplicity. The essay originally formed Part II of a collection entitled *The Spirit of Simplicity*. The title page of *The Spirit of Simplicity* attributes the person responsible for the book as "a Cistercian Monk of Our Lady of Gethsemani." Because of this anonymous designation, *The Spirit of Simplicity* is perhaps the least known of Merton's books. Written before Merton's meteoric rise to fame, the book is foundational to Merton's monastic scholarship and his continuing wide appeal.

Jean Leclercq OSB, Patrick F. O'Connell, and M. Basil Pennington OCSO have confirmed Merton's authorship of *The Spirit of Simplicity*. Merton and Leclercq began corresponding in early 1950. In a letter of October 9, 1950, Merton mentioned having sent him a copy of *The Spirit of Simplicity*. Though Merton regarded his particular contribution to *The Spirit of Simplicity* as "confused and weak," he saw their mutual exploration of the sources of monastic spirituality as extremely important.[3]

In 1970, Cistercian Publications reprinted Merton's essay "St. Bernard on Interior Simplicity." It appeared in a collection entitled *Thomas Merton on Saint Bernard*. Like most of Merton's writings, the book is still in print.

Patrick Hart OCSO was a colleague and onetime secretary for Thomas Merton. In the foreword to the reprint edition, Hart concluded that these studies,

> . . . are as relevant today as when they were written—perhaps more so. We are witnessing in our day a renewed interest in the contemplative aspects of the christian life. In fact the interest extends far beyond the monastic enclosure to the university campus, the market place and even the family household. Everywhere one hears the question: how can I lead a deeply contemplative life in the midst of my present activities?[4]

Introducing the collection, Leclercq commented on the enduring value of this area of Merton's scholarship. "This early Merton, already full of love and enthusiasm, still marked to some degree by ingenuousness, was building the solid foundation upon which would rise Merton the activist and social critic of the following decades."[5]

In the foreword to *The Spirit of Simplicity*, Merton introduced the simple life with the claim that simplicity is one of the outstanding characteristics of Cistercian spirituality and of Cistercian saintliness. Merton defined simplicity as a crucial monastic practice, along with humility, obedience, and love. Any person can live according to these spiritual precepts. The chief consequence was growth towards perfection of simplicity, a perfect union of wills with God, and a state of mystical union with God. Merton believed that anyone could attain such a "mystical marriage."[6]

3. *SC*, 25, letter of October 9, 1950.

4. Hart, "Foreword," *Thomas Merton on Saint Bernard*, 9.

5. Leclercq, "Introduction," *Thomas Merton on Saint Bernard*, 14.

6. *Thomas Merton on Saint Bernard*, 110, 156 n. 6.

Wanting to portray the Cistercians in a positive light, Merton offered simplicity as a key aspect of early Cistercians monasticism. The Cistercian movement emerged in Europe at a time of renaissance and reformation. The early Cistercians reacted negatively to the excessive power of the Abbey of Cluny in Burgundy. They objected that its church, constructed between 1088 and 1130, was taller than the Vatican. As such, it was the greatest ecclesiastical structure ever built in the West. It dominated the entire area.

Merton frequently quoted Bernard's *Apology to William of St. Thierry* as the *pièce justificative* in the controversy between Cluniac and Cistercian spirituality.[7] Of noble birth, William and his brother Simon studied at the Benedictine Monastery of Saint Nicaise at Reims. Both embraced the religious life and became abbots, Simon at St. Nicolas-aux-Bois in the diocese of Laon, and William at St-Thierry near Reims, where he implemented reforms associated with Pope Gregory VII and the Cluniac movement. A long-time friendship with Bernard led William to abdicate. He became a Cistercian at Signy where he wrote on the spiritual life until his death in 1148.

Part One of *The Spirit of Simplicity* includes Merton's translation and comments on the report of the 1925 General Chapter of the Order of Cistercians of the Strict Observance. Within the text are eleven plates of twelfth-century Cistercian monasteries and the plan for typical twelfth-century Cistercian church architecture. Part Two, "St. Bernard on Interior Simplicity," has selections from Bernard, Merton's commentary, and a three-page conclusion.

Merton highlighted Bernard's teaching on simplicity. In a treatise written in 1127, Bernard criticized the building of great structures and the comfortable lifestyle of the monks at Cluny, a Benedictine monastery. Bernard was scathing,

> Oh, vanity of vanities, whose vanity is rivaled only by its insanity! The walls of the church are aglow, but the poor of the Church go hungry. The stones of the church are covered with gold, while its children are left naked. The food of the poor is taken to feed the eyes of the rich, and amusement is provided for the curious, while the needy have not even the necessities of life.[8]

7. Knowles, *Cistercians and Cluniacs*, 18.
8. *Apologia* 28; *Works of Bernard of Clairvaux*, 1:65–66.

Merton did not dwell on Bernard's critique of Cluniac monasticism. He did emphasize that Bernard was "just as strong in castigating Cistercians, who were bordering on Pharisaism in their contempt of Cluny, as the easy-going Cluniacs themselves."[9]

The Pharisees were at various times a political party, a social movement, or a school of thought among Jews during the Second Temple period from 536 BCE–70 CE. Biblical accounts of the life of Jesus often portrayed in negative terms the Pharisees as living in accord with the letter of rabbinic law. Merton believed in the need to live out of the spirit as well as out of the letter of Benedict's teaching on simple living:

> when Cistercians build in fake, overdecorated gothic in prefer-
> ence to something on simple, functional modern lines, they are
> unconsciously contradicting the whole Cistercian tradition and
> ideal in their very attempt to preserve it. On the other hand, the
> more functional and less antiquarian our use of gothic styles, the
> more true will they be to the spirit of the purist Cistercian art.[10]

For early Cistercians, Merton observed, simplicity consisted in "*get-ting rid of everything that did not help the monk to arrive at union with God by the shortest possible way.* And the shortest possible way to arrive at union with God, who is Love, is by loving Him, in Himself, and in our brethren." Merton argued that, to attain charity, the love of God, the early Cistercians discarded everything, especially those "*means of getting to God that were less direct.*"[11]

Discerning the radical implications of the doctrine of simplicity, Merton observed how Bernard and other early Cistercians emphasized the need to simplify art, architecture, and life style. A monastic son of Bernard, Merton sought to recover this aspect of the *Rule* in ways relevant to twentieth-century Christians burdened with the worries of this life. Merton cited a key passage of the *Rule*, and its Biblical basis, "For nothing is as inconsistent with the life of *any* Christian as overindulgence. Our

9. Merton, *Spirit of Simplicity*, 44. Merton's use of the word pharisaism refers to hypocritical observance of the letter of religious or moral law without regard for the spirit of the law. The Pharisees constituted a party or school of thought among Jews during the Second Temple era (536 BCE–70 CE).

10. Ibid., 48.

11. Ibid., iii–iv, Merton's emphasis.

Lord says: *Take care that your hearts are not weighed down with overindul-gence. Luke 21:34*."[12]

Merton highlighted the relationship between his call for simplicity and his understanding of human nature.

> The whole aim of the cistercian life—and the Fathers of the Order are unanimous on this point—is to set men apart from the world that their souls may be purified and led step by step to perfect union with God by the recovery of our lost likeness to him.[13]

For Merton, practices such as simplicity, solitude, and silence helped monks come to perfect union of wills with God, by love. These custom-ary attributes of Cistercian asceticism were cornerstones by which anyone could claim her or his full humanity as a child of God in the image and likeness of God,

> St. Bernard has really vindicated the fundamental goodness of human nature in terms as strong as have ever been used by any philosopher or theologian. And if the first step in the Cistercian ascent to God is for the monk to *know himself* . . . the whole life of such a one will consist in *being himself*, or rather trying to return to the original simplicity, immortality and freedom which consti-tute his real self, in the image of God.[14]

Merton was developing a key idea. Contemplation strengthened people to claim one's true self and to resist cultural pressure to conform to a false self. Augustine called the true self a divine center, Calvin a divine spark, and other theologians, soul. For Merton, the real self or true self was the God-given center of our being. If we go to the heart of our lives and if we do not buy into the false claims of culture, we find the risen Christ, one with us, alive in us, and giving us strength to engage the pow-ers and principalities, even death.

Merton next discussed the idea of "intellectual simplicity." By this phrase he meant not only eliminating all that is superfluous, unnecessary, or indirect, but also concerning ourselves exclusively with "*the one thing necessary*—the knowledge and love of God, union with Him."[15] Merton acknowledged that intellectual simplicity is more than a matter of knowl-

12. *Rule* 39:8–9; 62, emphasis in original.

13. Merton, *Spirit of Simplicity*, 76.

14. Ibid., 89–90.

15. Ibid., 98.

edge. It prepared contemplatives for the deeper and more searching simplification of life that follows, namely, obedience, purification of the will and "perfect simplicity: union of Spirit with God."[16]

Merton described the process as follows: Cistercian simplicity begins in humility and self-denial, moves through the monastic vow of obedience, is perfected by love and culminates in a spiritual unity and peace. The Holy and Undivided Trinity was reflected not only in the souls of individuals, but also in the community. God was pleased to bend down and raise up those persons who move in the direction of simplicity. By their humility, they manifested unity in community. By their mystical prayer, they attained a closer and far more intimate union with God and bore such fruits of the Spirit as love.

Merton characterized the General Chapter of 1925 as a clarion call for the spiritual children of Benedict of Nursia and Bernard of Claivaux. He did not write *The Spirit of Simplicity* principally as an exercise in historical scholarship but as a way to focus on his search for the greatest desired end, namely, the knowledge of God and self. Through an uncluttered life, Merton envisioned attaining, ultimately, union with God.

Merton hoped to transform the spiritual testimony of eleventh- and twelfth-century monks into a practical treatise on simplicity. By entering into the fundamental spirit of simplicity of the first Benedictine and Cistercian saints, and ultimately holy women and men of all religions, Merton believed that the monks of Gethsemani should give up active works and all non-essentials to concentrate on living contemplatively. By implication, all Christians are to follow the path of simplicity, silence, solitude, and stillness.

Merton understood simplicity as an essential mark of our truest humanity. Merton returned to the sources of his community—the Holy Bible, *The Rule of Benedict*, and the earliest writings by Cistercians—as a cornerstone of post-Second World War monastic renewal in the United States. These sources inspired Merton and led an entire generation of readers to recover the wisdom of the so-called "desert saints." Merton discerned that the lives of the early Christian monastics of the deserts of Egypt and the Middle East revealed basic realities of the interior life. To highlight the wisdom of their teachings on faith, humility, love, meekness, self-denial, and simplicity, Merton collected an anthology of early

16. *Thomas Merton on Saint Bernard*, 153.

monastic sayings. He published this material in his book entitled *Wisdom of the Desert*.

The focus of early desert fathers and mothers of Christian monasticism was attaining "their own true self, in Christ." To achieve this, a Christian monk or nuns had to reject completely his or her false self, constructed under constraints of life in the world, and seek a way to God that was uncharted and freely chosen.[17]

Recovery of the earliest sources of Western monasticism can benefit all religious seekers. Private times of reading sacred Scripture, meditation, and living simply can nurture purity of life and awareness of mystical union with God. Simplification of one's personal life allows all Christians to journey through good and hard times with grace, joy, love, peace, and a sense of compassion for every living thing. Achieving "eternal union with the uncreated Simplicity that is the Triune God, the Holy One makes perfect in us as in our Fathers the image of that Simplicity."[18]

SIMPLICITY IN MERTON'S OTHER WRITINGS

As translator and commentator on classic monastic texts, Merton understood simplicity and simplification of life as crucial in the monastic journey. This emphasis on simplicity permeated his other literary activity as well. Merton explored the theme of simplicity in *Seeds of Contemplation*, published in 1948, and in *The Waters of Siloe*, a history of the Cistercian order published in 1949.

In *Seeds of Contemplation*, Merton offered a compelling collection of reflections. The book anticipated themes running throughout Merton's writing, notably his distinction between the false self and true self.

> For me to be a saint means to be myself. Therefore the problem of sanctity and salvation is in fact the problem of finding out who I am and of discovering my true self . . . To say I was born in sin is to say I came into the world with a false self. I came into existence under a sign of contradiction, being someone that I was never intended to be and therefore a denial of what I am supposed to be.[19]

Merton used various phrases to describe the false self: alienated, egocentric, exterior, illusory, and outward. For Merton the false self does

17. Merton, *Wisdom of the Desert*, 5–6.
18. Merton, *Spirit of Simplicity*, 138–39.
19. Merton, *Seeds of Contemplation*, 26–27.

not exist at any deep level of reality. As Merton wrote later in *New Seeds of Contemplation*, the "outer [false] self is nothing but an evanescent shadow . . . a garment that is cast off and consumed by decay."[20]

In *Seeds of Contemplation*, Merton described the true self as a full reflection of the image and likeness of God in each person. The monastery was simply one place in which to orient oneself to this one true good: love.

> To say that I am made in the image of God is to say that love is the reason for my existence: for God is love. Love is my true identity. Selflessness is my true self. Love is my true character. Love is my name.[21]

Merton stressed the centrality of seeking God. For Merton, God planted the seed of such desire in each person.

> For how can I receive the seeds of freedom if I am in love with slavery and how can I cherish the desire of God if I am filled with another and an opposite desire? God cannot plant His liberty in me because I am a prisoner and I do not even desire to be free. I love my captivity and I lock myself in the desire for the things that I hate, and I have hardened my heart against true love.[22]

Merton regarded Cistercian practices such as detachment and renunciation as essential to recover freedom and discover our true self. Merton observed that, because contemplatives cling to modest consolations that are given to beginners, many contemplatives never become great saints, never enter into close friendship with God, and never find a deep participation in God's immense joys.

> How many there are who are in a worse state still: they can never even get as far as contemplation because they are attached to activities and enterprises that seem to them to be important. Blinded by their desire for ceaseless motion, for a constant sense of achievement, famished with a crude hunger for results, for visible and tangible success, they work themselves into a state in which they cannot believe that they are pleasing God unless they are busy with a dozen jobs at the same time.[23]

20. *NSC*, 279–80.

21. Merton, *Seeds of Contemplation*, 47; Shannon, "Self," *Thomas Merton Encyclopedia*, 417–20.

22. Ibid., 7.

23. Ibid., 122.

Discussing renunciation, Merton appealed to many spiritual seekers of his generation: "Life in a Trappist monastery is fundamentally peasant life. The closer it conforms to the poverty and frugality and simplicity of those who have to dig their living out of the land, the more it fulfills its essential purpose, which is to dispose men for contemplation."[24]

While the time has passed during which one might characterize Trappist monasticism as peasant life, Merton's main point remains pertinent. Possessions, superfluous religious practices, and inane images are distractions. The contemplative must never lose sight of her or his simple desire for union with God. From such desire blossoms the experience of ecstatic union with God and of pure love. A person who has spent most of her or his life in simple tasks—making cheese, baking bread, repairing shoes, or contributing to community life in other ways—can be a far greater contemplative than Bible scholars or theologians. The latter may appear to have more time for meditation, contemplation, or prayer, yet they pay little attention to their own natural defects and eccentricities.

We simplify our lives by unencumbering our lives of all that detracts from this one good thing: the love of God, self, and others. Our attachments can get the best of us and prevent us from living into our truest self. Mass technological society can confuse people about what is unreal and what is truly real. For Merton, a truly humane society should depend for its existence on the inviolability of each person.

In his history of his monastic order, *The Waters of Siloe*, Merton emphasized the simplicity of Cistercian architecture:

> Cistercian architecture is famous for its energy and simplicity and purity, for its originality and technical brilliance. It was the Cistercians who effected the transition from the massive, ponderous Norman style to the thirteenth-century Gothic, with its genius for poising masses of stone in mid-air, and making masonry fly and hover over the low earth with the self-assurance of an angel. Yet, the Cistercians produced a far finer and purer Gothic than the ornate masses of columns and stained glass and flying buttresses that flourished all over western Europe, when the architects of the thirteenth century got drunk on the strong wine of their own virtuosity.
>
> The typical Cistercian church, with its low elevation, its plain, bare walls, lighted by few windows and without stained glass,

24. Ibid., 164.

achieved its effect by the balance of masses and austere, powerful, round or pointed arches and mighty vaulting. These buildings
filled anyone who entered them with peace and restfulness and
disposed the soul for contemplation in an atmosphere of simplicity and poverty.[25]

Later in the book, Merton returned to the theme of Cistercian architecture in relation to the surroundings in which the monks settled.

When the monks had found their homes, they . . . sank their roots
into the ground and fell in love with their woods. Indeed, this love
of one's monastery and its surrounding is something integral to
the Cistercian life. . . . It all adds up to one thing: peace, silence,
solitude. . . . So, from the very outset, even the site of a Cistercian
monastery is, or ought to be, a lesson in contemplation.[26]

In *No Man Is an Island*, published in 1955, Merton stressed that we
must see ourselves as human, like everyone else, with weaknesses, defi-
ciencies, and limitations. Merton understood that we are members of the
whole body within which each one of us has a purpose in life. Our task,
the task of each person, is to discover that life has a meaning and to live
in accord with that meaning. "The discovery of ourselves in God, and of
God in ourselves, by a charity that also finds all other men in God with
ourselves is, therefore, not the discovery of ourselves but of Christ."

For Merton, this was one of the most important and neglected elements of the interior life. Modern living made it very difficult to respond
to the reality that God is in all and is all. As a result, contemplation was—
and is—essential. Merton wrote,

. . . we do not see these things because we have withdrawn from
them. In a way we have to. In modern life our senses are so constantly bombarded with stimulation from every side that unless
we developed a kind of protective insensibility we would go crazy
trying to respond to *all* the advertisements at the same time![27]

A major theme in *No Man Is an Island* concerned the aim of the
contemplative life. It was to teach people to live in God and to find God all
around us, in all the things, in people with whom we live, and especially

25. Merton, *Waters of Siloe*, 14.

26. Ibid., 274–75.

27. Merton, *No Man Is an Island*, 33.

in ourselves. Merton stressed that we cannot live for others until we have first discovered God in ourselves. If we are to love others sincerely and with simplicity, we must first overcome the fear of not being loved. This could be done only when we "somehow strip ourselves of our greatest illusions about ourselves, frankly recognize in how many ways we are un-lovable, descend into the depths of our being until we come to the basic reality that is in us, and learn to see that we are loveable after all, in spite of everything."[28]

Merton makes a crucial point. When I claim my truest selfhood, I discover that I am beloved of God and capable of loving with something of God's love and unselfishness. Merton saw that this is a difficult work, done only by a lifetime of discipline, humility, and openness to God's Spirit. Merton held that those who led a genuinely contemplative life would nonetheless be able, by the grace of God, to cast off their false, exterior self and to find their real self. By contrast,

> Those who love their own noise are impatient of everything else. They constantly defile the silence of the forests and the mountains and the sea. They bore through silent nature in every direction with their machines, for fear that the calm world might accuse them of their own emptiness. The urgency of their swift move-ment seems to ignore the tranquility of nature by pretending to have a purpose. The loud plane seems for a moment to deny the reality of the clouds and of the sky, by its direction, its noise, and its pretended strength. The silence of the sky remains when the plane has gone. The tranquility of the clouds will remain when the plane has fallen apart. It is the silence of the world that is real. Our noise, our business, our purposes, and all our fatuous state-ments about our purposes, our business, and our noise: these are the illusion.[29]

In *Thoughts in Solitude* (1958), Merton observed that every person has the capacity to establish a rhythm of life marked by personal simplicity and times when one is being alone. One need not become a monk to go to wilderness places:

> [T]he "unreality" of material things is only relative to the *greater* reality of spiritual things. . . .

28. Ibid., 202.
29. Ibid., 257.

The Desert Fathers believed that the wilderness has been created as supremely valuable in the eyes of God precisely because it had no value to men . . .

Look at the deserts today. What are they? The birthplace of a new and terrible creation, the testing-ground of the power by which man seeks to un-create what God has blessed. Today, in the century of man's greatest technological achievement, the wilderness at last comes into its own. Man no longer needs God . . . . When man and his money and machines move out into the desert, and dwell there, not fighting the devil as Christ did, but believing in his promises of power and wealth, and adoring his angelic wisdom, then the desert itself moves everywhere. Everywhere is desert. Everywhere is solitude in which man must do penance and fight the adversary and purify his own heart in the grace of God.[30]

Merton wrote that each person can embrace the ways of the desert saints of the first Christian centuries. Everyone could find his or own wilderness places in living a simple life. "The more we are content with our own poverty the closer we are to God for then we accept our poverty in peace, expecting nothing from ourselves and everything from God."[31]

Here, Merton stressed that poverty is not so much a monetary concept, but rather a portal to freedom and a source of hope. When one knows that she or he has found her or his calling, that person stops thinking about how to live and begins to live. Simplification of life allows one to hear God, find God, and measure life by the embrace of God. "Solitude . . . has to be a communion in something greater than the world, as great as Being itself, in order that in its deep peace we may find God."[32]

Merton concluded that the gifts of silence, stillness, and solitude can enrich every life. He taught that the sky is our prayer, the birds are our prayer, and the wind in the trees is our prayer. God is all and in all. So discovering God, one responds with gratitude. The natural response to perceiving life in such a way is gratitude. Welling up from a life given to simplicity and solitude, we praise God who enables us to share in the Divine Nature and thereby become one with the God of infinite love.

In *Monastic Peace*, also published in 1958, Merton stressed that a true contemplative life is simply a deep penetration and understanding of

30. Merton, *Thoughts in Solitude*, 17–20.

31. Ibid., 29.

32. Ibid.,85.

ordinary Christian living. Anyone can experience the most wonderful of all miracles: God living in us.

> St. Bernard of Clairvaux expanded and implemented the thought of St. Benedict when he called the monastery a school of charity. The main object of monastic discipline, according to St. Bernard, was to restore man's nature created in the image and likeness of God, that is to say created for love and for self-surrender.[33]

One goes into the wilderness not to escape others but to find them in God. In a well-known passage, Merton recounted his experience around 1958 at the corner of Fourth and Walnut in Louisville, Kentucky. As recorded in *Conjectures of a Guilty Bystander*, Merton re-iterated his rejection of monasticism as flight, as follows:

> but the conception of "separation from the world" that we have in the monastery too easily presents itself as a complete illusion: the illusion that by making vows we become a different species of being, pseudo angels, "spiritual men," men of interior life, what have you.
>
> Certainly these traditional values are very real, but their reality is not of an order outside everyday existence in a contingent world, nor does it entitle one to despise the secular: though "out of the world" we are in the same world as everybody else, the world of the bomb, the world of race hatred, the world of technology, the world of mass media, big business, revolution, and all the rest. We take a different attitude to all these things, for we belong to God. Yet so does everybody else belong to God We just happen to be conscious of it, and to make a profession out of this consciousness. But does this entitle us to consider ourselves different, or even *better* than others? The whole idea is preposterous.[34]

Merton characterized his monastic calling as *fuga mundi*, a phrase that meant flight from the world. By use of the phrase *fuga mundi*, Merton did not mean he had rejected the world to live a life indifferent to life. He did not refuse to know anything about the world. Rather, his "no" was a "rejection of all standards of judgment which imply attachment to a history of delusion, egoism, and sin."[35] Many of the values of society still seemed idiotic, trivial, and onerous to Merton. If anything, the image of a

33. Merton, *Monastic Peace*, as published in *Monastic Journey*, 77.

34. *CGB*, 141 (156–57).

35. Merton, *Seeds of Destruction*, xii–xiii.

society that provided happiness through a life of luxury and that needed to be protected by bombs remained "repugnant" to Merton.[36]

Merton came to understand that one goes to the monastery not because it is there that one can be holier than other people can. Rather, one goes there to discover one's true self in relation to God, nature, and others. Merton observed, "One of the greatest paradoxes of the mystical life is this: *that a man cannot enter into the deepest center of himself and pass through that center into God, unless he is able to pass entirely out of himself and empty himself and give himself to other people in the purity of a selfless love*."[37]

WHY MERTON ON SIMPLICITY MATTERS

For fifteen hundred years, *The Rule of St. Benedict* has offered Christians a way of living in moderation. Nowhere in the spirituality of St. Benedict is there anything that imposes a particular system of practices on believers or an aesthetic for the church. Each person, each monk or nun, and each community must find his or her own way. However, without simplicity one cannot fully carry out the task assigned them in the church or the world.

Merton's thinking on simplicity remains important in three areas: humanism; a growing protest against some forms of technology; and Merton's emphasis on simplicity in religious art. The following paragraphs briefly explore these themes.

First, Merton traced the development of Christian humanism to medieval Europe, notably the twelfth and thirteenth centuries, a period when historians have discerned the emergence of the idea of the self. Merton cited the School of Chartres for its scholars who were deeply intrigued by the natural world; the School of St. Victor for its motto, "learn everything, you will find nothing superfluous"; and St. Thomas Aquinas for his openness to Aristotle, the Arabs, and the claims of reason and nature.[38]

For Merton, monastic culture and classic Christian humanism emphasized love, forgiveness, and the common good. By contrast, narcis-

---

36. *CGB*, 47.

37. *NSC*, 64, emphasis Merton's.

38. Merton, "Christian Humanism," essays collected as Part III of *Love and Learning*; O'Connell, "Humanism," *Thomas Merton Encyclopedia*, 214–15.

sism, depersonalization, and totalitarian regimes have marked modern secular society. Merton saw Nazi Germany and Stalinist Russia as extreme examples of a universal problem. Merton called upon humanists around the world to come together in new ways to foster a more human and desirable future.

Merton often returned to this theme. In a talk on Marxism and technology, Merton explored issues around plans to establish a new monastery in Latin America. Merton identified one problem he saw with Marxism, namely, depersonalization. Merton explained, "Marxist political totalitarianism, especially in Russia, . . . is a sensitive area. Another sensitive area is the area of the intellectuals in Iron Curtain countries like Poland and Czechoslovakia; that is an area of sensitive dialogue because these people are reacting, they're fighting back against this bureaucratic Marxism. This is what you are going to run into in Chile."[39]

Merton insisted on the importance of monastic simplicity. At a time that many people were reacting against bureaucracy and totalitarianism, he welcomed that many Russians and Chinese persons were reacting to a mindless acceptance of the technological, bureaucratic machine. Merton opined that the future of Marxism in Russia might be decided in the struggle between the rigid organizational types and the freewheeling types. "There are tendencies at work, here as well, with the organizational, bureaucratic types. People want to loosen it up."[40]

In the paper he delivered at the monastic conference just before he died in Thailand, Merton talked of the need to replace self-centered love with an other-centered love. In the process by which a Christian ceases to see self not simply as an individual ego, one becomes "fully open to all other persons because ultimately all other persons are Christ."[41]

To love others, we must first know ourselves, bridling monsters deep in the depths of our being including illusions fed by corporate advertising, greed, and other forces of self-destructiveness. Especially since the end of the Second Great War, many have understood humanity as traveling towards some sort of earthy paradise filled with stuff. Non-attachment is not particularly descriptive of our lives as non-monks. We have ignored

39. Tape cited with permission from the Merton Legacy Trust and the Thomas Merton Center at Bellarmine University. Most of the recording is from Gethsemani tape 161, Track 1, dated June 19, 1966.

40. Ibid.

41. Merton, *Asian Journal*, 334.

the implications for ourselves, and for society generally of our present economic and social assumptions and practices.

Merton encouraged people to tame their own ambitions, cravings, and passions. As people do so in appropriate ways and use God's given talents mindfully, they move towards a unity and an awareness of their truest self. Merton wrote of healing in lives that are otherwise fragmented and wounded. As we share in the limited supply of created goods, we no longer impose a false difference between others and ourselves.[42]

Merton characterized such healing as freeing. In "Hagia Sophia," he wrote of the discovery of "an invisible fecundity, a dimmed light, a meek namelessness, a hidden wholeness. This mysterious Unity and Integrity is Wisdom . . . at once my own being, my own nature, and the Gift of my Creator's Thought and Art within me. . . ."[43]

Second, Merton criticized a society organized around machines. Technology had come to characterize and control our lives and therefore constituted a death urge. Drawing on his reading of Lewis Mumford, Jacques Ellul, and others, Merton expressed concern that technology could lead people to ignore basic human needs. He criticized the nonsense of making technology an "ultimate value."[44]

Finally, Merton manifested a passionate interest in the intersection of the sacred and the aesthetic. Son of two artists, Merton lectured on sacred art in 1954. He wrote several articles on art.[45]

Merton's understanding of the arts found their way into Catholic liturgical art and worship. Among those influenced by Merton was Frank Kacmarcik. Simplicity, meaningful proportions, timelessness, enduring quality, poetry of light, and visual silence marked his work in design for myriad Catholic churches of their architectural setting and furnishings. In these areas, Kacmarcik was arguably the most important Catholic consultant in the United States during the mid-twentieth century. Kacmarcik

42. *NSC*, 47.

43. *CP*, 363.

44. *Dancing in the Water of Life*, 166, entry for November 16, 1964.

45. "Absurdity in Sacred Decoration," and "Sacred Art and the Spiritual Life," *Disputed Questions*; "Art and Worship," partially published as "Seven Qualities of the Sacred"; "Answers on Art and Freedom"; *Raids on the Unspeakable*, reprinted in Hart, *Literary Essays*, hereafter *LE*; "Reality, Art and Prayer;"; "Notes on Sacred and Profane Art," 24–32.

spent considerable time at the Abbey of Gethsemani, where he designed two of Merton's books, *Monastic Peace* and *Nativity Kerygma*.[46]

Without exaggerating Merton's ongoing legacy in this area, Cistercians continue to emphasize simplicity in the arts. A new Trappist monastery in Bohemia, designed by the minimalist architect, John Pawson, elicits a sense of peace and serenity for those who visit.

REFLECTIONS

In a pastoral message on the church's mission, Bishop Oscar Romero of El Salvador (1917–1980) wrote that the idolatry of wealth and private property inclines persons towards "having more" and lessens their interest in "being more." The absolutism of wealth encourages the selfishness that destroys communal bonds among all God's people. It also prevents people from sharing the goods that God has made for all and produces in the all-possessing minority an exaggerated pleasure in stuff.[47]

Bishop Romero was but one of many prophets who have drawn attention to much that is missing in our "developed" lifestyles in Europe and North America. In the mid-1990s, comedian Bill Cosby spoke in Memphis, Tennessee. Cosby was star of the situation comedy *The Cosby Show*, which aired on television from 1984–1992. High school students sold tickets for the show. The reward for the ones who sold the most tickets was an opportunity to be on stage with Cosby. One young person asked Cosby if the comedian had one piece of advice for his generation. "What would you do about the culture of despair, drugs, guns, and violence that so infects my high school?" Cosby replied at once. "Change the object of desire."

A story that I heard while in Colombia in 2009 encapsulates my understanding of our need to change the object of desire. Peter Cousins translated the story. He was a British volunteer serving with the Fellowship of Reconciliation (FOR), an international pacifist organization that provides non-violent, protective accompaniment of people at risk from violence in Colombia. The story goes as follows,

46. Interview with Kacmarcik, May 12, 2003. There are scattered references to him in Merton's journals and letters.

47. Romero, *Voice of the Voiceless*, 133.

Once upon a time, the father of a well-to-do family took his son on a trip to the countryside, determined to show him how poor the families in the area were. They stayed in the house of a humble rural family for a day and a night. They shared their meals and their periods of rest together. When the journey was over, and they were back at home, the father asked his son, "What did you think of the trip?" "Very beautiful, dad!" "Did you see how poor people can be?" "Yes!" "And what did you learn?"

"I saw that we have a dog at home, and they have four. We have a swimming pool which runs from the wall halfway down the garden; they have a river which never ends. We have some imported light bulbs in our room; they have millions of stars which shimmer all night long. Our patio stops at the neighbour's wall; their patio is the horizon. They have time to chat and be a family; you and mum have to work all the time and I almost never see you." When he had finished, his father was dumbfounded. And the boy added, "Thanks, dad, for showing me how rich we can become!"

What we are grateful for, we cherish. North America is a consumer society. Overall, North Americans are preoccupied with money. We are in a rush. We are addicted to size because we confuse more for better. We hallow youth and depreciate the wisdom of our elders. We are also experiencing the breakdown of community, the degradation of the self-worth of people, and the idolization of things. Despite material prosperity and a boom in religious activity, a malaise of materialism infects many individuals.

The monastic life offers an alternative understanding of life, according to which God is the principal object of desire. Monks, nuns, and myriad people influenced by monastic values do not see the material world as an end in itself. However, they do recognize the need to live fully within the material world. They know that it is in the real world where they come to know and love God. They create places of beauty. They appreciate what is good. To support themselves, they value and make products of quality.

Once, when on retreat at the Abbey of Our Lady of Gethsemani, I was helping with the Christmas mailing of fudge and fruitcakes, a major source of income for the community. I asked if the monks distilled their own bourbon for use in these products. "No," I was told, "we use the premium bourbon whisky made in Kentucky. We know quality."

The monastery is but one context that offers space and time for people to experience God. As I have heard monks and nuns describe their calling, they seek primarily to live lives consecrated to God. By doing so, they can "justly claim to be public servants in a special, spiritual sense. They are helping to preserve the nation's liberty by keeping the nation in contact with God, who is the giver of liberty."[48]

Thomas Merton characterized the monastery as a school of charity. Monks and nuns live this out in practical ways. After completion of the novitiate, monks and nuns give their possessions to the poor, or they make a formal donation of them to the monastery. Some monks have shared that they were told not to get rid of their "stuff" too quickly in case they did not make it through the novitiate![49]

Perhaps more significantly, monks and nuns love others. Above all, they share their lives with members of the community. They also share their lives with those who come to their communities, and with those whom the communities serve.

Carved over the portals of the temple to Apollo, the sun deity in ancient Delphi, in Greece, are two mottos that anticipate themes that later came to dominate the writings of Thomas Merton: "Moderation in all things," and "Know thyself."

Nearly three millennia later, Thomas Merton concluded that humankind had violated both precepts. From the margins of a culture gone awry, Merton warned that enough is enough. Discover your true self. Come to your senses. You are about to plunge over a precipice. Do not imitate the small, mouse-like lemmings that, as their numbers soar, scatter in all directions and in large numbers self-destruct.

A proverb says, "Wherever there is excess, something is lacking."[50] Merton's monastic spirituality accents the right use of God's gifts and offers an antidote to the malaise of modernity. To a busy, over-stressed, and complex world, Merton directs contemporary spiritual seekers to a path of equanimity, peacefulness, and moderation. The new monastics seek to follow this path outside the monastery, using the good things of life in moderation, living well, and promoting the common good.

---

48. Hart quoting Merton, Foreword to Cunningham, *Thomas Merton, Spiritual Master*, 2.

49. Email, Paul M. Pearson, April 12, 2010.

50. Chittister, *Wisdom Distilled from the Daily*, 197.

FIVE

Thomas Merton, Guide to the Right Use of Technology

It is the peculiar office of the monk in the modern world to keep alive the contemplative experience and to keep the way open for modern technological people to recover the integrity of their own inner depths.

—Thomas Merton, "Monastic Experience and East-West Dialogue,"
    Asian Journal

In this chapter, we continue our exploration of monastic culture. Especially during the 1960s, Thomas Merton wrote and gave several talks in which he reflected on this period in history as a time of great technological innovation. He articulated keen insights on what he called "the right use of technology to serve the real needs of modern man."[1]

Merton's concern for the right use of technology developed at a time of prevalent and growing anxiety about technology and its role in the abuse of people's human rights, in war, and by its impact upon the environment. Merton read books by thoughtful writers anxious about social changes engendered by new technological developments. Merton's growing discomfort intensified after 1964 when he read a pamphlet entitled *The Triple Revolution*, which subsequently grew into a textbook that went through more than one edition.

The first revolution had to do with cybernetics. The second concerned new forms of weaponry that people had developed. The authors

---

1. *CGB*, (284).

of *The Triple Revolution* believed such weapons cannot win wars, but they can and do obliterate civilization. The third revolution concerned the universal demand for full human rights.[2]

Signatories of *The Triple Revolution* included thirty-two prominent thinkers. They included activists Todd Gitlin and Tom Hayden of the Students for a Democratic Society and Bayard Rustin, organizer of the August 28, 1963, March on Washington; economists Michael Harrington, author of *The Other America*, Robert Heilbroner, author of *The Great Ascent*, and Robert Theobald, author of *Free Men and Free Markets*; and 1962 Nobel peace laureate Linus Pauling.

At the time, *The Triple Revolution* generated a great deal of commentary. Martin Luther King Jr. was one of many prominent individuals who responded to the pamphlet. Dr. King preached on the theme in several sermons and explicitly mentioned the three revolutions in a sermon, "Remaining Awake through a Great Revolution." He preached this sermon on March 31, 1968, at the National Cathedral in Washington, DC only a few days before his death.

Comments on the three revolutions generally focused on the effects of technology. Many serious thinkers regarded the three revolutions of such magnitude that society's response to them was proving very inadequate. The authors addressed their concerns to President Lyndon B. Johnson. On April 6, 1964, Lee C. White, Assistant Special Counsel to the President, replied that the President was taking steps to deal with the areas of poverty, unemployment, and technological change.

For Merton, *The Triple Revolution* offered an excellent starting point from which to diagnose and ameliorate a pattern of illness in the United States and elsewhere, namely, distortion of our true humanity. Failure to develop a spirituality by which people might resist negative consequences of technology has since given rise to diverse symptoms of human distress. It is worth returning to the 1964 statement.

We may read Merton's reaction to the pamphlet as a reflection of his wider concern to refuse to surrender to the exalted place of technology in Western society. His comments provide a useful filter by which we may read and understand Merton's views on technology. Especially during the 1960s, he wrote frequently on the subject. As one of the leading Catholic intellectuals of his period, Merton's writings on this theme have proved prophetic. By calling the wider church to engage seriously the realms of

2. Perrucci and Pilisuk, "The Triple Revolution."

science and technology, Merton highlights an ethical norm. Technology must serve humankind. The well-being of people must take precedence over efficiency and outputs.

MERTON ON *THE TRIPLE REVOLUTION*

In March 1964, Wilbur H. (Ping) Ferry, Vice President of the Center for the Study of Democratic Institutions in California, sent Merton a copy of *The Triple Revolution*. Replying to Ferry on March 23, 1964, Merton wrote that the message of *The Triple Revolution* was "urgent and clear and if it does not get the right reactions (it won't) people ought to have their heads examined (they won't). (Even if they did, it would not change anything.)" He added, "We are in for a rough and dizzy ride, and though we have no good motive for hoping for a special and divine protection, that is about all we can look for." Merton expressed concern that so-called Christians were totally invested in a "spiritually and mentally insolvent society."[3]

A key phrase in the pamphlet, cybernetic revolution, referred to the combination of the computer and automated self-regulating machines. The pamphlet concentrated on this phenomenon because authors anticipated possible abuses of computer systems in the other two arenas, war and human rights. The authors stated that a new era of production had begun. Its principles of organization were as different from those of the industrial era as those of the industrial era were different from the agricultural era. The authors identified a key challenge in the modern industrial engineering and production model. It failed to take into consideration its unintended and unplanned side effects.

The signatories worried that machines can achieve potentially unlimited production without humans. They anticipated that industry progressively would require less human labor, contribute to the loss of jobs and lead to the reorganization of the economic and social system. The authors also recognized a historic paradox, that a growing proportion of the population subsisted on minimal incomes, often below the poverty line, at a time when sufficient productive capacity was available to supply the needs of everyone.

Conventional economic analysis denied or ignored the existence of this inner contradiction. With others, African Americans had marched in Washington for freedom and jobs, yet many were falling behind.

3. *HGL*, 216.

OCCUPY WALL STREET.

Unemployment was far worse than the figures indicated. The gap between rich and poor was growing. This division of people threatened to create a human slagheap. The authors could not tolerate the development of a separate nation of the poor, unskilled, and jobless living within another nation of the well off, the trained, and the employed.

The authors called for a new consensus and for major changes in values and institutions. The authors called for policies that anticipated the probable long-term effects of the triple revolution such as the large-scale displacement of workers, inadequate public resources for human services, and environmental degradation. The authors also proposed interventions that would address as a priority the needs of jobless or under-incomed people and those fearful for their future.

Merton shared the conviction of the authors of *The Triple Revolution* that humanity was at a historic moment. Merton called for a fundamental reexamination of existing values and radical action.

As early as March 1963, Paul Peachey proposed the idea of a retreat to Merton. Peachey was Executive Secretary for the Church Peace Mission, a peace organization that began as an outgrowth of a conference on the "Church and War," held in Detroit in May 1950. The goal of the group was to challenge as many Christians as possible not to make or use weapons of war and to dedicate themselves to the removal of the social, economic, and moral causes of war.

John C. Heidbrink, secretary for ecumenical relations of the Fellowship of Reconciliation (FOR), encouraged Merton to take a lead role in hosting the retreat at the site of his future hermitage. In a letter of September 17, 1964, Heidbrink wrote to Merton expressing the hope that A. J. Muste, former Executive Director of the FOR, might attend along with Martin Luther King Jr. and another civil rights leader, Bayard Rustin. Merton mentioned this possibility in a letter of October 17 to Ping Ferry. On October 29, Heidbrink wrote to Merton, "Bayard Rustin is yet to finalize the change of plans required if he is to come: but he is doing his darnedest." Heidbrink did not mention King attending.[4]

Most of the group arrived at the Abbey of Our Lady of Gethsemani on the morning of November 18, 1964. Participants included Ferry, Mennonite theologian John Howard Yoder, A. J. Muste, and John Oliver Nelson, onetime national FOR chairperson. Catholics included Dan

4. Email, Gordon Oyer, May 3, 2010; Merton to Ferry, October 17, 1964, *HGL*, 219; journal entry, November 17, *DWL*, 167.

Berrigan, Phil Berrigan, John Peter Grady, Tom Cornell, and Jim Forest, who with Tom Cornell was then involved with a FOR affiliate, the Catholic Peace Fellowship. Heidbrink had back surgery and could not attend. He had asked Peachey to fill in for him but he too was unable to attend the Gethsemani gathering.

Sessions began that afternoon. During formal comments at the opening of the retreat, Merton began by explaining the purpose of the gathering, as follows:

> We are hoping to reflect together during these days on our common grounds for *religious dissent and commitment* in the face of the injustice and disorder of a world in which total war seems at time inevitable, in which few seek any but violent solutions to economic and social problems more critical and more vast than man has ever known before.

Merton asked, *"By what right* do we assume that we are called to protest, to judge, and to witness?"* He affirmed that people protest because we have to, for *within me there is something like a burning fire shut up in my bones; I am weary with holding it in, and I cannot* (Jer 20:9). Merton further asked the group to consider whether technological society is by its very nature oriented to self-destruction or whether it can by contrast be regarded as a source of hope in the building of a new sacral order, a millennial "city" in which God is manifest and praised by free and enlightened people.

Merton prayed that this latter outcome emerge. However, he did not believe at the time that technology was morally or religiously promising. "Does this call for reaction and protest; if so, what kind? What can we really do about it?"[5]

As a partial response to these questions, Merton called for *metanoia*. By this Greek word, he did not mean conversion, as translators often misinterpret. Merton had in mind total personal transformation and *conversatio morum* (conversion of life), a phrase in *The Rule of Saint Benedict* (58.17). Merton called for a radical turn to the gospel of peace. People must sacrifice, suffer, and participate in redemptive non-violent protest.

5. Merton, "Retreat, November, 1964," *Thomas Merton on Peace,* 259–60. Cornell, *Fellowship,* 23; Mott, *Seven Mountains,* 406–7.

In terms of protest, Merton expected that, "the future will depend on what we do in the present."[6] As basis for reflection, Merton introduced excerpts from his Gandhi anthology.

Mennonite theologian John Howard Yoder commented that Christians must live the gospel, pure and simple. Yoder proclaimed the Cross, the unique element that Christianity brings to the mystery of the pursuit of peace and justice in a world ruled by perverse power. Dan Berrigan said, "The church's fearfulness is our confession of unconvertedness."[7] Ping Ferry led a discussion of *The Triple Revolution* and introduced some of the books of the French thinker Jacques Ellul, notably his *The Technological Society* (1964) and *Propaganda: The Formation of Men's Attitudes* (1965). The French subtitle of the first book suggested Ellul's negativity with respect to technology: *La technique ou l'enjeu du siècle,* "the stake of the century," a pessimism reflected at times in Merton's critique of the technological culture in which he lived.

From first-hand accounts, the retreat proved to be near legendary and a watershed experience. In a letter to FOR coordinator for religious groups, John C. Heidbrink, who had helped organize the meeting but could not attend, Merton wrote,

> I think we all felt it was a great experience. I will not use the world "meaningful," as I have heard this so much lately that the only bell it rings is the one for nausea. But certainly I think we were in contact with reality and truth in a way that is not met with every day. Thanks be to God for it. I would sum it up in two words: (a) a sense of the awful depth and seriousness of the situation; (b) a sense of deeper and purer hope, a hope purified of trust in the technological machinery and the "principalities and powers" at work therein.

Merton characterized the retreat as a "last fling," as many of his superiors were not favorable to his continuing to engage in such activity and to cut back in retreats and writing.[8]

The retreat did not shape the specific ways by which retreatants reacted to the culture of technology. Writing to Charles Cameron, a twenty-year old student reading theology at Christ Church College of Oxford

6. Merton, *Gandhi on Non-Violence,* 74.

7. Quoted by Forest, "A Great Lake of Beer," 120.

8. *HGL,* 417, letter of November 26, 1964.

University, Merton commented, "we came out with no solution to anything except a hope that is so close to despair that it seems to be one and the same thing."[9]

The retreat did encourage most of the participants to join in antiwar protests. Many of them would serve time in prison. Merton was an exception. In a letter of March 19, 1967, to theologian Rosemary Radford Ruether, he explained he saw his life as one of cultivation and expansion of the senses. He could participate in political life in a way that made sense to him.

> In actual fact, is there anything you can do in the city, more effectively than I can do in the country, to stop the war in Vietnam? Except perhaps march with a sign in front of the White House (which is something I too ought to be allowed to do). But in reality are we not reduced to pretty much the same gestures, with pretty much the same hope of achieving anything? My negative ideas about political life today are trying precisely to say that political action is too often rendered futile by the massive corruption and dishonesty and fakery which neutralize it everywhere. But I do not mean by that to say that political action is ineffective and hopeless: just that something else is needed. Same with technology: it is not evil, but it is not beyond all criticism either. If used cynically and opportunistically for power and wealth, it becomes a disastrous weapon *against* humanity and is the instrument by which the demons crush and humiliate and destroy humanity.[10]

Merton had first corresponded with Ruether after reading an article by her on the church in the world. The exchange took place when Merton was again wrestling with the question of whether he should leave Gethsemani. At the time, Ruther was then twenty-nine years old. Thus, the correspondence took place at a time when she was just at the beginning of her intellectual career as a thinker, writer, and teacher. Though separated by more than twenty years in age, Merton responded to her as an equal. He subsequently entrusted her with several black ink Zen drawings that he had done. When Merton died, she honored his request not to exploit the drawings commercially but to use them for some social good.

---

9. *RJ*, 334, Merton to Cameron, letter of November 29, 1964.

10. *At Home in the World*, 43–44.

She used them for an auction to raise money for the defense of Dan and Phil Berrigan, anti-war activists facing conspiracy charges.[11]

In that he did not join movements or take to the streets, Merton was not an activist. This was not simply a matter of obedience. Merton believed in the need, ethically and personally, to define his limits. For Merton, this meant excluding sloganeering and joining causes. Rather, as Merton expressed in late 1962 in a letter to Jim Forest, "there is a genuine reality, totally opposed to the fictions of politics." Merton explained that the necessary first step along the way of purifying, humanizing, and somehow illuminating the world was to emphasize spirituality.

> We have to pray for a total and profound change in the mentality of the whole world. What we have known in the past as Christian penance is not a deep enough concept if it does not comprehend the special problems and dangers of the present age. Hair shirts will not do the trick, though there is no harm in mortifying the flesh. But vastly more important is the complete change of heart and the totally new outlook on the world of man. . . . The great problem is this inner change. . . . [Any peace action has] to be regarded . . . as an application of spiritual force and not the use of merely political pressure. We all have the great duty to realize the deep need for purity of soul, that is to say the deep need to possess in us the Holy Spirit, to be possessed by Him. This takes precedence over everything else.[12]

He cautioned against a temptation of peacemakers, to seek immediate results. Wanting peacemakers to witness for peace, justice, and truth through compassionate living, Merton explained in another letter to Forest,

> Do not depend on the hope of results. . . . It is so easy to get engrossed with ideas and slogans and myths that in the end one is left holding the bag, empty, with no trace of meaning left in it. And then the temptation is to yell louder than ever in order to make the meaning be there again by magic. . . . As for the big results, they are not in your hands or mine, but they can suddenly happen, and we can share in them: but there is no point in building our lives on this personal satisfaction, which may be denied us and which after all is not that important. . . . The great thing, after all, is to live, not to pour out your life in the service of

11. Ruether, "Introduction," ibid., xix.

12. Online: http://www.jimandnancyforest.com/2006/05/02/mertons-advice/

a myth: and we turn the best things into myths. If you can get free from the domination of causes and just serve Christ's truth, you will be able to do more and will be less crushed by the inevitable disappointments. . . . The real hope . . . is not in something we think we can do, but in God who is making something good out of it in some way we cannot see. If we can do His will, we will be helping in this process. But we will not necessarily know all about it beforehand.[13]

Merton offered similar reflections in a letter dated October 10, 1967, to Dan Berrigan,

In my opinion the job of the Christian is to try to give an example of sanity, independence, human integrity, good sense, as well as Christian love and wisdom, against all establishments and all mass movements and all current fashions which are merely mindless and hysterical. . . . The most popular and exciting thing at the moment is not necessarily the best choice.[14]

Merton genuinely worried that many peace activists succumbed to the rush and pressures of modern life. Merton warned that to allow one to be carried away by a multitude of conflicting concerns, to commit oneself to too many demands, to undertake too many projects, and to want to help everyone in everything is to yield to a pervasive contemporary form of violence. It is cooperation in violence. It destroys the fruitfulness of one's work because it kills the root of inner wisdom that makes work fruitful.[15]

Merton responded to *The Triple Revolution* by analyzing the three revolutions as separate but linked. The cybernation revolution invalidated the general mechanisms of the political economy that evolved through the industrial revolution. As machines took over production, they would absorb an increasing proportion of resources while the people who are displaced become dependent on minimal and unrelated government measures such as social security, welfare payments, or unemployment insurance. The resulting misery could give way to political chaos and undermine civil liberties.

13. Ibid.
14. *HGL*, 98.
15. *CGB*, 86.

Merton also observed that new weapon systems cannot win wars, but they could obliterate civilization. Merton anticipated a trend away from the deployment of armed troops in combat and towards the use of powerful weapons of mass destruction that could terrorize and destroy an enemy. This was also the theoretical basis of the London blitz and the strategic bombing of both Germany and Japan by the Allies. Rather than causing morale to break, these bombing served only to harden the resolve of the bombed people. Merton warned that modern warfare is planned and fought not by people alone, but also by "mechanical computers."[16]

People were feeling the full impact of the weapons revolution. Governments at every level had reduced public services like schools, parks, roads, homes, decent cities, and clean air and water. At the same time, government funding seemed unlimited for the development and deployment of new weapon systems around the world. Wars around the world entailed real costs in human and material terms. In contemporary parlance, you could not pay for guns and butter.

With deep pessimism, Thomas Merton responded to such threats as thought control, formalized mechanization of the economy, preemptive attacks, and "unquestioning belief in machines and processes which characterizes the mass mind."[17] Merton expressed concern about the spiritual disruption that would occur if humans come to base our moral or political decisions on computers. He saw a very serious danger in which most of our crucial decisions may turn out to be no decisions at all, but only the end product of conjectures and games fed to us by computers. He decried "a depressingly inane magazine article" on "the mechanical output" of thinking machines. "[J]ust wait until they start philosophizing with computers!"[18]

Merton anticipated a movement towards a "more and more collectivist, cybernated mass culture."[19] His nightmarish vision included such areas as the arts and religion. In "A Letter to Pablo Antonio Cuadra concerning Giants," Merton addressed the Nicaraguan poet and editor of the newspaper *La Prensa* with his concern about "a Christianity of money, of action, of passive crowds, an electronic Christianity of loudspeakers and

16. Merton, "Nuclear War and Christian Responsibility," 43.

17. Merton, "Introduction," *Breakthrough to Peace*, 11–13.

18. *CGB*, 8 (17).

19. Ibid, 258 (282).

parades. Magog (a symbol of the United States) is himself without belief, cynically tolerant of the athletic yet sentimental Christ devised by some of his clients, because this Christ is profitable to Magog."[20]

DEFINING AND EVALUATING TECHNOLOGY

In June 1966, Merton gave several talks on technology, partially transcribed and included as appendices in this book, at the Abbey of Our Lady of Gethsemani. He disavowed any special competency or originality on the subject of technology. He explained that technology derives from the Greek *techne* (an art or craft) and *logia* (the systematic treatment of) and generally refers to tools, techniques, or systems of organization and production that have as their intended consequence a solution for a single problem.

Merton understood as positive the idea that people have available scientific knowledge and research that they may apply to changing the natural environment into an artificial environment for some purpose, and ultimately for the common good. Merton saw the technological revolution as therefore revolutionizing the relationship of humankind to the environment. People are "creating a completely artificial environment to replace a natural environment. That's not an essential part of the definition, but that is what happens. That's what technology does."[21]

Merton identified several characteristics of technology in the modern world that he believed dangerous, notably asking right questions about the meaning of technology. The right question is not whether a technology works, whether it will benefit anyone, or if it will increase profits. No, the right question is this: what is the essence of technology? Not what it does, but what it means, and is it right.

Speaking of the potential misuse of technology in modern warfare, Merton explained that any understanding of technology that is not aligned with ethics is diabolical. For Merton, there was something the matter with a theology that fails to address the real problems of life and actually to come to grips with them. Technological innovation may not be

---

20. *CP*, 382.

21. Transcript is an appendix; also, Merton, "Technology," *Collected Essays* 6, Bellarmine Archives, 53–59.

heretical, but Merton insisted that there is something profoundly wrong with anything that could lead to the destruction of millions of people.

For Merton, modern people display a Faustian attitude towards life. Faust is the protagonist in a classic German tale that tells of a highly successful scholar who makes a deal with the devil in exchange for unlimited knowledge and worldly pleasure. In Merton's usage, the Faustian legend recalls the three temptations of Jesus in the desert. Offered three paths of self-sufficiency, authority over the earthly kingdoms, and unlimited godlike power, Jesus refuses to surrender his integrity by making a deal with the devil. Similarly, modern people face contemporary forms of the same temptations: self-sufficiency, power, militarism, and wealth. Merton exhorted people to honor God and to live into community with love.

Merton approached technology as inherently neutral. People can use technology for good or evil outcomes. Discernment makes a difference. The malevolent intent and destructive potential of some technologies require self-limitation. Indeed, for Merton some technologies that were developed could have been stopped and should have been refused.

To evaluate technology, Merton outlined broad-brush guidelines in the passage already quoted at the start of this chapter. Subsequently, especially in his journals, letters, and poetry, Merton articulated several specific ethical criteria: 1) valuing human personality; 2) promoting the common good; 3) protecting the health (including the psychic health) and well being of people; and 4) exercising skepticism towards so-called experts. Merton especially worried about the power and wealth concentrated among those who controlled technological innovation.

Merton saw technology as a fact of modern life, a necessity for modern living, and an enormous influence on the monastic life. According to Merton, *The Rule of St. Benedict* taught that monks were to respect tools and to honor artisans and craftspeople (*Rule*, chapters 31, 32, and 57). "St. Benedict never said the monk must *never* go out, *never* receive a letter, *never* have a visitor, *never* talk to anyone, *never* hear any news. He meant that the monk should distinguish what is useless or harmful from what is useful and salutary, and *in all things* glorify God." [22]

Later in *Conjectures of a Guilty Bystander*, Merton returned to themes that he believed characterized the freshness, freedom, broadness,

---

22. *CGB*, 6 (15), Merton's emphasis

and healthiness of early Benedictine life. "St. Benedict's principle is that the Rule should be moderate."[23]

Three Baskets of Concern: Destruction, Distortion, and Distraction,

What specifically bothered Merton about technology? We may gather Merton's concerns in three baskets.

Destructive Developments

In the first basket, Merton believed that technology threatened human survival. Humankind had over-reached itself in such areas as military hardware and environmental pollutants.

Unintended and potentially destructive consequences of modern science and technology constitute the first basket of Merton's concerns regarding technology. He understood that he lived during revolutionary times. By the nineteen sixties, Merton had in mind a profound spiritual crisis manifested throughout the world in desperation, cynicism, violence, conflict, self-contradiction, ambivalence, and fear. He decried an obsessive attachment to images, idols, slogans, and programs that only dull the general anguish for a moment until it bursts out in more acute and terrifying form:

> We do not know if we are building a fabulously wonderful world or destroying all that we have ever had, all that we have achieved!
>
> All the inner force of man is boiling and bursting out, the good together with the evil, the good poisoned by evil and fighting it, the evil pretending to be good and revealing itself in the most dreadful crimes, justified and rationalized by the purest and most innocent intentions.
>
> Man is all ready to become a god, and instead he appears at times to be a zombie. And so we fear to recognize our *kairos* [time of fulfillment] and accept it.[24]

Merton saw specific manifestations of the times—computers, racism, violation of human rights, war, militarism, and the eclipse of nature—as

23. Ibid., 82–83 (96).
24. Ibid., 55 (67).

incompatible with the norms of God. Merton wrote, "Certainly there is great risk for a nation which is still playing cowboys and Indians in its own imagination but with H-Bombs and Polaris submarines at its disposal!"[25]

Merton acknowledged the many achievements of science and technology. But priorities of the day did not enthuse him. When, on his forty-sixth birthday, an ape was sent into space, Merton was not impressed. He discerned that what was at stake was not a human good, as apologists for the space program argued, but rather the militarization of space. From Mars or the moon we will perhaps someday blow up the world:

> . . . Tra la. Push the buttons, press the levers! As soon as they get a factory on Mars for banana-colored apes there will be no guilt at all.
>
> I am forty-six years old. Let's be quite serious. Civilization has deigned to grace my forty-sixth birthday with this marvelous feat, and I should get ribald about it? Let me learn from this contented ape. He pressed buttons. He pulled levers. They shot him too far. Never mind. They fished him out of the Atlantic and he shook hands with the Navy.[26]

Distortion of Our True Humanity

In the second basket, Merton cautioned that an uncritical embrace of engineering and technology distorts our true humanity. In a lecture on technology, he observed that a crucial point emerging from such documents as the Dogmatic Constitution in the Modern World (*Lumen Gentium*) was that technology must serve humankind. Technology must serve the interests of real people.

For Merton, technological society would not produce faith. He saw this as an outcome of prayer and contemplation. Merton saw no reason to be a monk if he was not able to develop a consciousness different from that experienced outside the monastery. For people to recover their capacity to have faith and to live more humanly, they should seek radical healing, one path to which is contemplation.[27]

Merton believed that, by regarding engineers and technologists as arbiters of the future, humankind had ceased fully to love God, self, and

25. *LE,* 169.

26. *CGB,* 49 (61).

27. Merton, *Life and Holiness,* 106–7; *Thomas Merton in Alaska,* 126.

neighbor. Beginning in the late eighteenth and early nineteenth centuries with the industrial revolution, new technologies had degraded the human spirit and reduced humanity to the condition of a machine responding automatically to diverse stimuli, notably those generated by political demagogues and by modern mass media.

Specifically, how did technology so distort our true humanity? Merton believed that technology could easily manipulate the false self. Technology contributes to alienation from our pilgrimage to our truest selfhood. Merton addressed this in a Chilean magazine *Punto Final*:

> There is a danger of technology becoming an end in itself and arrogating to itself all that is best and most vital in human effort: thus humans come to serve their machines instead of being served by them. . . . The more corrupt a social system is, the more it tends to be controlled by technology instead of controlling it. The intimate connection between technology and alienation is and will remain one of the crucial problems we will need to study and master in our lifetime. Technology means wealth and power but it bestows the greatest amount of wealth and power upon those who serve it most slavishly at the expense of authentic human interests and values, including their own human and personal integrity. Life in the United States shows this beyond question. But unfortunately, the rest of the world secretly or overtly wishes to become like the United States.[28]

Merton concluded this reflection by observing, "What a tragedy that would be." Merton's editorial comment reflected his appreciation of diversity. It also revealed awareness that earth's carrying capacity will not sustain indefinitely the material prosperity of the rich world. His social location led Merton to be very critical of the United States during turbulent times.

Merton often worried that technology prevents our discovering of our truest selfhood. Merton frequently stressed that what really matters in life is our journey, or pilgrimage to claim our true humanity. "Our real journey in life is interior: it is a matter of growth, deepening, and of an ever greater surrender to the creative action of love and grace in our hearts."[29] Merton defended contemplation as a path to realize one's true self:

28. "Answers for Herman Lavin Cerda"; reprinted in English translation, *Merton Annual* 2 (1989) 6–7.

29. *RJ*, September 1968 Circular Letter, 118.

In an age where there is much talk about "being yourself," I re-
serve to myself the right to forget about being myself, since in any
case there is very little chance of my being anybody else. Rather
it seems to me that when one is too intent on "being himself" he
runs the risk of impersonating a shadow.

Yet I cannot pride myself on special freedom, simply because
I am living in the woods. . . . We all live somehow or other, and
that's that. It is a compelling necessity for me to be free to embrace
the necessity of my own nature.[30]

Divertissements, Diversions, and Distractions

As a third basket of concern, Merton thought technology had become for
many a distraction, or *divertissement*, the function of which is to stoke our
false self through acquiring money, satisfying our appetite for status or
justifying society, "My country right or wrong" thinking. Merton believed
that technology anesthetizes individuals and plunges them in the warm,
apathetic stupor of a collectivity. These forces threatened *shalom*, a God-
given condition of balance, harmony, and integrity.

Merton believed that society seeks to distract or divert our attention from the reality that we are God's beloved. We live more fully, more
humanly, when we discover we are God's beloved. In the words of a song
sung by Bobby Darin, "if anybody asks you who I am, tell them I'm a child
of God."

Even Gethsemani was not immune from the technological forces
of the modern world. Monks worked overtime. Increased busy-ness and
business heightened Merton's ongoing search for solitude. Merton culti-
vated an attitude of skepticism for machines. He chafed at excessive or
unnecessary innovation and a negative impact of technology on the pace
of life at Gethsemani.

In 1955, new machines speeded cheese production on which the
monks depended for their livelihood. The influx of orders excited everyone, but Merton commented sarcastically that, with sales booming, the
monks had finally justified their existence.[31]

30. "Day of a Stranger," *Thomas Merton Reader*, 431–32.
31. *SS*, 356.

Merton recognized that people living in any age could follow *The Rule of St Benedict*. Though not written for a technological society, Merton urged adaptation of the *Rule* for a technological culture. In talks on technology that he gave at Gethsemani, Merton acknowledged the need for the monastery to take into account the fact that technology had a deeply revolutionary impact on monastic life. If this was not done, "we're going to be running a museum, with a lot of air conditioning and fans on the side, but it is going to be a museum with people sitting around in funny costumes in air-conditioned rooms and kidding themselves that they haven't anything to do with technology, which is absurd. So what we have to do, we have to face this fact."

Merton struggled personally with transparency, integrity, and authentic Christian living in a world that robes Christian selfhood in secular clothing. As early as 1938, Merton worried about what he wanted to be. He suggested to Robert Lax that he wanted to be a "good Catholic."

Lax responded, "What you should say is that you want to be a saint."

Thinking this was a little weird, Merton said, "How do you expect me to become a saint?"

Lax responded simply, "By wanting to."[32]

Merton returned to this theme. In *Seeds of Contemplation*, Merton observed that for him to become a saint meant to discover his true self. The problem of sanctity and salvation weighed heavily on Merton. He saw technology as distorting true human freedom. Merton eschewed aspects of modernity and followed an alternative spiritual path, one that enabled him to find God at the center of his truest selfhood.

Merton's antidote to technology was in no way unique. For example, in his 1953 book *Nothing but Christ: A Benedictine Approach to Lay Spirituality*, Killian McDonnell OSB observed,

> When we contrast the intimacy of our life in God with the love of distraction which is so characteristic of our modern life we see how much distraction is an obstacle to our growth in God. Distraction has been commercialized and streamlined to satisfy each and every possible novel whim. Sometimes we pay a high price for an evening of distraction. Not that recreation is unimportant. But if the whole of life, its end and very meaning, is defined and described in terms of play and distraction, then something is radically wrong. Recreation should be of such a kind

32. *SSM*, 238.

that it does not impede the "re-creation" of the soul in the image of God, it should be as noble, in its way, as the calling of man to divine life; it should relieve man of his tensions, but not make him forget God. Even at play man must "have the awe of God before his eyes."[33]

Merton did not reject technological innovation that enhanced life at Gethsemani. He understood that it was in the nature of a monastery to use all gifts wisely. On September 21, 1949, Merton reported a new machine that aided the monks in their agricultural work. "Things have changed greatly in the six years since I was a novice. But since there is much more work, we can do with a few machines."[34] In a February 16, 1965, journal entry, Merton welcomed new power lines and with them tools that eased the workload of his brothers and allowed him to have electricity in his hermitage. "I was glad of American technology pitching in to bring me light," but he had no brief for an excess of useless technology.[35]

In a December 12, 1962, letter to Ray Livingston of Macalester College in St. Paul, Minnesota, Merton wrote that he had to some extent abandoned any intransigent position of complete hostility to machines as such.[36] Having come to accept the value of a camera and jet planes, Merton observed how helpful a tape recorder was. "It is a very fine machine and I am abashed by it. I take back some of the things I have said about technology."[37]

In spite of the Christian elements that survive in the West, Merton believed that he lived in an essentially secular, if not atheistic society. The dominant culture of the West at best tolerates God and religion. Prevailing values such as materialism, status, and power distract people from Christian values and prevent them from receiving God's grace. As a cure, Merton taught that we come to live in God's care. Only then can we resist *divertissements*, even those in monastic life.[38]

33. McDonnell, *Nothing but Christ*, 19. Killian McDonnell OSB met Merton in 1956 at St. John's Abbey in Collegeville, Minnesota. McDonnell visited Gethsemani. *TTW*, 81, 85, entries for December 31, 1960, January 3, 1961.

34. *SJ*, 241.

35. *DWL*, 206.

36. *Witness to Freedom*, 246, hereafter *WF*.

37. *Learning to Love*, 222, entry for on April 22, 1967.

38. "Notes for a Philosophy of Solitude," *Disputed Questions*, 178; *SS*, 352, entry for December 6, 1959.

Merton worried about the impact of technology on human relationships and freedoms. French thinker Jacques Ellul's discussion of mass society especially influenced Merton. For Ellul, having things imparted a false sense of security. Thus, Merton criticized frivolous materialism:

> The tragedy of a life centered on "things," on the grasping and manipulation of objects, is that such a life closes the ego upon itself as though it were an end in itself, and throws it into a hopeless struggle with other perverse and hostile selves competing together for the possessions which will give them power and satisfaction. Instead of being "open to the world" such minds are in fact closed to it and their titanic efforts to build the world according to their own desires are doomed in the end by the ambiguity and destructiveness that are in them. They seem to be light, but they battle together in impenetrable moral darkness.[39]

Merton wrote that technology had the capacity to numb a person to the danger of confusing means and ends. The reification or worship of anything other than God was, for Merton, idolatry,

> Technology was made for man, not man for technology. In losing touch with being and thus with God, we have fallen into a senseless idolatry of production and consumption for their own sakes. We have renounced the act of being and plunged ourselves into *process* for its own sake. We no longer know how to live, and because we cannot accept life in its reality life ceases to be a joy and becomes an affliction.[40]

Peering into an abyss, Merton could be quite despairing. He believed that the fixation with technology in the West blinds people to the reality of the spiritual world. Technological civilization such as people now live is without angels or God. Machines now exercise the function of shaping human consciousness, desire, and priorities. Angels and God used to play this role. Today it is hard if not impossible to find God, angels, self, or neighbor.

39. *Zen and the Birds of Appetite*, 82.
40. *CGB*, 202 (222), Merton's emphasis.

Merton's Prophetic Diagnosis

Welling up with compassion for a world caught up in pursuit of the false self, a world of hallucinogenic drugs, consumerism, propaganda, technology, and war, Merton sought to bring people to their senses. To shape an alternative vision, Merton probed the monastic traditions as well as other religions, world-views, communal experiments, and twentieth-century literature. Especially significant was his role in introducing myriad readers to the spiritual teachings of southern and east Asia, of Islam, and of the ancient wisdom of Africa, Australasia, and native America. Imaginatively, Merton also mediated his knowledge of traditional knowledge systems and modern technology through art, photography, literary criticism, and poetry.

Believing that technology had evolved to such an extent that some form of religious idealism was necessary to sustain humanity, Merton did not look primarily to organized religion for hope. He turned to contemporary artists and poets. In an article on "Art and Freedom," Merton observed, "Society benefits when the artist liberates himself from its coercive or seductive pressures. Only when he is obligated to his fellow man in the concrete, rather than to society in the abstract can the artist have anything to say that will be of value to others."[41]

Merton doubted that technology could deliver what people expected, a new world of progress, prosperity, and peace. Rather, technology would usher in a new kind of jungle, an electronic labyrinth. Merton worried about forces that threatened ultimate disaster. In an exchange with Lord Northbourne, hereditary landowner, farmer, and author of *Religion in the Modern World*, Merton laid out his belief that technological society could be redeemed. His letter formed the basis of an essay entitled "Redeeming the Time." The letter offers a succinct summary of Merton's thoughts on technological society, ecology, and the place of contemplation in finding balance in life. Merton observed,

> More and more I become aware of the gravity of the present situation, not only in matters of tradition and discipline and the spiritual life, but even as regarding man and his civilization. The forces that have been at work to bring us to this critical point have now apparently completely escaped our control (if they ever were un-

41. *Raids on the Unspeakable*, 172.

der it) and I do not see how we can avoid a very great disaster, by which I do not mean a sudden extermination of the whole race by H-bombs, but nevertheless a general collapse into anarchy and sickness together. In a certain sense, the profound alterations in the world and in man that have resulted from the last hundred years of "progress" are already a disaster, and the effects will be unavoidable. In such a situation, to speak with bland optimism of the future of man and of the Church blessing a new technological paradise becomes not only absurd but blasphemous. Yet at the same time, this technological society still has to be redeemed and sanctified in some way, not simply cursed and abhorred.[42]

Merton's letter was one of a number of occasions in which he reflected on the Second Vatican Council and the renewal of the Catholic Church. Merton hoped that the church would somehow inspire humanity to overcome false expectations associated with science and technology and to work for a culture of peace. This culture of peace could be the fruit of the convergence of diverse cultures, including the ancient wisdom of our elders, those who live in pre-modern, traditional societies.

As a way to reflect on culture and society, Merton continued to express himself in poetry. *Emblems of a Season of Fury* (1963) contained some of Merton's most moving poems with ethical force. The lead poem, "Why Some Look Up to Planets and Heroes," was eerily topical. Merton looked at the space program of the United States. It expended enormous sums of money for purposes Merton deemed irrelevant to human need. Technology had become an end in itself; computers had come to be thinking machines.

Merton's prophetic power was evident in a poem entitled, "And the Children of Birmingham." Merton focused on the deaths of four children when demonstrations took place after the bombings of a motel and a civil rights leader's home. On September 15, 1963, a Ku Klux Klan group bombed the 16th Street Baptist Church. The racially motivated bombing resulted in the deaths of four girls, Addie Mae Collins (aged 14), Denise McNair (aged 11), Carole Robertson (aged 14), and Cynthia Wesley (aged 14). Twenty-two other people were injured, one of whom was Addie Mae Collins' younger sister, Sarah.

In a prose poem, "Chant To Be Used in Processions around a Site with Furnaces," Merton commented on the technological sophistication

42. *WF,* 313–14, letter written Easter, 1965.

of the Nazis. "I was born into a Catholic family but as these people were not going to need a priest I did not become a priest I installed a perfectly good machine it gave satisfaction to many." He concluded his meditation with a warning, "Do not think yourself better because you burn up friends and enemies with long-range missiles without ever seeing what you have done." Merton did not merely condemn the Nazis. As in his early novel, *Journal of My Escape from the Nazis*, which appeared posthumously in 1969, Merton indicted the whole of Western civilization.[43]

In a prose poem entitled "Hagia Sophia," Merton wrote of the appearance of his "sister, Wisdom" during four of the daily times of common prayer at the Abbey of Gethsemani: dawn, the hour of *Lauds;* early morning, the hour of *Prime*; high morning, the hour of *Terce*; and sunset, the hour of *Compline*. Merton explored alienation of the individual and the breakdown of communication between the individual and God, leading ultimately to the breakdown in community and communion. Whatever positive things Merton wrote elsewhere about technology, Merton was critical here and throughout his later poetry.

The collection *Emblems of a Season of Fury* included "A Letter to Pablo Antonio Cuadra Concerning Giants," a prose poem that used symbolism to analyze the "emptiness of technological man." Merton likened technology to a genie summoned out of the depths of human confusion, a "complacent sorcerer's apprentice who spends billions on weapons of destruction and space rockets when he cannot provide decent meals, shelter, and clothing for two thirds of the human race." Merton asked, "Is it improper to doubt the intelligence and sincerity of modern man?"[44]

Merton acknowledged that it was "not accepted as a sign of progressive thinking to question the enlightenment of the twentieth century barbarian." However, he could not be silent, as were the "stool pigeons and torturers whose most signal claim to success is that they have built so many extermination camps and operated them to the limit of their capacity."[45]

Ezekiel 38 and 39 mentioned Gog, king of Magog. Revelation 20:8 used the two names as symbols of the gentile nations mobilized against the church. For Merton, Gog and Magog were symbols of the United

---

43. *CP,* 346–49; *In the Dark before Dawn,* 119–22.

44. Ibid., 372.

45. Ibid., 373.

States and Soviet Union. For Merton, the greatest sin of the Russian and American empires was not merely their greed, cruelty, moral dishonesty, and infidelity to truth, but above all their unmitigated arrogance towards the rest of humanity.[46] With great urgency, Merton was saying, be not like these giants.

Elsewhere, Merton commented, "It is taken for granted that the U.S. is universally benevolent, wise, unselfish and magnanimous in her dealings with Latin American countries." Merton concluded that this is not the case.[47] With stunning language and visual imagery, Merton explored a new world coming into being. In an essay on "Poetry and Contemplation," Merton reflected on his identity as poet, contemplative, and co-creator with God:

> In an age of science and technology, in which we find ourselves bewildered and disoriented by the fabulous versatility of the machines we have created, we live precipitated outside ourselves at every movement, interiorly empty, spiritually lost. . . . At such a time as this, it seems absurd to talk of contemplation. . . . The contemplative is not just a person who sits under a tree with legs crossed, or one who edifies herself or himself with the answer to ultimate and spiritual problems. He or she is one who seeks to know the meaning of life not only with one's head but with one's whole being, by living it in depth and in purity, and thus uniting himself to the very Source of Life. . . . the whole world and all the incidents of life tend to be sacraments—signs of God, signs of God's love working in the world.[48]

Thomas Merton was not a Luddite. The Luddites were English working class people who, early in the nineteenth century, opposed the introduction of new wide-framed automated looms that could be operated by cheap, relatively unskilled labor. This resulted in the loss of jobs for many skilled textile workers who protested—generally peacefully—the introduction of new tools for textile production. The ruling classes suppressed any resistance violently.

Merton did not oppose technology per se. The following excerpt from an essay on communication and communion expresses Merton's nuanced thinking about science, technology, and religion:

46. Ibid., 380.
47. *Secular Journal*, 47–48.
48. Merton, *LE*, 339–40, 345.

If man is to recover his sanity and spiritual balance, there must be a renewal of communion between the traditional, contemplative disciplines and those of science, between the poet and the physicist, the priest and the depth psychologist, the monk and the politician.

Certainly the mere rejection of modern technology as an absolute and irremediable evil will not solve any problems. The harm done by technology is attributable more to its excessive and inordinately hasty development than to technology itself. It is possible that in the future a technological society *might* conceivably be a tranquil and contemplative one. . . . But one thing is certain, if the contemplative, the monk, the priest, and the poet merely forsake their vestiges of wisdom and join in the triumphant empty-headed crowing of advertising men and engineers of opinion, then there is nothing left in store for us but total madness.[49]

Merton appreciated technologies that blessed his life and added joy to the lives of others. He valued appropriate uses of technology, a position he shared with Gandhi. Merton liked simple technology, which accounts for his fascination with Shaker furnishings. Even as he spent much of the last years of his life in a hermitage, Merton resourcefully used simple technologies at his disposal—notably those of the publishing world—to communicate his vision of a better world.

Merton read widely in contemporary literature, including progressive Catholic thinkers on science and technology like Teilhard de Chardin. In Merton's observations on technology, one discerns a provisional shift from embrace to warning against an obsession with the new. Merton worried that neither scientist, nor technologist, nor artist, nor poet could save humankind. Contemporary fetishisms like pseudo-mysticism, technology, and violence were leading in an ultimately fatal direction. In an article entitled, "The Angel and the Machine," Merton observed that God and God's angels alone have such power to save. He continued,

Surely, if we are to rebuild the temporal order by the dedication of our own freedom and our science to truth and to love, we need our good angels to help us and to guide us. Who knows? Maybe our technology itself calls for angelic guardians who are ready to come if we let them. We need not fear that they will revive obsessions that died with the Middle Ages. It is not for us to imagine

49. Merton, "Symbolism: Communication or Communion," *New Directions in Prose and Poetry*, 15; also published in *Love and Living*, 79, Merton's emphasis.

them, to explain them, to write them bodily into the details of our blueprints. It is for us to trust them, knowing that more than ever they are invisible to us, unknown to us, yet very powerful, very propitious and always near.[50]

Merton was prescient about the growing reach of technology. In a circular letter written for Lent 1967, he expressed awareness of the effects of the cybernation revolution. Merton decried the way society diverts resources away from helping the needy. He dismissed President Johnson's "war on poverty" as "a sheer insult to the people living in our Eastern Kentucky Mountains." Merton therefore took aim at the "universal myth that technology infallibly makes everything in every way better for everybody. It does not."[51]

Merton acknowledged that technology can be good and that humanity has an absolute obligation to use means at our disposal to help people otherwise living in utter misery and dying like flies. He warned about negative externalities, or effects on people whose interests were ignored and probably not taken into account. For example, modern drugs like penicillin and other medical advances save lives, but our abuse of these have decreased their effectiveness. Similarly, modern agriculture can enhance our ability to feed starving people, but the excessive use of chemical fertilizers has often resulted in the degradation of water supplies used by people throughout an entire ecosystem.

Merton recognized that technology has the capacity to make the world better for millions of persons. Yet Merton saw that those in powerful positions instead used technology to enrich big corporations, spray Vietnamese with napalm, and threaten people with genocide.

Twenty years later, the Cistercian M. Basil Pennington mentioned the impact this letter had on readers. Some felt Merton had been too negative about technology. Pennington believed that Merton wrote what people needed to hear at the time.[52] Merton spoke truth to the powers and principalities of his day. He envisioned the Spirit of God bringing about a new world in which all might live more humanly.

---

50. "The Angel and the Machine," *Merton Seasonal*, 6.

51. *RJ*, 98.

52. Pennington, *Thomas Merton, Brother Monk*, 189–90.

REFLECTIONS

One Monday in June 1999, full of excitement, I arrived at the Abbey of Our Lady of Gethsemani for my third retreat there. Having departed Memphis in the wee hours of the morning, I retired around 8:00 that evening. I woke up early the next day, at 3:00 AM. Hardly conscious, I dressed and made my way to the balcony of the chapel for *Matins* and *Lauds*, the early morning prayers. I picked up a copy of the psalms for the day and made my way to the front pew.

By this time, I had become relatively familiar with the routine. Benedictine prayer is at once regular and communal. Yet, as is true for any community, I could expect the unanticipated.

On this particular morning, several monks in white robes had already gathered. However, I was surprised that several Tibetan Buddhist monks in yellow-orange robes were also present.

Through the week, the Christian and Buddhist monks chanted together as part of an interreligious vigil that grew out of the historic meeting in 1968 of Thomas Merton and Tenzin Gyatso, the fourteenth Dalai Lama. The monks produced a compact disk entitled *Compassion*. The recording recalled the legacy of two men who united Eastern and Western religions in compassion.

His Holiness the Dalai Lama wrote a message on the cover. "The world has become smaller and smaller. In spite of different traditions, different beliefs, we all have a common goal and one common responsibility. That is to make a common effort to achieve peace, world peace, peace through inner peace and a meaningful life."

Since that week at the Abbey of Our Lady of Gethsemani, I have frequently listened to the compact disk during personal contemplation, introspection, and meditation. I quietly join with the monks and chant Psalm 19:1–8:[53]

> The command of the Lord is clear, (*Cantor*)
> It gives light to the eye. (*all; refrain; repeats at end*)

---

53. From Psalm 10 to Psalm 148, the numbering adopted here follows the Hebrew Bible and is one figure ahead of the Greek and the Vulgate versions. These join 9, 10, also 114, and 115, but divide both 116 and 147 into two.

The heavens proclaim the glory of God, (*all*)
And the firmament shows forth the work of God's hand.

Day after day takes up the story,
And night after night makes known the message.

No speech, no words, no voices heard,
Yet their span extends through all the earth,
Their words to the utmost bounds of the world.

There God has placed a tent for the sun,
It comes forth like a bridegroom coming from his tent,
Rejoices like a champion to run its course.

At the end of the sky is the rising of the sun,
To the furthest ends of the sky is its course,
There is nothing consumed from its burning heat.

The inexpensive recording of the Psalm stimulates the forces of love and gratitude necessary for true transformation. It speaks commandingly to the soul and irresistibly induces, on the part of many listeners, a sense of serenity and peace with God.

In his study of gifts, creativity, and the artist in the modern world, Lewis Hyde, former director of creative writing at Harvard University, discusses a cardinal property of the gift: whatever we have been given must be given away again, not kept. Or if it is kept, something of similar value should be given away. The only essential is this: the gift must always move.[54]

The recording has blessed my life, a gift that I eagerly share with others. As with any true gift, I accomplish this when I play the compact disk in workshops, talks, and worship settings. Sometimes, I loan it to friends. Through its capacity to generate adoration of God, who alone is Holy, who alone is Lord, the recording and playing of *Compassion* materialize for me as appropriate technologies.

54. Hyde, *The Gift*, 4.

In a role something like that of a physician, Merton contributed significantly to the conversation engendered by discussion under way in the 1960s about technology. Merton made the following diagnosis.

> We are living in the greatest revolution in history . . . a profound spiritual crisis of the whole world, manifested largely in desperation, cynicism, violence, conflict, self-contradiction, ambivalence, fear and hope, doubt and belief, creation and destructiveness, progress and aggression, obsessive attachments to images, idols, slogans, programs that only dull the general anguish . . . Our times manifest in us a basic distortion, a deep-rooted moral disharmony against which laws, sermons, philosophies, authority, inspiration, creativity, and apparently even love itself would seem to have no power.

Merton characterized "our sickness" as "the sickness of disordered love," a "self-love that realizes itself simultaneously to be self-hate and instantly becomes a source of universal, indiscriminate destructiveness."[55]

Merton traced the sources of the crisis of Western civilization, and more precisely of European civilization, to ideas prevalent in the nineteenth century when people came to believe in indefinite progress, in the supreme goodness of the human person, and in the capacity of science and technology to achieve infinite good despite their historical and consistent misapplication. Merton challenged these principles. He believed that technology had contributed to the creation of a culture that is not livable for humankind. As evidence, Merton cited the abject misery of the poor, the problem of racism, and a crude materialism without spirit. "The fact that most believe, as an article of faith, that we are now in a position to solve all our problems does not prove that this is so. On the contrary, this belief is so unfounded that it is itself one of our greatest problems."[56]

Merton never ceased to struggle with the allure of technology or to warn others about its effects. Out of solidarity with marginalized peoples, Merton offered a vision of a better world.

Merton still speaks to the disquiet of at least four groups of readers. First, Merton opens a window into Christian contemplative traditions and other spiritual traditions that provide an antidote to modern technological society. He also guides spiritual seekers to practices that may

55. *CGB*, 55 (66–67).
56. Ibid., 60–61 (73–74).

help them in times during which materialism and noise have become a tsunami. Merton also pronounces a prophetic word for those who pronounce an anathema on leaders of any society preparing for war, violating human rights, or abusing the environment. Finally, he anticipates the new monastic movement.

Two generations ago, living out of his Trappist calling, Thomas Merton began to delineate the contours of a revolutionary way by which Christians might live more faithfully and resist such aspects of Western culture antithetical to Christianity as individualism, materialism, and anti-intellectualism. Merton wanted many people to explore alternative forms of communal living and contemplative practices. He thought ordinary people in the world should be able to fulfill their calling as children of God by adopting monastic practices such as contemplative prayer.

Merton acknowledges that technological change is a reality. As humanity develops newer technologies, Merton invites us to consider carefully the choices before us, to use technology mindfully to meet basic human needs, to refuse to acquiesce to evil, to find community, and to honor God. In this prescription, Merton was truly prescient. He warned humanity about a disastrous trajectory along which he understood the reigning science-technology paradigm to be headed. In the preface to a collection entitled *Faith and Violence: Christian Teaching and Christian Practice*, Merton told a Hassidic tale of Baal-Shem-Tov.[57] By recounting the story, Merton signaled his sense of urgency.

> Two men were traveling through a forest. One was drunk, the other was sober. As they went, they were attacked by robbers, beaten, robbed of all they had, even their clothing. When they emerged, people asked them if they got through the wood without trouble. The drunken man said, "Everything was fine; nothing went wrong; we had no trouble at all!"
>
> They said, "How does it happen that you are naked and covered with blood?"
>
> He did not have an answer.
>
> The sober man said: "Do not believe him: he is drunk. It was a disaster. Robbers beat us without mercy and took everything we had. Be warned by what happened to us, and look out for yourselves."

57. Merton, *Faith and Violence*, ix.

Be warned! Merton cautioned about the mindless doings of the heedless ones among us. He sensed a "responsibility to be in all reality a peacemaker in the world, an apostle, to bring people to truth, to make my whole life a true and effective witness to God's Truth." Merton invites all his readers to obey life, and the Spirit of Life that calls us to harvest many new fruits for which the world hungers, fruits of hope such as we may never have seen before. With these fruits, we shall build communities of love rooted and grounded in a power greater than our own.[58]

58. *SS*, 149, entry for December 27, 1957; *Raids on the Unspeakable*, 160.

SIX

Thomas Merton on Care of Earth

The Lord God is present where the new day shines in the moisture on the young grasses. The Lord God is present where the small wildflowers are known to Him alone. The Lord God passes suddenly, in the wind, at the moment when night ebbs into the ground. He Who is infinitely great has given His children a share in His own innocence. His alone is the gentlest of loves: whose pure flame respects all things.

God, Who owns all things, leaves them all to themselves. He never takes them for His own, the way we take them for our own and destroy them. He leaves them to themselves. He keeps giving them all that they are, asking no thanks of them save that they should receive from Him and be loved and nurtured by Him, and that they should increase and multiply, and so praise Him.

He saw that all things were good. . . . All things belong to Him. They owe Him everything and they can repay Him nothing. They exist in Him with an uncreated existence, holy and pure, infinitely above them.

—Thomas Merton, *Sign of Jonas*

A crucial aspect of Thomas Merton's monastic life anticipates a priority of the new monasticism. Merton cared deeply for the plot of God's earth given to the monks of Gethsemani. His writings captured eloquently a sense of the sacred throughout the entire range of God's good earth. As a Catholic priest and an ecological philosopher, Thomas Berry observed in his foreword to a collection of Merton's writings on nature, "Everywhere we find ourselves invaded by the world of the sacred. Such was the experience of Thomas Merton. Such is the wonder that he is communicating to us."[1]

A crucial aspect of my retreats at the Abbey of Our Lady of Gethsemani has been time alone in the natural world surrounding the monastery. Forests, fields, and streams abound. There is a pond with fish. On occasion, I have brought fishing gear. Though I have never caught anything, I have used un-barbed hooks. I have been prepared to release any catch.

Depending on weather and season, one can tramp through snow amidst leafless trees, bask in sunshine, or see flowers and grain ready for harvest. If one chooses to climb one of the knob hills, one can enjoy a panoramic view that extends north through Kentucky woodlands to the shores of the Ohio River; east to the Appalachians; west to an area of caves and farmland; and south to the Mississippi Delta.

Once, a monk escorted me after breakfast to the hermitage where Merton spent his last years. Over the door to the hermitage was one word, "Shalom," peace. A small sign adorned an empty chair on the porch with the words, "Bench of Dreams." Nearby were the wheel and cross often associated with the hermitage, thanks to an iconic photograph that Merton took.

Even though I never met him in person, I have sensed Merton accompanying me while I have explored the Abbey's grounds. In some measure after 1951, when Abbot James named him forester, Thomas Merton was responsible for the health of the forests. The work entailed restoration of the woodlands that had been previously clear-cut. During this short-lived assignment, Merton developed knowledge and skills that enabled him to become a competent naturalist. Merton also wrote about his sense of intimate connection with the land and the place of the natural world in his experience of solitude, stillness, and silence.

For Merton, a favored vantage point for observing nature was a fire tower. From that and other places in the woods, Merton read, meditated, and incorporated nature centrally into his life of prayer. Throughout his journals, he recorded prayers that revealed his deep love of the natural world. In *Conjectures of a Guilty Bystander*, Merton offered the following prayer, which expressed his understanding of connection with God and the whole of creation, "to God the Father on the Vigil of Pentecost":

1. Foreword to Merton, *When the Trees Say Nothing*, 18.

Today, Father, this blue sky lauds you. The delicate green and or-
ange flowers of the tulip poplar tree praise you. The distant blue
hills praise you, together with the sweet-smelling air that is full
of brilliant light. The bickering flycatchers praise you with the
lowing cattle and the quails that whistle over there. I too, Father,
praise you, with all these my brothers, and they give voice to my
own heart and to my own silence. We are all one silence, and the
diversity of voices.

You have made us together, you have made us one and many,
you have placed me here in the midst as witness, as awareness,
and as joy. Here I am. To me the world is present, and you are
present. I am a link in the chain of light and of presence. You
have made me a kind of center, but a center that is nowhere. And
yet also I am "here," let us say I am "here" under these trees, not
others.[2]

Kathleen Deignan, a sister of the Congregation of Notre Dame, observes that the voice of Merton that we hear in such passages is that of
a creation mystic. For Sister Deignan, as in many other matters of the
sacred, Merton is a spiritual master for twenty-first-century readers,

offering a way to practice the art of natural contemplation by
reading with delight and awe the scripture of creation unfolding
moment by moment all about us. With him we enter into the liturgies of rain and autumn and dawn, discovering our own "thin
places" where earth becomes diaphanous to Eden and finding
there the sanity and refreshment that brings us true vitality.[3]

Merton believed that we who benefit from the industrial revolution
are responsible for the ecological crisis that had begun to manifest itself
during his lifetime. He traced the historical roots of our predicament to a
philosophical worldview according to which people have come to regard
nature as having no reason to exist except to serve humans. Merton rejected commonplace ideas that God gave humans limitless rule of the created order; or that humans could develop technologies to fix any problem
in nature. For Merton, such thinking was rash, misguided, and arrogant,
a word used by contemporary theologian Sallie McFague to characterize

2. *CGB*, (177).
3. "Introduction," *When the Trees Say Nothing*, 41.

the way by which contemporary Western people presently understand nature.[4]

Merton saw mindless behavior by humans as contributing directly to the ongoing and potentially life-ending destruction of the very habitats upon which humans and all other organisms depend. In response, he proposed two primary courses of action. First, humans must acknowledge our interconnection with nature. Second, we need to recognize that we are custodians of creation. We are to care for the earth and for every creature.

Merton affirmed these two broad priorities as an outgrowth of his monastic calling. Reading journals and letters written over the course of twenty-seven years at the Abbey of Our Lady of Gethsemani, we see Merton developing a comprehensive ecological ethic and living by its implications for his life and potentially for the lives of his readers.

INTERCONNECTION WITH NATURE

Merton's journal entries are replete with careful observations about the seasons, the elements, plants, and creatures. In an entry dated April 13, 1963, Merton notes,

> Two superb days. When was there ever such a morning as yesterday? Cold at first, the hermitage dark in the moonlight (I had permission to go up right after Lauds), a fire in the grate (and how beautifully firelight shines through the lattice-blocks and all through the house at night!) Then the sunrise, enormous yolk of energy spreading and spreading as if to take over the sky. After that the ceremonies of the birds feeding in the dewy grass, and the meadowlark feeding and singing. Then the quiet, totally silent day, warm mid morning under the climbing sun. It was hard to say psalms: one's attention was totally absorbed by the great arc of the sky and the trees and hills and grass and all things in them. How absolutely true, and how central a truth, that we are purely and simply *part of nature,* though we are the part which recognizes God. It is not Christianity, indeed, but post-Cartesian technologism that separates man from the world and makes him a kind of little god in his own right, with his clear ideas, all by himself . . . And one can be "part of nature" surely, without being Lady Chatterley's lover.[5]

4. McFague, *Super, Natural Christians,* 66.

5. *TTW,* 312, Merton's emphasis.

Merton underscored the need to recognize our interdependence with all creation. He highlighted the phrase "part of nature." By this, he affirmed the intrinsic value of nature and our relationship to the natural world. Merton wrestled with the total innocence, and sometimes the total ignorance of people in relationship to the natural world. He sounded a call for humility and realism in our relationship with the cosmos.

The previous day, Merton had come upon a titmouse, a small resident bird. It lay dead on the grass, perhaps through his action. Having dumped some calcium chloride on a couple of anthills—not as an insecticide but as something to move the ants elsewhere—Merton pondered his role in the death of the bird. "What a miserable bundle of foolish idiots we are! We kill everything around us even when we think we love and respect nature and life."[6]

Merton continued this line of reflection. Denial of our part in nature has resulted in the madness and cruelties of Nazism and in people who are sick with junk and drugs. People needed to recognize how well God has made all things and the sacredness of all life.

A few months before Merton recorded these thoughts in his journal, Rachel Carson published the fruit of research regarding the disruptive influence of DDT on nature. Her work appeared in three installments in *The New Yorker* and then in a single volume entitled *Silent Spring*. The articles and book stirred a firestorm of controversy and launched the modern environmental movement. As much as any single piece of writing can take such credit, *Silent Spring* led to specific, significant pieces of legislation.

Through a friend, Anne Ford, Merton secured a copy of the book. After reading it, Merton wrote Rachel Carson and commended her for "contributing to a most valuable and essential piece of evidence for the diagnosis of the ills of our civilization."[7] Merton identified areas that resonated with the alarms Carson had sounded. "The awful irresponsibility with which we scorn the smallest values is part of the same portentous irresponsibility with which we dare to use our titanic power in a way that threatens not only civilization but life itself." He saw the need to address a "*consistent pattern*" that runs through every aspect of life—culture, economy, "our whole way of life"—and to arrive at a "clear, cogent statement of our ills, so that we may begin to correct them." Otherwise, humans might

6. Ibid.

7. *WF*, 70–72, letter dated January 12, 1963.

direct their efforts to superficial symptoms only. This risked aggravating the sickness: "*the remedies are expressions of the sickness itself.*"

Merton characterized the root cause of the problem as a subconscious hatred of life as such and a death wish. He went on to name a calling he shared with Carson, namely that of being an "eye of the body." He wrote that humanity is part of not only nature, but also of the whole created order. This transcends nature. For Merton, people must maintain a delicate balance. This entailed using nature wisely, understanding the interconnection of humans with the entire cosmos, and not misusing our wisdom and technical expertise.

Merton commended Carson for her analysis. He lifted up *Silent Spring* as illustrating an area in which humankind is going in the wrong direction. He saw her book as "a most salutary and important warning. I desperately hope that everyone who has a chance to help form public opinion on these vital practical matters may read your book . . . and the connection between what you say and the vastly more important problem of nuclear war: the relationship is so terribly close." Merton then offered a concrete example:

> We don't like the looks of a Japanese beetle. We let ourselves be convinced by a salesman that the beetle is a dire threat. It then becomes obvious that the thing to do is exterminate the beetle by any means whatever even if it means the extermination of many other beings which have not harmed us and which even bring joy into our lives: worse still, we will exterminate the beetle even of it means danger to our children and to our very selves. To make this seem "reasonable" we go to some lengths to produce arguments that our steps are really "harmless." I am afraid I do not relish the safety of the atomic age, but I hope I can use it to attain to a salutary detachment from life and from temporal things so that I can dedicate myself entirely and freely to truth and to my fellow man. A dangerous situation after all has certain spiritual advantages. Let us hope that we may be guided effectively by the right directions.

After signing the letter, Merton added a postscript. He indicated that he would like to write to Carson about some of the problems faced at the Abbey of Our Lady of Gethsemani. He mentioned cedar trees dying out unaccountably and a plague of bagworms.

There is no evidence that Carson replied or that they corresponded further. Merton wrote this letter before he started to keep every letter he received and carbon copies of every letter he typed and mailed. He kept a carbon of this one because he was thinking of using it as an appendix to the *Cold War Letters*, a collection that went beyond the specific topics of war and peace.[8]

In a lecture on technology, transcribed and included as an appendix to this book, Merton addressed the issue of insecticides. For Merton, the insecticide problem was a concrete example of how challenging the application of a new technology can be for a society that rejects the values of the Bible. Merton believed that technology, like theology, should help people live well. Both should take into account the wonderful interrelationship between the Creator and all creatures.

Custodianship of Nature

Merton communicated his concern for earth care in an exchange with Barbara Hubbard of the Center of American Living in New York City. Responding to a letter from her, Merton renewed his concern about the precariousness of the future. He believed that people must make life-affirming decisions. However, these are "not likely to emerge from a thought system that is largely programmed by unconscious death drives, destructiveness, greed . . . [and] the wanton taking of life and exploitation of others." Merton identified as crucial that "we are still problems to ourselves."[9]

A few weeks later, Merton again responded to another letter from Barbara Hubbard. He identified two essential components of an ethical consciousness that he believed were needed if people were to transcend "the sclerotic fixation on norms that are given by the past." He called first for a millennial consciousness that anticipates God's realm breaking in and the withering away of state systems as they existed. He identified many arenas where he detected elements of such a millennial consciousness: Marxism, Black Power, Cargo Cults, Catholic Church *aggiornamento*, liberation theology, and the realms of science and business.

Merton called for an ecological consciousness. Merton was emphatic: "look out! . . . We are not alone. We belong to a community of living beings and we owe our fellow members in this community the respect and

8. Shannon, "Preface," *Cold War Letters*, xxiii; Paul M. Pearson, email, February 24, 2010.

9. *WF*, 73, letter of December 23, 1967.

honor due to them." From this affirmation of human interconnection with the whole of creation, Merton cited theologian Albert Schweitzer to make the point that all life is sacred. Merton also quoted environmentalist Aldo Leopold, who articulated an earth ethic based on expanding the Golden Rule. "A thing is right when it tends to preserve the integrity, stability, and beauty of the biotic community. It is wrong when it tends otherwise."[10]

In a review of a book by Roderick Nash, *Wilderness and the American Mind*, Merton observed that people are blind to contradictions of our existence. He noted, for example, that citizens of the United States live by a frontier mentality despite lacking a frontier or being a predominantly rural people. As pioneers, we are both product and destroyer of the wilderness. We are oblivious to our power to reduce the wilderness to something else—farm, village, road, canal, railway, mine, factory, city, an urban nation, and a globalized world—and to the logical progression by which this will ultimately lead to destruction of the planet.

Merton found paradoxical humanity's current situation in a highly advanced technological society. Humans—at least the majority who live in the rich northern tier of nations of Europe and North America—are affluent, unsurpassed in power, and in control of our surroundings. Yet these very people are ambivalent towards the consequences of our cultural values. Our very condition is replete with self-contradictions, especially in the way humans approach wild places.

On the one hand, humans benefit from their firm attachment to values that inexorably demand the destruction of the last remnants of wildness. On the other hand, if someone suggests that our addictive behavior is itself a symptom of a sickness in ourselves, we dismiss the one who sounds a note of realism as some sort of kook rather than as a prophet.

Merton boldly affirmed that the "ambivalence of the American Mind toward nature is "rooted in our Biblical, Judeo-Christian tradition."[11] Merton remarked that what drives our wanton behavior is neither genuinely Biblical nor Jewish, nor Christian. While Merton might have added that no valid basis exists in the holy texts of any religion for the degradation of the natural world, he continued by acknowledging that a nominally-Christian kind of culture has resulted in a "manichean hostility toward created nature." This approach, dualist in its metaphysics,

10. Ibid., 74, letter of February 16, 1968, quoting but not referencing directly Leopold, *Sand County Almanac*, 262.

11. Merton, "Wild Places," 42, here and for the discussion that follows.

existed for Merton at a deep and unconscious level. It was a form of popular, superficial, and one-sided "Christian worldliness" that, in its hidden implications, was ultimately and profoundly destructive of nature and of God's creation.

Merton accepted Roderick Nash's argument that the Bible provided the Puritans grist for the mill for a tradition of repugnance towards nature in the wild. The Puritans regarded the "hideous and desolate wilderness of America as though it were filled with conscious malevolence against them. They hated it as a *person*, an extension of the Evil One, the Enemy opposed to the spread of the Kingdom of God." This Puritan ethos shaped the growth of "American capitalist culture . . . firmly rooted in a secularized Christian myth and mystique of struggle with nature." Merton observed that the basic article of faith in this mystique is that you prove you are worthy by overcoming and dominating the natural world. You justify your existence and attain bliss by transforming nature into wealth. Until it is thus transformed, nature is useless and absurd. With self-deprecating wit, Merton wrote that "anyone who refuses to see this or acquiesce in it is some kind of half-wit—or, worse, a rebel, an anarchist, a prophet of apocalyptic disorders."

Merton saw that a second theme is superimposed on this mystique. Essentially, it is that of America the beautiful. "America which must be kept lovely. . . . So don't throw that beer can in the river, even though the water is polluted with all kinds of industrial waste. Business can mess up nature, but not *you*, Jack!"

In his review article, Merton delineated an alternative trajectory to that which dominates attitudes toward nature in the United States. Merton highlighted the Transcendentalists, who reversed the Puritan prejudice against nature and began to teach that in the forests and mountains God is nearer than in the cities.

To those who listen, woodland silence whispered a message of sanity and healing. While the Puritans had assumed that humans, being evil, would only revert to the most corrupt condition in the wilderness, the Transcendentalists held that since people are naturally good, and the cities corrupting, people needed contact with nature in order to recover their true self.

Alert to the fact that such a narrative can be reduced to a cliché, Merton studied the prophetic work of Henry David Thoreau and showed that an ecological consciousness goes far deeper than a mere surface enthusiasm for scenery and fresh air. According to Merton, Thoreau and other transcendental writers produced a philosophy of balance. Wildness must be preserved. If it is not, humankind will self-destruct while destroying nature in the process. Merton took note of Thoreau's belief that not every part of a human existence should be brought under rational and conscious control. He believed that reducing all nature to a profit motif risked ending in savagery and dehumanization. The price of turning green forests into asphalt jungles was precisely this: savagery for its own sake.

For Merton, the absence of an ecological consciousness in United States history has contributed to great evils not only in the past, but also in the present. These included the genocide of First Peoples, the near extinction of bison, the enslavement of African peoples, and, in his time, the dangers of radioactive fallout and of atomic waste as potentially destructive outcomes of the military and industrial forces at work in North America.

As an alternative trajectory, Merton held up Aldo Leopold. In his classic *A Sand County Almanac*, Leopold offered perhaps the best example of how humans should approach the current problems of technology and ecology. Calling it "one of the most important moral discoveries of our time," Merton cited Leopold's "ecological conscience" as being "centered in an awareness of man's true place as a dependent member of the biotic community."[12]

In his second letter to Barbara Hubbard on December 23, 1967, Merton returned to a key ecological principle. "A thing is right when it tends to preserve the integrity, stability, and beauty of the biotic community. It is wrong when it tends otherwise." In light of this principle, Merton concluded that an examination of the social, economic, and political history over the last hundred years in the United States would be a "moral nightmare, redeemed only by a few gestures of good will on the part of those who obscurely realize that there *is* a problem. Yet compared to the magnitude of the problem, their efforts are at best pitiful: and what is more, the same gestures are made with great earnestness by the very people who continue to ravage, destroy, and pollute the country. They honor the wilderness myth while they proceed to destroy nature."[13]

Merton asked if an ecological conscience, essentially a "peace-making conscience," could become effective in the country of his day. At the

12. Ibid.

13. Ibid., 44.

time, the situation was bleak. For Merton, the country seemed to be more and more oriented to war making than to addressing the urgent moral need to live out of an ecological conscience. Merton did not hold much cause for hope. Meanwhile, he did affirm that some people wear a "little yellow and red button" that proclaims "celebrate life!" Merton bore witness to this exhortation in his life.

By these less than promising words, Merton revealed his sense of despair with not only the human condition, but also his own life. Merton had always affirmed the monastery and the witness of contemplatives as providing an effective antidote to counteract the technological onslaught. In his Preface to the Japanese edition of *Seeds of Contemplation*, Merton wrote:

> Science and technology are indeed admirable in many respects and if they fulfill their promises they can do much for man. But they can never solve man's deepest problems. On the contrary, without wisdom, without the intuition and freedom that enable man to return to the root of his being, science can only precipitate him still further into the centrifugal flight that flings him, in all his compact and uncomprehending isolation, into the darkness of outer space without purpose and without objective.[14]

Yet by 1966, when *Conjectures of a Guilty Bystander* appeared, Merton had become deeply worried that monastic institutions were having their mission and effectiveness weakened by the adoption of "modern production technologies."[15] If the monastery was to be a continual foretaste of paradise until Christ's second coming, then it is our duty to continue the work of creation by tending the garden. For, the garden, the wilderness, and the natural world more generally are essential for contemplation and growth in relation to God and one's truest self.

In an essay called "Wilderness and Paradise," which first appeared in *Cistercian Studies* in 1967, Merton concluded:

> If the monk is a man whose whole life is built around a deeply religious appreciation of his call to wilderness and paradise, and thereby to a special kind of kinship with God's creatures in the new creation, and if technological society is constantly encroaching upon and destroying the remaining "wildernesses" which it

14. *Honorable Reader*, 92.
15. St. John, "Technological Culture and Contemplative Ecology," 179 and *CGB*, 25.

nevertheless needs in order to remain human, then we might suggest that the monk, of all people should be concerned with staying
in the "wilderness" and helping to keep it a true "wilderness and
paradise."[16]

Merton affirmed that a monk should be anxious to preserve and
share the wilderness with those who come out from the cities and enjoy
sitting under trees and climbing mountains. God ordered the world in
such a way that it is good for people to dwell from time to time in wilderness places and to see themselves as protectors of these places.

In a marginal note left in one of his last working notebooks kept
while at the hermitage at Gethsemani, Merton expressed a sense of what
was at stake if we do not care for the earth and for all that dwell on earth.

> The dreadful fact that I was born into this world at the very
> moment when the whole thing came to a head (and) it is precisely
> in my lifetime that civilization has undergone this massive attack
> from within itself. My whole life is shaped by this . . . it presses on
> the brain with a [near] darkness.[17]

Over forty years have passed since Merton recorded these observations. In
the years since Rachel Carson, Thomas Merton, and others began to call
for people to walk on earth more lightly, we are learning that we cannot
sustain our socioeconomic and cultural patterns indefinitely. The prevailing cultural mood in North America encourages people to define success
and happiness by how much we consume, how much we travel, how rich
our diet, how big our house, or how fancy our car. The dominant model
of economic growth is seductive. It has benefitted some Europeans, some
North Americans, and some people in newly rich countries. However, the
fixed resources of a finite planet will never allow a world population that
has surpassed 6.7 billion humans to share in the prosperity of a few.

Merton encouraged readers around the world to examine critically
the consumer system of the rich countries of Australasia, Europe, and
North America. He believed it is fatally flawed. It makes people fat and
sick, shortens lives, increases stress and social isolation, and wreaks havoc
on the global and local environments.

Merton was a pioneer in calling for a new ecological consciousness.
However, he did not live long enough to delineate a concrete action plan.

16. *Monastic Journey*, 196.

17. Cited by Lotz in "Thomas Merton and Technology."

He did point in the right direction by calling on humans to recover paradise, at both local and global levels, personally and in our communities. Merton sensed the very dark, ominous, and desperate manner by which an ecological crisis could envelop the earth, as it has.

REFLECTIONS

Humanity has created "needs" that cannot be sustained. Like most North Americans, I live in chains. These are not prison doors behind which governments incarcerate or kill women and men for reason of conscience. These are not barbed wire fences that confine refugees to their camps. These are more invisible chains of affluence. They prevent me from discerning their evil effects on me and on many persons around me.

The chains lead me to worship false gods and, as the Epistle of James states, they are a major cause of war. Here and elsewhere among wealthy nations, people must confront the reality that our abundance depends on control of global resources. We North Americans have aided and abetted a process that has plunged the poor nations into a succession of traumatic and catastrophic crises.

The gap between the rich and poor continues to widen. The degradation of earth continues unabated. If anything, the pace of destructive change is accelerating. By military means, the U.S. and its allies are affecting change in Iraq, Afghanistan, Sudan, Colombia, and elsewhere. Meanwhile, Brazil, China, India, a newly united Europe, and other countries confront the U.S. as competitors for resources and power. Earth's resources cannot sustain the consumption of resources by the richer countries of the world, including the U.S., or those who would mimic the material success of the rich.

Many have suggested that the churches are on the eve of a second reformation. If this proves to be the case, the new reformation will be international rather than regional, and it will potentially have an even more powerful impact than that of the sixteenth century. Thomas Berry characterized the focus of such a reformation as one that will bring into being a "mutually enhancing human-Earth relationship."[18]

In the 1990s, a global social movement successfully gave new life to an ancient Biblical idea called Jubilee. In just one North American city,

18. Berry, 2006 interview quoted by Assadourian, "Rise and Fall of Consumer Cultures," 16.

Memphis, Tennessee, a coalition of over a thousand religious bodies came together and undertook several initiatives. These included the following: 1) Participating congregations contributed $1.00 per member for early intervention on behalf of infants at risk. One program used the funds to strengthen learning skills of at-risk pre-school children and to offer parenting skills to mothers and fathers. 2) People worked (unsuccessfully) to eliminate the Tennessee sales tax on food and (successfully) to implement a Living Wage campaign for full-time city and county workers. 3) The coalition supported local groups monitoring toxic wastes. 4) A Jubilee campaign promoted education in the areas of eco-justice, anti-racism, and inter-ethnic relations.

The Jubilee idea appeared in a Biblical text. Leviticus 25 spelled out the details of a mutually enhancing and sustainable human-earth relationship. Though it is possible ancient Israel never implemented Jubilee legislation, it was more than a utopian ideal. The Hebrew prophets who put forward the idea sought to ensure that everyone lived with a guaranteed minimum of economic means and thereby could actualize God's will for society. In Ezekiel 46, Isaiah 61, and other texts, the prophets drew attention to Jubilee practices, as did Jesus. In Luke 4:18–19, he said the time of Jubilee was at hand.

Few Christians or Jews know about Jubilee practices. It is not hard to guess why. Jubilee justice envisions a periodic and fundamental restructuring of economic relations for all creation! Ancestral lands must be returned to the original inhabitants. Financial debts must be cancelled. Freedom from slavery must be granted. The land must periodically lie fallow. Farm animals must regularly have a year off.

Jesus did more than announce that God's commonwealth of justice was breaking in. He called for action. He told a rich young man to give what he had to the poor (Mark 10:17–22). He blessed Zacchaeus when the tax collector offered restitution to those he had defrauded (Luke 19:1–10).

In this latter story, Jesus dispelled three myths about what it meant to be a righteous person. First, when Jesus went to the home of a sinner he demonstrated that holiness is this-worldly as well as otherworldly. Second, he affirmed that charity is inadequate. Zacchaeus did not simply give a handout. He repaid his debts and more. Zacchaeus knew he could not follow Jesus while continuing to enjoy the economic benefits of systemic evil. He had to repent, give reparations publicly, and live in a new way. Third, Jesus proved again that God's love is not a scarce commodity. Jesus came to seek and save *all* that are lost.

Imagine the reactions of politicians or bankers if Jews and Christians pressed home the implications of queries such as these. Who owns the land? Who profits from its resources?

I am describing a fundamental restructuring of economic relations among all people and in relation to the earth, which sustains life. Jubilee sees humans, non-humans, and the whole of creation as part of the drama of redemption. The fate of the earth is bound up with the whole of creation. It is as though God knew that human greed, which caused our expulsion from paradise, would lead to imbalance. Some would accumulate more than others; disparities would grow. So every fifty years, a grand leveling should take place.

A crucial dimension of the Jubilee ideal is reconciliation between indigenous peoples and colonizers. We need a new way of living together peacefully. On trips to Israel and Palestine, I have visited *Neve Shalom/ Wahat al-Salam*. It is a *moshav* in which Palestinians and Israelis live together. This is a form of cooperative living that offers more independence for the people than a *kibbutz*, another kind of community. In the case of *Neve Shalom/Wahat al-Salam*, families occupy their own farmland and homes. However, the land belongs to no one but the Holy One. Purchasing and selling are done collaboratively. Everyone learns both Hebrew and Arabic. Children of all faith communities go to school together. Families meet together to discuss the problems that they face and how individuals and families could effect change, rather than relying on the government.

Finally, Jubilee justice entails forgiveness. Jubilee justice requires restitution rather than an attitude of forgive-and-forget. The Jubilee justice agenda involves land being restored to its original owners and lessening the poverty gap.

In my vision of a future world house, we have a color plan. It is green, because, unless we take care of the environment and address the serious problem of global warming, we seal our own doom. In my world house, as in any house, we have some rules: we beat our swords into plowshares, feed the hungry, clothe the naked, periodically forgive debt, welcome the stranger, take care of the widow, and visit those in prison. We do not kill or exploit each other. We have to have family meeting times and places, like the United Nations, where we try to work out differences and solve problems. We fix structural problems of racism, poverty, materialism, and militarism, or the world house is in danger of collapse. Whatever our problems, we focus on prevention and not simply on treatment. We immunize children so they will not become disabled or die from disease. We launch terrorism prevention initiatives to address the root causes of terrorism. We value the lives of soldiers, try to love enemies, and are concerned about civilians who are killed or injured in military actions done in our name. In my world house, there are no guns to inflict suffering or instill fear. With justice, people live in peace, unafraid.

With these words, I am echoing Nobel Peace Prize laureates from Martin Luther King Jr. of the United States (1964) to Shirin Ebadi of Iran (2003) and Wangari Maathai of Kenya (2004). All have called for a new awareness of our interconnection with the created world, including one another. As we take the lead, building cultures of peace, our leaders will follow.

Jubilee entails release from every form of bondage and imprisonment. It requires challenging the powers and principalities (church, nation-state, corporation, patriarchy) whose values conflict with God's dream for creation. It means the meek really will inherit the earth, wolf and lamb one day will lie together in peace, the hungry will have plenty to eat, the rich turned away. A new heaven and a new earth are on the way. One day every tear will be dried.

God's dream must be lived to sustain our own well-being and all life on earth. Heeding the inherent wisdom of Merton and the new monastics, we should use God-gifted resources efficiently because many of these are nonrenewable. For example, petroleum has many beneficial uses. Yet all we do is burn it up rather than develop alternative sources of renewable energy.

All things are connected. The natural world has value for humankind that no scientist can synthesize, no economist price, and no technology replace. Whatever we do to the earth, we do to ourselves. As Merton warned, if humans continue to destroy our remaining wild places, to neglect our farmland, woodlands, coastal areas, and deserts, and to use up our resources, we will ultimately end life as we know it and destroy the earth.

SEVEN

The Root of War Is Fear

The present war crisis is something we have made entirely for and by ourselves. There is in reality not the slightest logical reason for war, and yet the whole world is plunging headlong into frightful destruction, and doing so with the purpose of avoiding war and preserving peace! This is a true war-madness, an illness of the mind and the spirit that is spreading with a furious and subtle contagion all over the world.

— Thomas Merton, *The Catholic Worker*, October 1961

As an undergraduate student at the University of California at Berkeley from 1961 to 1965, I lived through one of those rare periods in which movements changed society and people made a difference. The campus simmered with the fervor of the Civil Rights, the Feminist, the anti-Vietnam War, the anti-Nuclear, and the Free Speech movements. We believed we could change the world and promote the common good. We were also aware of the danger to the whole world that the economic life of the United States and of other highly developed nations was in large measure centered on the production of weapons, missiles, and other technologies of mass destruction. Many of us saw that comfortable life styles had made it easy for many people to ignore or to be passive regarding the military-industrial complex and anticipated the consequences of such developments. Some prophets warned about the breakdown of community, the erosion of civic consciousness, the degrading of democracy, and the immorality of modern warfare.

I saw utter disaster looming but struggled with the problems as they personally affected me. Should my conviction that United States involvement in the war in Vietnam was wrong lead me to protest through legal means only? Should I participate in an act of civil disobedience? If I did so, how might my being arrested affect my future career?

As I wrestled with these questions, someone gave me copies of two issues of *The Catholic Worker*. The October 1961 issue had an article by Thomas Merton. It was entitled "The Root of War Is Fear." The November 1961 issue included another article by Merton, "The Shelter Ethic." The effect on me of reading these two essays was catalytic. Somehow, Merton seemed to reach out to me personally as friend and spiritual advisor.

Merton's essays encouraged me to accept active non-violence as the only legitimate way to establish God's peace in a world of violence and to join demonstrations against United States military intervention in southeast Asia. I read other writings by Merton, and these had a decisive impact on my decision to attend Colgate Rochester Divinity College rather than to go to law school, as I had planned.

As a seminary student, I received a deferment from military service. Courses in the Bible, history, and ethics confirmed my growing pacifist convictions. On April 4, 1967, Martin Luther King Jr. spoke at the Riverside Church in New York and urged ministers to give up ministerial immunity and to do alternative service as conscientious objectors. After I read Dr. King's speech, with needed support from my future wife Nancy, I gave up my seminary exemption, went before my draft board, registered as a conscientious objector, and offered to do alternative service. In my application, I cited passages in the Bible as well as such contemporary figures as Thomas Merton and Martin Luther King Jr. as the intellectual sources of my conscientious objection.

The United States was using a lottery system. I had a number that likely exempted me from the draft. Nevertheless, the draft board accepted my request and authorized my going overseas with the United States Department of State with a particular focus on international development.

Today, the United States and many of its allies are fighting wars that seem as unending as the war in Vietnam that many of my generation of war resisters opposed. The nations of the world continue to develop and build powerful weapons of mass destruction. The advocacy by Merton and King of peace and non-violence remains fresh and relevant. Read today along with Dr. King's April 4, 1967 address, Merton's writings on war, peace, and non-violence may serve to inspire a new generation weary of war to seek to build a culture of peace rooted in justice and active peacemaking.

MERTON ON WAR AND PEACE

From the start of his autobiography, *The Seven Storey Mountain*, Thomas Merton expressed awareness that war was absurd. "Not many hundreds of miles away from the house where I was born, they were picking up the men who rotted in the rainy ditches among the dead horses and the ruined seventy-fives, in a forest of trees without branches along the river Marne."[1]

During his secondary education at Oakham, Merton was a member of the debating society. On one occasion, Merton defended Gandhi's non-violent campaign for Home Rule for India. It was not clear if this reflected a deeply held value to which he had come at the time. His teacher may simply have assigned him to the side of the debate that he argued.

On February 9, 1933, students at Oxford University in England discussed and by 275 votes to 153 adopted the following resolution: "That this House will in no circumstances fight for its King and Country." The Oxford Union debate reflected a growing popularity of pacifism, manifested in the Oxford Peace Pledge, which Merton signed in early 1934, and in organizations such as the Fellowship of Reconciliation and Peace Pledge Union. In the journal he began to keep, Merton decried war. In a journal entry on June 16, 1940, Merton observed that no one likes war. He continued,

> if I don't pretend, like other people, to understand the war, I do know this much: that the knowledge of what is going on only makes it seem desperately important to be voluntarily poor, to get rid of all possessions this instant. I am scared, sometimes, to own anything, even a name, let alone a coin, or shares in the oil, the munitions, the airplane factories. I am scared to take a proprietary interest in anything, for fear that my love of what I own may be killing somebody somewhere.[2]

1. *SSM*, 3. The "ruined seventy-fives" refers to French artillery. The 75-mm M-1897 was still regarded as the best field gun in the world twenty years after World War I ended.

2. *RM*, 232.

Merton did not describe his spirituality as pacifist. In 1940, the U.S. Congress adopted a Selective Service Training Act. On March 19, 1941, Merton registered, declaring himself a "partial conscientious objector." He requested that he serve only in a noncombatant role. He argued that he would not "kill men made in the image of God when it is possible to obey the law (as I must) by serving the wounded and saving lives . . . or by the humiliation of digging latrines, which is a far greater honor to God than killing men." In November, he received his classification, 1-B, unfit for medical reasons.

In early December 1941, Merton received a notice to re-appear before his draft board. This had a remarkable effect of clarification. As he wrote in his journal, "before I got this surprise notice from the Draft Board I had a great desire, for the cloister. After the notice I also got *confidence* in the vocation!"[3]

In poetry and prose written between 1941 and 1961, Merton frequently discussed peace, in part as a spiritual quality. He observed that a person not at peace with or within himself or herself is not likely to achieve peace in the world. In *Seeds of Contemplation*, Merton opened chapter 9, entitled "The Root of War Is Fear," with a discussion of the concept of virtue. He noted, "I have very little idea of what is going on in the world." He continued:

> At the root of all war is fear: not so much the fear men have of one another as the fear they have of *everything*. It is not merely that they do not trust one another: they do not even trust themselves. If they are not sure when someone else may turn around and kill them, they are still less sure when they may turn around and kill themselves. They cannot trust anything, because they have ceased to believe in God.
>
> Will you end wars by asking men to trust men who evidently cannot be trusted? No. Teach them to love and trust God; then they will be able to love the men they cannot trust, and will dare to make peace with them, not trusting in them but in God.
>
> For only love—which means humility—can cast out the fear which is the root of all war.[4]

Merton concluded this chapter by affirming the importance of loving people and God above all. Rather than hating people one thinks make

3. *RM*, 467, entry for December 2, 1941, Merton's emphasis.
4. *Seeds of Contemplation*, 71–73, Merton's emphasis.

war, one should hate the appetites and the disorder of one's own soul. According to Merton, these are the causes of war.

At Gethsemani, Merton had many ways to follow world events, including his wide reading, visitors, conversations with novices, and letters from numerous correspondents. Writing in the mid-1950s, Merton highlighted the relationship between "Being and Doing." Merton urged readers first to find God in oneself, owning one's limitations and learning to commune with oneself before trying to commune with others. "All men seek peace first of all with themselves. . . . A man who is not at peace with himself necessarily projects his interior fighting into the society of those he lives with, and spreads a contagion of conflict all around him."[5]

In the early 1960s, as the world seemed to move closer to nuclear war, Merton had a sense of déjà vu. The forces were similar to those that erupted in World War II. Merton was not prepared to be silent even though he must have known that to speak out would bring him into conflict with those in authority in his order. As Merton-scholar William Shannon observed in introducing a collection of Merton's writings on peace, "At the time no Catholic priest or bishop—at least none well known—had spoken out against war. Roman Catholics by and large were a patriotic lot."[6]

Articles and books on war, peace, and other social issues began to pour from Merton's pen. In 1961, Merton totally rewrote "The Root of War is Fear," first published twelve years earlier, and included it as chapter 16 of *New Seeds of Contemplation*. Merton kept several paragraphs from the earlier publication but reframed the context of his reflections. Rather than discussing love, trust, and peace as personal virtues, Merton focused on a different concern. "When the whole world is in moral confusion . . . everyone is becoming more and more aware of the widening gulf between good purposes and bad results, between efforts to make peace and the growing likelihood of war." Merton affirmed that principles such as love, trust, and peace should govern not only personal moral conduct, but "also apply in the wider area of the state and in the whole community of nations."[7]

The censors approved this publication. Immediately on receiving that approval, Merton then sent it to Dorothy Day for possible publication

5. *No Man Is An Island*, 120–21.

6. Shannon, "Introduction," *Passion for Peace*, 2.

7. *NSC*, 114–17.

in *The Catholic Worker*. In his letter to her, Merton mentioned that he had added material "to situate these thoughts in the present crisis."[8]

The additional material amounted to three long paragraphs that the censors had not seen. The essay appeared in the October 1961 issue of *The Catholic Worker*. Merton opened, "The present war crisis is something we have made entirely for and by ourselves. There is in reality not the slightest logical reason for war, and yet the whole world is plunging headlong into frightful destruction, and doing so *with the purpose of avoiding war and preserving peace!*"

For Merton, this was "true war-madness, an illness of the mind and the spirit that is spreading with a furious and subtle contagion all over the world." Merton directed his concern especially towards the United States, of all the countries that are sick the one that is most "grievously afflicted." He saw the futility of people preparing shelters when, in the case of nuclear war, they would simply bake inside slowly instead of burning up quickly by exposure to a nuclear flash. He expressed concern that, "This is a nation that claims to be fighting for religious truth along with freedom and other values of the spirit. Truly we have entered the 'post-Christian era' with a vengeance. Whether we are destroyed or whether we survive, the future is awful to contemplate."[9]

Merton explored the place of the Christian in the circumstances of the day. He rejected several options clearly. For Merton, the Christian should not simply prepare for the destruction of earth, nor should he or she cry wolf. Rather, the duty of the Christian was to strive to do the one task that God has laid before humanity in the world at that time. This task was to work for the total abolition of war.

Merton urged Christians to become active in every possible way. They should struggle against war by mobilizing every resource available to them: study, prayer, sacrifice, and restraint of our instinct for violence or aggression in relations with others. "Everything else is secondary, for the survival of the human race itself depends on it. We must at least face

8. HGL, 140. Shannon discusses this in introducing the essay in *Passion for Peace: The Social Essays*, 11.

9. "The Root of War is Fear," *Passion for Peace*, 11–19. The January 1, 1962 issue of *Fellowship*, a publication of the Fellowship of Reconciliation, reprinted this version of the article.

this responsibility and do something about it. And the first job of all is to understand the psychological forces at work in ourselves and in society."[10]

Merton's essay "The Shelter Ethic" appeared the following month in *The Catholic Worker*. He addressed the question about the legitimacy of defending one's safety in a fallout shelter by keeping others out at the point of a gun. Merton sought to focus the discussion in the midst of what he deemed "the most crucial moral and spiritual crisis the human race has ever faced during its history." He affirmed the right of individuals to protect their lives, but he also cautioned against "creating a very dangerous mentality and opening the way to moral chaos if we give the impression that from here on out it is just every man for himself, and the devil take the hindmost." Exploring the ethic of the Sermon on the Mount, Merton concluded, "Love and Mercy are the most powerful forces on earth."[11]

In 1962, Merton published two books in which he emphasized the responsibility of Christians to be peacemakers in the world. The first was *Original Child Bomb*, the literal translation of one of the poetic names the Japanese found for the bomb that destroyed Hiroshima on August 6, 1945. The subtitle of the work, *Points for Meditation to Be Scratched on the Walls of a Cave*, underscored Merton's conviction that few survivors of atomic war would live.

The book, a prose poem, provided a summary of actions that culminated in the decision by United States President Harry S. Truman to use nuclear weapons at Hiroshima on August 6, 1945, and Nagasaki on August 9, 1945. Merton communicated his dismay toward these events. He believed that decision makers ignored a classic criteria, for the just conduct of warfare, namely, the protection of civilians. At Hiroshima, "70,000 people were killed right away or died within a few hours. Those who did not die at once suffered great pain. Few of them were soldiers."[12] Merton wove in details on the efforts of the government of Japan to arrange a negotiated surrender and of the attitude of Japanese military leaders who believed "that the war should continue until everyone was dead."[13]

Merton concluded with two final points on the contemporary significance of the events. "As to the Original Child that was now born,

10. Ibid.,13.

11. "The Shelter Ethic," *Passion for Peace*, 20–26.

12. *Original Child Bomb*, point 32.The prose poem also appeared in Merton's *Collected Poems*, 291–302, and in an anthology, Charters' *Portable Sixties Reader*, 108–18.

13. Ibid., point 4.

President Truman summed up the philosophy of the situation in a few words. 'We found the bomb' he said, 'and we used it.' Since that summer many other bombs have been 'found.'" Merton observed, "At the time of writing, after a season of brisk speculation, men seem to be fatigued by the whole question."[14]

Merton discussed the question of Christian responsibility in the face of possible nuclear war with James Laughlin, his publisher at New Directions. Together, they conceived a book that New Directions published in 1962 with the title *Breakthrough to Peace*. Merton and Laughlin sought to highlight the danger and even the imminent threat of nuclear war. Although Merton carried out the responsibilities of an editor, he was not so designated. He did contribute an introduction and an essay entitled "Peace: A Religious Responsibility." Lewis Mumford, Tom Stonier, Norman Cousins, Erich Fromm and Michael Maccoby, Howard E. Gruber, Gordon C. Zahn, Walter Stein, Herbert Butterfield, Alan Forbes Jr., Joost A. M. Meerloo, and Jerome D. Frank contributed the eleven other essays included in the book.

Another article, "Target Equals City," brought Merton into conflict with the Cistercian censors who had to provide their imprimatur before Merton sent off what he wrote for publication. In April 1962, the Abbot General, the highest authority in the Order, forbade Merton to publish anything further on the issue of war and peace. That Merton might complete some of his writing projects, Abbot James Fox delayed before communicating this directive to Merton about six weeks. Merton did not publish the essay during his lifetime.

During this burst of writing on war and peace, Merton drafted a third book, *Peace in the Post-Christian Era*. Merton did not send it to a major publisher. He doubted whether the censors would approve its publication. Merton did arrange for a mimeograph version of the manuscript. Several hundred copies circulated. In 1967, Merton's superiors lifted the general ban on Merton publishing in the area of peace. However, Merton did not revisit the manuscript. In 2004, Orbis Press published the book.

Read today, Merton's forbidden book provides a timely call to work "not merely to prevent the destruction of the human race by nuclear war" but also to convince people "that every possible effort must be made for the abolition of war." This remains an imperative even though, as Merton

14. Ibid., points 40–41.

acknowledged forty years earlier, "this may be extraordinarily difficult . . . we have still time to do something about it, but the time is running out."[15]

In 1963, Merton received a peace award. Unable to receive the Pax Medal in person, he wrote that he was "in the rather awkward position of receiving a prize for doing what is only the plain and obvious duty of a reasonable human being who also happens to be a Christian. It is like getting a medal for going to work in the morning, or stopping at traffic lights, or paying one's bills."[16]

Merton went on to observe that he had written and said nothing that Pope John XXIII did not say in his encyclical *Pacem in Terris*. Merton publicly affirmed that *Pacem in Terris* was a call upon the conscience of every reasonable human person on the face of the earth. "Each one of us has a strict obligation to work for world peace, for the peaceful arbitration of all disputes, and for the peaceful settlement of the social, international, interracial, religious, economic and political problems. . . ."[17]

Despite the ban on Merton publishing on social issues, several avenues remained open by which Merton explored issues of war and peace. He read. He prayed. He corresponded with activists. He joined the Catholic Peace Fellowship (CPF), an affiliate of a leading pacifist body, the Fellowship of Reconciliation. He encouraged those who resisted the growing involvement of the United States in the war in Vietnam, for example, Dorothy Day of the Catholic Worker Movement and Dan and Phil Berrigan.

In 1964, with pacifist David Dellinger, Dan and Phil Berrigan helped write a "declaration of conscience" urging young men to resist conscription into the armed forces. A year later, they joined with Yale chaplain William Sloane Coffin Jr. and others in a coalition of church persons called Clergy and Laity Concerned about Vietnam. From 1967 to 1975, the Berrigans were part of a network of Catholic radicals who either helped to plan or inspired non-violent actions against the war in Vietnam. Specific actions were kept stringently non-violent by small groups of people who were willing to take responsibility for them, including facing jail time. The planning for the actions was always a series of spiritual retreats in

---

15. Merton, *Peace in the Post-Christian Era*, 158, 162.

16. "In Acceptance of the Pax Medal, 1963," in Zahn, *Non-violent Alternative*, 258.

17. Ibid.

which those who finally acted did so out of a firm personal commitment to non-violence.

CPF members concentrated on building up the organization's membership base, securing funds, and played a role behind the scenes pressing the Second Vatican Council to condemn the nuclear arms race and to legitimate the right of Catholics facing the draft to claim CO status. CPF faced considerable obstacles. These included members of the Catholic hierarchy, clergy, and laity who condemned communism and assented to traditional Catholic support for just war theory. Pope John's *Pacem in Terris* and Vatican II documents such as the *Pastoral Constitution on the Church in the Modern World* provided Catholic pacifists a needed theological framework to overcome such constraints.

Anti-Vietnam War activists resisted through raids on draft-board offices and burning of draft cards. For example, on May 17, 1968, nine Catholic protesters walked into a Catonsville, Maryland, draft board office and burned hundreds of selective service records with homemade napalm. The incident jolted public conscience and became a play on Broadway called "The Trial of the Catonsville Nine."

One specific action left Merton aghast. On November 10, 1965, Roger Allen LaPorte committed suicide by self-immolation to protest United States involvement in the Vietnam War. While Merton did not hold the CPF responsible for this tragedy, he sent telegraphs to Dorothy Day and Jim Forest asking that his name be removed from a list of CPF sponsors. In a journal entry, Merton observed, "The world has never been so sick. Demonstrations. Counter-demonstrations . . . [yet] the war in Viet Nam goes on and the only effect of the demonstrations is that the general run of people get scared and accept the war because at least it is familiar!"[18] Subsequently, Merton reconciled with CPF and FOR members.

Though he never described himself as a pacifist, Merton shared with them an unwavering commitment to peace. Merton's passion for peace grew from his conviction that God's realm of justice and peace is already here. Peace is available for those who seek it and for those who strip away all that is not peace or prevents peace from manifesting itself.

The key insights of Merton's writings from this period are not dated, so it is more difficult to place them within a temporal context. However, Merton generally believed that people must still work to create conditions

18. *DWL*, 315, entry for November 11, 1965.

in which people can reclaim their truest self and, recovering their lost humanity, live into God's realm of peace. No less important early in this century is Merton's contribution linking contemplation with active non-violence and peacemaking. Though his superiors thwarted Merton in some measure, he expressed his opposition to the immorality of modern warfare with clarity and wisdom. Humanity still faces the threat of nuclear annihilation. Merton's prophetic writing on the danger can move a new generation of readers to refuse to allow persons in positions of leadership to lead humanity to ruin. In words of *Breakthrough to Peace*, "We have to make ourselves heard."[19]

MERTON ON GANDHI AND NON-VIOLENCE

Gandhi died in 1948. Before my generation, born in the 1940s, knew anything about Gandhi, many of us were reading Thomas Merton, arguably the most successful religious author in North America or perhaps the world. Merton not only fueled my passion for victims of war and injustice but also provided a tool for working to establish God's peace in a world of violence. His anthology *Gandhi on Non-Violence: Selected Texts from Mohandas K. Gandhi's Non-Violence in Peace and War* is a compilation of texts in five sections, with an introduction, notes, and index. The book provided an entry-level source book of Gandhi's life and legacy. It led me to read more of Gandhi's writings as well as Louis Fischer's biography of Gandhi.

Merton's interest in Gandhi went back to the London Round Table Conference in November and December 1931. Merton was then a high school student in Britain. In his dorm, Merton insisted Gandhi was right in championing India's independence from Britain. Someone rebutted that British rule was a purely benevolent, civilizing enterprise for which the Indians were not suitably grateful. Infuriated at the complacent idiocy of this line of reasoning, Merton persuaded no one.[20] Draft resistance and horror at a world marked by genocide and other evils contributed to Merton's decision in December 1941 to become a monk, but it was not

19. *Passion for Peace*, 122.

20. Merton, "A Tribute to Gandhi," *Seeds of Destruction*, 222–23. In *SSM*, 269, Merton only mentions Gandhi in reference to prayer.

until late in the 1950s that he returned to an active interest in writing on Gandhi.

By the late 1950s, Merton was again reading widely in Eastern religion. Over the last decade of his life, he wrote five books on Eastern religions, *Gandhi on Non-Violence* (1965); *The Way of Chuang Tzu* (1965); *Mystics and Zen Masters* (1967); *Zen and the Birds of Appetite* (1968); and, posthumously, *The Asian Journal of Thomas Merton* (1973). Through this deep engagement with the living spiritualities of Asia, Merton assumed a new calling, that of nurturing a new world into being, one free of bombs, racism, the worst effects of technology, media, big business, intolerance, and other evils. Though superiors in his monastic order attempted to silence him, Merton had come to believe that the writings of a contemplative monk must be relevant to the issues of the day. He held that the contemplative life is not, and cannot be, a mere withdrawal, a pure negation, a turning of one's back on the world.

Merton's prophetic writings spoke to a new generation of youth. He concluded that Gandhi spoke more to situations he faced than anyone else.[21] Merton wrote "A Tribute to Gandhi," an essay that appeared in two publications: *Ramparts*, established in 1962 by Edward M. Keating as a Catholic literary quarterly, and *Seeds of Destruction*, published in 1964 and regarded by Merton as his "most non-understood book" because his essay on race did not hew to the "liberal party line."[22]

For Merton, Gandhi was unlike all other world leaders of his time. Gandhi's life was marked by wholeness and wisdom, integrity, spirituality, and consistency that the others lacked or manifested, only in reverse. For Merton, Gandhi was consistent and faithful in resisting the dynamism of evil and destruction.[23]

Merton asked, "What has Gandhi to do with Christianity?" Gandhi esteemed Jesus and understood that for a Christian, problems of political and social existence are *inseparably* religious and political at the same time.[24] Merton compared Christian and Hindu terms such as *leitourgia* (liturgy, public service) and *dharma* (duty, right action); *agape* (love) and *satyagraha* (holding on to truth). For Merton, Gandhi was more Christian

21. *HGL*, 143, Cold War Letter 11, December 20, 1961 to Dorothy Day; *TTW*, 69, entry for October 12, 1960. Mott, 290; *SS*, 156, entry for January 16, 1958.

22. *SC*, 264, letter to Father Illtud Evans, February 8, 1965.

23. *Seeds of Destruction*, 225.

24. Ibid,. 226, Merton's emphasis.

than many Christians. "Gandhi remains in our time as a sign of the genuine union of spiritual fervor and social action in the midst of a hundred pseudo-spiritual crypto-fascist, or communist movements in which the capacity for creative and spontaneous dedication is captured, debased and exploited by false prophets."[25]

For Merton, the power of Gandhian non-violence grew from its religious underpinnings; that is, for Gandhi, non-violence was a way of life and not merely a strategy. Gandhi knew the value of solitude. He fasted, observed days of silence, did retreats and was generous in listening to and communicating with others. For Merton, Gandhi recognized the impossibility of being a peaceful, non-violent person if one submits passively to the insatiable requirements of a society maddened by overstimulation and obsessed with the demons of noise, voyeurism, and speed.[26]

Reviewing Merton's *Seeds of Destruction* in the *Book Week*,[27] Martin E. Marty of the University of Chicago asserted that Merton, despite his admiration for Gandhi and King, contributed nothing to help solve a problem identified by many students of Christian non-violence. How does one relate justice to love, King's Jesus to King's Gandhi? In "Negro Violence and White Non-Violence," Merton defended his "pessimistic prophesy." Two and a half years after the review initially appeared, Marty retracted his statement in letters published in the *National Catholic Reporter*. Marty conceded the need for non-violence. Also writing in the *National Catholic Reporter*, Richard Horchler observed that Merton was trying almost desperately to say *something*, anything, to spark a dialogue with the world outside the monastery. Seen in that light, Merton's essay on Gandhi was an expression of responsibility, part of its love and anguish.[28]

Merton's second essay, "Gandhi and the One-Eyed Giant," first appeared in *Jubilee*, and subsequently served to introduce his anthology on Gandhian non-violence. For Merton, one of the significant aspects of the life of Gandhi was his discovery of the East through the West. Like so many other educated Indians, Gandhi received a completely Western education. He was an "alienated Asian" and thought of himself as a white man without

25. Ibid., 229.

26. Ibid., 232.

27. *Book Week* January 17, 1965, 4.

28. *National Catholic Reporter* 3 (September 6, 1967) 8; *Learning to Love*, 283, entry for August 30, 1967; personal discussion with Martin E. Marty, October 5, 2006; *Commonweal* 81 (March 12, 1965), 766.

ceasing to be a "Nigger." Continuing, Merton observed that Gandhi was unusual in that he found something good not only in the West, but also in Asia. Through his acquaintance with writers like Thoreau, Tolstoy, and Jesus, Gandhi made connections with his own Hindu tradition and with such concepts that had universal significance as *dharma* and *satyagraha.* [29]

According to Merton, Gandhi came to believe that the central issue of the time was acceptance or rejection of a basic law. This was the law of love. Traditional religions made the truth of this law known to the world. For Merton, Gandhi committed his whole life to seeking to build a more peaceful and just world struggling through love in action. "If love or non-violence be not the law of our being, the whole of my argument falls to pieces." [30]

For Gandhi and Merton, *ahimsa* (non-violence) is not a way to seize power. Rather, non-violence transforms relationships and brings about a peaceful transfer of power, freely, without compulsion, and for the good of all concerned. People recognize the need for change through lives marked by a non-violent lifestyle.

Leading the non-violent movement by which India gained independence from the United Kingdom, Gandhi maintained that *satyagraha* or truth force was not merely a technique, but rather a way of life in which the *satyagrahi* exercises power through love and the strength of truth. Refuting those who saw non-violent action only as a means by which the weak come to power, Gandhi saw non-violence not as a policy of passive protest or cloak for impotent hatred that does not dare to use force. Rather, non-violent activists must express love and strength. For Merton, this was a noble and effective way of defending one's rights. Not merely a private affair, *ahimsa* required that the means of all political action be consistent with desired results.

In the first section of *Gandhi on Non-Violence*, Merton summarized key "Principles of Non-Violence." According to Merton, Gandhi understood nonviolence as an effective principle for social action because it is in deep accord with human nature. For Gandhi, to be human was to hold to an innate desire for peace, justice, order, freedom, and personal dignity. All people should be willing to engage in the risk of living by *ahisma*

29. "Gandhi and the One-Eyed Giant," *Gandhi on Non-Violence*, 3–4.
30. *Seeds of Destruction*, 234; *Gandhi on Non-Violence*, 25 (I-121).

(non-violence) because violent practices have proved not only bankrupt, but also capable of bringing about the extinction of life.

Gandhi did not believe that non-violence was simply an effective basis for social action. He also saw non-violence as the basic law of our being, something that everyone can learn and practice. Gandhi did not expect everyone to practice non-violence perfectly, but, "given the proper training and proper generalship, non-violence can be practiced by the masses of mankind. *Non-violence is the supreme law.* During my half a century of experience I have not yet come across a situation when I had to say that I was helpless, that I had no remedy in terms of non-violence."[31]

Gandhi understood non-violence as a way of love. The practitioner of non-violence should not measure his or her success by whether or not she or he achieves some objective, for example, freeing India from British rule. Rather, a non-violent resister to British rule in India may count as success his or her ability to respond to every situation with love and with assurance of the unfailing assistance of God sustaining the individual throughout difficulties that would otherwise be considered insurmountable.[32]

In the second section entitled "Non-Violence: True and False," Merton presented Gandhian emphasis on the extraordinary difficulty by which activists sustain a stance of non-violence. Such supernatural valor is available only through spiritual practices such as prayer. Courage demands nothing short of the ability to face death with complete fearlessness and to suffer without retaliation. Non-violence is meaningless and impossible without belief in God and spiritual practice.

Gandhi offered Jesus as the model of non-violent resistance. "Jesus lived and died in vain if He did not teach us to regulate the whole of life by the eternal law of love. . . . Jesus was the most active resister known perhaps to history. This was non-violence par excellence."[33]

Exploring the political scope of non-violence, Merton stressed that Gandhi did not envision a tactical non-violence confined to one area of life or to an isolated moment. Gandhi's non-violence was a creed that embraced all of life in a consistent and logical network of obligations. Merton saw Gandhian non-violent direct action as a way to address specific issues

31. Ibid., 25 (I-168, I-172), Gandhi's emphasis.
32. Ibid., 25–26 (I-175).
33. Ibid., 26, 40 (I-181; II-16).

that readers in the United States faced in the early 1960s, the threat of nuclear annihilation, how to struggle against evil, and how to build a world
at peace on a basis other than exclusivism, absolutism, and intolerance.
"There is no escape for any of us save through truth and non-violence. I
know that war is wrong, is an unmitigated evil. I know too that it has got
to go. I firmly believe that freedom won through bloodshed or fraud is no
freedom."[34]

Merton included a passage that addressed the situation in the United
States of young men facing conscription for service in the armed forces.
"Merely to refuse military service is not enough. . . . Non-cooperation in
military service and service in non-military matters are not compatible."[35]
Merton also included a passage in which Gandhi called for disarmament.
"Peace will never come until the great powers courageously decide to dis-
arm themselves."[36]

In the final section of the anthology of Gandhi quotes, "The Purity
of Non-Violence," Merton summarized five essential elements of how to
act non-violently:

1. It implies not wishing ill.
2. It includes total refusal to cooperate with or participate in activities
   of the unjust group, even to eating food that comes from them [for
   example, Gandhi's 1930 salt campaign]:
3. It requires a living faith in the God of love and acting in love for the
   good of all persons.
4. Who practices non-violence must be ready to sacrifice everything
   except honor.
5. It must pervade *everything* and not be applied merely to isolated acts
   only.[37]

Merton noted Gandhi's call for the formation of non-violent volunteer corps. These peace brigades would interpose themselves in situations
of violent conflict. Volunteers could not carry any weapons. Members of a
peace brigade must be easily recognizable. They must know the essentials
of first aid and be acquainted with all the residents of the locality. Finally,

34. Ibid., 52 (I-75).
35. Ibid., I-106, I-108.
36. Ibid., 53 (I-176).
37. Ibid., 64 (I-119), Gandhi's emphasis.

Gandhi believed the volunteers should pray with the Name of God and persuade others who believe to do likewise.

Gandhi and Merton were aware of antecedents of such non-violent initiatives. For example, in 1927, FOR and the Religious Society of Friends (Quakers) sent a delegation to intervene in a conflict in Nicaragua. The International Fellowship of Reconciliation also sponsored an Ambassadors of Reconciliation program through which traveling secretary Muriel Lester, a friend of Gandhi who hosted his 1931 stay in London, and Toyohiko Kagawa of Japan, toured China. Afterwards, they sought to make Japanese citizens and the government aware of the impact of the "Rape of Nanking" and other war crimes.

Merton believed that humanity was at a historic moment and needed to undertake a fundamental re-examination of existing values. He also believed that radical action was needed. Many activists visited or corresponded with Merton. He encouraged individuals like the musician Joan Baez. He sent a copy of his Gandhi book to James Douglass, a young Catholic in the anti-nuclear movement and later the author of several books that drew on Merton and Gandhi's writings. Merton encouraged the Student Non-violent Coordinating Committee, Students for a Democratic Society, and Black Power advocates. Merton also sent a copy of his Gandhi article in *Seeds of Destruction* to Sister M. Emmanuel de Souza e Silva, who worked in the slums of Rio de Janeiro and translated the essay and other books by Merton into Portuguese.[38] He encouraged Leilani Bentley, a college freshman from Mulliken, Michigan, to read *Gandhi on Non-Violence,* even though he was aware that non-violence was no panacea, even in India.[39] In 1968, Merton sought to meet disciples of Gandhi during his pilgrimage to India.[40]

Although he was not a street activist, Merton helped form the people who joined the non-violent movements of the 1960s. He thus contributed to the process by which Gandhian ideas generated collective action. Merton sought to ensure that the motivations or ideologies of young activists were compatible with Gandhi's legacy.

In the 1960s, the powerful in the United States lost connection with the depths of popular culture and resisted the reform impulse of young

38. HGL, 192.

39. RJ, 252, letter to Therese Lentfoehr, September 28, 1965; p. 346, letter to Leilani Bentley.

40. *Asian Journal,* 35 et passim.

activists. Converging with parallel risings of young people around the world, the uprising of youth challenged illegitimate authority and groped toward new codes of common life and new principles by which to transform society. Merton helped make Gandhi accessible to youth acting for social change non-violently.

Today, people confront an environmental crisis, a growing gap between rich and poor, war, and other issues. The legacies of Gandhi and Merton still can contribute to building communities engaged in nonviolent action. If humanity is to survive, people must be the change they want to see, as Gandhi wrote.[41] In an essay, "Blessed Are the Meek, The Christian Roots of Non-violence," Merton summarizes the theory and practice of non-violence. His seven points are no less relevant today than when Merton wrote the essay in the 1960s:

1. "Nonviolence must be aimed above all at the transformation of the present state of the world." Merton believed that nonviolence was far more than a strategy. Christians must live out of the nonviolent ethic of Christ as a way of life and eschew becoming too political, which happens when one is drawn into a power struggle and identifies too much with one side or another in the struggle.

2. "The nonviolent resistance of the Christian who belongs to one of the powerful nations and who is himself in some sense a privileged member of world society will have to be clearly not *for himself* but *for others*, that is, for the poor and underprivileged." Merton cited the struggle of African Americans as a possible exception, but he insisted that even in this case, the starting point of resistance should be the struggle for truth, *satyagraha*, through nonviolent means.

3. "In the case of nonviolent struggle for peace—the threat of nuclear war abolishes all privileges." Merton urged that those in the United States carried a special burden. Nonviolent resisters should avoid facile and fanatical self-righteousness and refrain from dramatic, self-justifying gestures.

4. "Perhaps the most insidious temptation to be avoided is one which is characteristic of the power structure itself: this fetishism of im-

---

41. McCluskey, Online: http://student.vwc.edu/~chronicle/2_11_00/index.htm. "Gandhi Shares Family Legacy," reports this quote in a speech by Arun Gandhi, Virginia Wesleyan College, February 8, 2000.

mediate visible results." As a spiritual director to activists, Merton cautioned against depending on the hope of results. The work of the peacemaker is essentially an expression of humility.

5. "Christian nonviolence is convinced that the manner in which the conflict for truth is waged will itself manifest or obscure the truth. To fight for truth by dishonest, violent, inhuman, or unreasonable means would simply betray the truth one is trying to vindicate." Merton did not support some measures of anti-war activists, such as self-immolation or burning draft records. While Merton stressed that there is no room for passivity, neither is there a place for violence. Merton highlighted Pope Paul VI's words before the United Nations General Assembly in 1965, "let the weapons fall from your hands. You cannot love with offensive weapons in your hands."

6. "A test of our sincerity . . . is this: are we willing to *learn something from the adversary*? . . . Nonviolence has great power, provided that it really witnesses to truth and not just to self-righteousness." Merton saw adversaries as human persons with rights. He insisted that it is important to be ready to see some good in adversaries and to agree with some of their ideas. One who is engaged in nonviolent resistance can discover one's own truth in a new light by being open-minded towards the views of others.

7. "Christian hope and Christian humility are inseparable." Merton's vision of peace was at once spiritual—peace with God in Christ—and practical. Grounded and rooted in God's peace, men and women could actualize the spiritual reality in life.[42]

Merton welcomed Pope John XXIII's encyclical *Pacem in Terris* and much of the work of Vatican II. In his own writing, Merton quoted *Pacem in Terris*. He believed that the Second Vatican Council followed its teachings when it insisted on human values. One was to trust that there are radical possibilities in every person for peace and order provided the right conditions exist. For Merton, the Christian contributes to creating these conditions "by preferring love and trust to hate and suspiciousness" and

42. *Passion for Peace*, 248–59; first published in English in *Fellowship*, May 1967; reprinted in Wink.

by engendering an attitude of simplicity and openness that can "break down barriers of suspicion that had divided men for centuries."[43]

Merton saw his writing as in tune with the new emphases of the Catholic Church. This was especially true in his unfolding relationship with people of other faiths. Merton wrote a prayer, read in the U.S. House of Representatives by Congressperson Frank Kowalski on April 12, 1962, in which he asked God to "bless our earnest will to help all races and peoples to travel, in friendship with us, along the road to justice, liberty and lasting peace."[44] This prayer reflects Merton's enduring commitment to live in harmony with people nurtured by diverse spiritual traditions that foster compassion, reconciliation, solidarity, and understanding.

MERTON ON DIALOGUE

Dialogue means conversation coupled with embrace. The English comes from the Greek *dialogos* and *dialegesthai*, "through the word," meaning such practices as compassionate listening, forgiving, and loving others. Broadly, dialogue is an embrace of the world, in part through words. Dialogue wells up from our being in such a way that the practitioner holds all life very close. If one understands dialogue as speaking words or discussing amiably in an open or pleasant manner, one misses the significance of dialogue as something fundamental to a peaceful lifestyle.

In the early pages of *Conjectures of a Guilty Bystander*, Merton offered several reflections that indicated his commitment to dialogue as embrace. The first followed a discussion of several Latin American poets whose mild temper, Franciscan way of life, and respect for all living things moved Merton and prompted his re-reading of Proverbs 8 on the gifts of wisdom.

> One has either got to be a Jew or stop reading the Bible. The Bible cannot make sense to anyone who is not "spiritually a Semite." The spiritual sense of the Old Testament is not and cannot be a simple emptying out of its Israelite context. Quite the contrary! The New Testament is the fulfillment of that spiritual content, the fulfillment of the promise made to Abraham, the promise that

---

43. Ibid., 256.
44. Ibid., 328.

Abraham believed in. It is never therefore a denial of Judaism, but its affirmation.[45]

This passage reflects Merton's deep respect for the people Israel, Jewish scriptures (the Psalms and prophetic books of the Bible especially), correspondence with three Jewish scholars, Rabbi Abraham Heschel, Hasidic scholar Zalman Schachter, and the psychoanalyst Erich Fromm, and his reading Rolf Hochhuth's *The Deputy*, which Merton considered "a bad play" that nonetheless raised a crucial question for Merton: is the Catholic Church so concerned with preserving power and influence that it understands its duty to God and humankind with its duty for self-preservation at any cost?[46]

Merton shared with Karl Barth a deep concern to overcome the separation between the Christian and Jewish communities. By this separation, Merton believed, the Christian community had suffered and opened a way for the growth in Germany of Nazi anti-Semitism. For Merton, to deny the truth of The Other was to deny the humanity of The Other.

The second passage of *Conjectures of a Guilty Bystander* arose during a time when Merton was reading works by several Russian Orthodox intellectuals including Nicholas Berdyaev, Sergius Bulgakov, Paul Evdokimov, Vladimir Lossky, and Vladimir Soloviev. In the following passage, Merton advanced a strategy for transparency and openness to others.

> If I can unite *in myself* the thought and the devotion of Eastern and Western Christendom, the Greek and the Latin Fathers, the Russians with the Spanish mystics, I can prepare in myself the reunion of divided Christians. From that secret and unspoken unity in myself can eventually come a visible and manifest unity of all Christians. If we want to bring together what is divided, we can not do so by imposing one division upon the other or absorbing one division into the other. But if we do this, the union is not Christian. It is political, and doomed to further conflicts. We must contain all divided worlds in ourselves and transcend them in Christ.[47]

45. *CGB*, 14.

46. "The Trial of Pope Pius XII: Rolf Hochhuth's *The Deputy*," in *LE*, 162–67.

47. *CGB*, 21, Merton's emphasis.

Merton continued by touching a wide variety of subjects, including thoughts on Marx, on technology, and a proper understanding of the Christian approach to the world.

> Gandhi once asked: "How can he who thinks he possesses absolute truth be fraternal?
>
> Let us be frank about it: the history of Christianity raises this question again and again.

Aware that the Dalai Lama was anxious that Buddhist monks be trained in knowledge of Western culture and religion, Merton argued that Christian monks (and those of other religions) reexamine the tradition of maintaining a certain distance or detachment from the world and "acquire a healthy and articulate respect for the modern world."[48]

We can trace Merton's interest in other religions and cultures from at least as early as 1930 when, as a student at Oakham, he defended the right of the Indians to rule their own country. His reading in 1956 included books on Gandhi and China. By the late 1950s, Merton was practicing yoga, exploring Zen, and studying the Sufis and Shakers. As always, he read prodigiously, notably, books by the Japanese Zen scholar Daisetz Teitaro Suzuki (1870–1966). Merton admired Suzuki's works and hoped to collaborate with him on a book dealing with the desert saints and the Zen masters. In 1960, Merton sent Suzuki translations from the *Verba Seniorum*, which became *The Wisdom of the Desert* and which Suzuki used in an exchanged published as Part II of *Zen and the Birds of Appe*tite (1968).

For Merton, the papacy of John XXIII and the Second Vatican Council opened the possibility of addressing issues of religious pluralism, racial justice, and peace. As he wrote on the latter subjects, he was profoundly disappointed when his superiors categorically denied his request to publish essays in which the pope said exactly what he was saying himself.

In dialogue with non-Christians, Merton believed he must maintain a sense of his own identity as a Christian. At the same time, he believed that God has not been silent among people other than ancient Israel, and that Christians have much to gain as they study the wisdom of Asia.

In an essay entitled "Christian Culture Needs Oriental Wisdom," Merton observed how much Greek philosophy and Roman law contrib-

48. Ibid., 44, 46.

uted to the actual formation of Christian culture and Christian spirituality. Had early Christianity made a similar use of Oriental philosophy and religious thought from the very start, "Western Christian thought would have been immeasurably enriched and deepened." Continuing, Merton highlighted the point that the values hidden in Oriental thought have deep affinities with Christian values and can help lead to a deeper and wiser understanding of the Christian tradition. "A Christian culture that is not capable of such a dialogue would show, by that very fact, that it lacked catholicity."[49]

In an essay entitled "A Christian Looks at Zen," Merton observed that there are differences between Christianity and Buddhism. For Merton, finding areas of common ground was no easy task, not least because of the immense variety of forms of thought, experience, worship, and ethics of the two religions. Merton saw Zen as a practice by which one makes use of ordinary, everyday human experience as material for a radical transformation of consciousness, including the experience of suffering, love, and the search for wisdom. Merton sought not so much to understand, but rather to look, to be mindful, and just to see what is right before him, as a practitioner, without adding any comment, interpretation, judgment, or conclusion. Acknowledging that this approach might seem very remote from Christianity, which is definitely concerned with a message, Merton highlighted the importance of direct experience in the Bible. Merton concluded that it is "quite possible for Zen to be adapted and used to clear the air of ascetic irrelevancies and help us to regain a healthy natural balance in our understanding of the spiritual life. . . . Though few Westerners will ever actually come to a real understanding of Zen, it is still worth their while to be exposed to its brisk and heady atmosphere."[50]

Merton opposed forms of contemplation that stressed the conceptual. He liked the Zen stream of Buddhist practice, notably the traditions of the Rinzai sect, which sought to break down the disciple's desire to define concepts, to do analysis, or to want to make formal progress in the religious life. In Zen, there are riddles that appear to be nonsense. Merton quotes a Zen Master who nonchalantly said to his disciple, "If you meet the Buddha, kill him!"[51] Merton uses this example to demonstrate that

49. As published in *A Thomas Merton Reader*, ed. Thomas McDonnell, 302–3.

50. *Zen and the Birds of Appetite*, 58.

51. Ibid., 44.

Zen in its essence offers no explanations of reality. Zen is content simply to see.

In early 1964, D. T. Suzuki's secretary wrote Merton that the Zen master would be in New York City during the month of June but that, given Suzuki's advanced age, there would be no chance of his coming to Gethsemani. In the light of Merton's studies of Zen, Abbot James Fox gave reluctant permission to Merton to meet Suzuki provided that he limit his time there to a few days and that he would not get in touch with old friends. Merton kept these commitments. He did see a Van Gogh exhibit at the Guggenheim. Twice he said Mass alone at Corpus Cristi Parish where he had been baptized twenty-six years earlier. He had two sessions with Suzuki, frail, deaf, but lively, and responsive. They meditated and drank tea together. As Merton left, Suzuki said, "The most important thing is Love." By this, Merton understood Suzuki as intending to sum up all that he had ever written, experienced, or said.[52]

The experience of returning to New York awed Merton. More important, Suzuki authenticated Merton's understanding of Zen and gave Merton confidence in his studies of Zen.[53] In a letter to Dame Hildelith Cumming, an English Benedictine nun, Merton expressed pleasure that Suzuki considered him his "favorite disciple" in the U.S.[54] Merton hoped Suzuki would return to the United States, but Suzuki's age made this impossible.

About this time, Abbot Fox allowed Merton to withdraw to a hermitage. This enabled him to write more, but this move also precluded any travel. Fox refused Merton permission to attend a Zen conference in Japan.

Merton welcomed the opportunity for more time for meditation and study. He continued to receive some visitors. He described his pilgrimage on earth as a quest for the "promised land" and "paradise." For Merton, paradise symbolized freedom and creativity. It also entailed a "personal encounter with the stranger seen as our other self."[55]

Another dimension of Merton's quest to understand otherness was his exploration of native American, tribal African, and aboriginal

52. *Mystics and Zen Masters*, 41; *Zen and the Birds of Appetite*, 62.
53. *Springs of Contemplation*, 140.
54. *SC*, 223, letter of July 22, 1964.
55. Merton, *Mystics and Zen Masters*, 111.

Australian sources. Merton called for recovery of ancient wisdom of first peoples, "Our task now is to learn that if we can voyage to the ends of the earth and there find *ourselves* in the aborigine who most differs from ourselves, we will have made a fruitful pilgrimage."[56] For Merton, failure to embrace the wisdom of the elders is an error. "Neither the ancient wisdoms nor the modern sciences are complete in themselves. They do not stand alone. They call for one another."[57]

In October 1964, he received Marco Pallis, a scholar of Buddhism, as a guest at Gethsemani. They talked at length on Zen and Tibetan Buddhism. The Buddhist monk Thich Nhat Hanh also visited Merton. Nhat Hanh made a profound impression on Merton and the whole community. Nhat Hanh delighted the monks of Gethsemani when he explained that during the period of the Buddhist novitiate, novices did not meditate. "Before you can meditate, you've got to learn how to close doors."[58]

On January 13, 1968, the Gethsemani community elected Dom James's successor Flavian Burns. Around the same time, Merton received an invitation from Jean Leclercq to attend an interfaith monastic gathering in Bangkok at the end of the year. At the time that he received this invitation, on March 16, he was wrestling with many invitations, including one from Dan Berrigan to go to Vietnam.

By mid-year, Merton gave up any thought of going to Vietnam and leaned towards attending the Bangkok gathering. For Merton, this was an especially attractive opportunity, as it would take place in Asia at a time of growing savagery in the Vietnam War. Struggling to find a way to have an impact for peace, Merton also saw the opportunity to go to Asia as one that would open doors, for example, through visiting Tenzin Gyatso, the fourteenth Dalai Lama, in India.

The new abbot granted Merton permission to attend. On October 15, 1968, Merton left for Asia not as an ordinary tourist. Rather, his was an interior journey of the heart. As Merton travelled, he kept notes. Had he lived, he would have published a book different from *The Asian Journal*. However, the notes and the addresses he delivered appeared after his death. This has enabled successive generations of readers to follow his deep engagement with people of other faiths and ideologies.

56. Ibid., 112, Merton's emphasis.
57. Merton, *Gandhi and Non-Violence*, 1.
58. Mott, 454.

Merton had profound moments of dialogue, notably with Tenzin Gyatso, the Dalai Lama, from November 4–8, 1968. In his journal, Merton characterized their three meetings as "very warm and cordial . . . at the end I felt we had become very good friends and were somehow quite close to one another. I feel a great respect and fondness for him as a person and believe, too, that there is a real spiritual bond between us."[59]

For the fourteenth Dalai Lama, the time with Merton proved significant. Writing in the *New York Times* for May 25, 2010, he recalled,

> An early eye-opener for me was my meeting with the Trappist monk Thomas Merton in India shortly before his untimely death in 1968. Merton told me he could be perfectly faithful to Christianity, yet learn in depth from other religions like Buddhism. The same is true for me as an ardent Buddhist learning from the world's other great religions.
>
> A main point in my discussion with Merton was how central compassion was to the message of both Christianity and Buddhism. In my readings of the New Testament, I find myself inspired by Jesus' acts of compassion. His miracle of the loaves and fishes, his healing and his teaching are all motivated by the desire to relieve suffering.
>
> I'm a firm believer in the power of personal contact to bridge differences, so I've long been drawn to dialogues with people of other religious outlooks. The focus on compassion that Merton and I observed in our two religions strikes me as a strong unifying thread among all the major faiths. And these days we need to highlight what unifies us.

As well, Merton also had profound moments of mystical encounter, notably at Polonnaruwa in Ceylon, now Sri Lanka, where Merton gazed at several statues: a reclining Buddha, two seated Buddhas, and a standing Buddha. In the peace and silence of the figures, Merton felt "knocked over with a rush of relief and thankfulness." Looking at these figures, he felt "suddenly, almost forcibly, jerked clean out of the habitual, half-tied vision of things and an inner clearness, clarity, as if exploding from the rocks themselves, became evident and obvious. . . . I don't know when in my life I have ever had such a sense of beauty and spiritual validity running together in one aesthetic illumination."[60]

59. *Asian Journal*, 125, entry for November 8, 1968.
60. *Asian Journal*, 233–35, entry for December 4, 1968.

In a letter to Joseph Tjo Tchel-oung, a seminary student in Seoul, Korea, Merton expressed gratitude for his having translated *Seeds of Contemplation* into Korean. Merton wrote of his deep interest in Oriental philosophy, an interest that he believed helped prepare him to understand Christianity, which in many ways is alien to the aggressive, materialistic, and pragmatic world of the West. "We must never forget that Christianity came to the west from the Orient. . . . Christ is the fulfillment of the latent desires and aspirations of all religions and all philosophies. One must transcend them all to come to Him: yet in Him one finds all that was good and true in every other religion."[61]

REFLECTIONS

Peacemaking, non-violence, and dialogue are at once essential practices, and a way of life. There has been a good deal of contemporary discussion about the meaning of difference. People craft "The Other" in different images. For example, Europeans once tended to project the image of nobility upon people of color. This idea of the noble savage gave way, subsequently, to the image of "the primitive," an idea foundational to the racist contamination of Christianity in the West. When we are at peace, when we practice non-violence, when we engage in dialogue, when we meet people on their own terms, religion becomes *a* if not *the* source of embrace. *When the Spirit of truth comes, he will guide you into all the truth; for he will not speak on his own, but will speak whatever he hears, and he will declare to you the things that are to come* (John 16:13).

The converse is that, when we do not recognize and appreciate The Other, religion becomes *a* if not *the* source of friction. Adah Price, the daughter of a missionary in a contemporary novel, *The Poisonwood Bible*, writes, "Illusions mistaken for truth are the pavement under our feet. They are what we call civilization."[62] To paraphrase words of the musical *South Pacific*, we have to be taught very carefully to hate.

In *Conjectures of a Guilty Bystander*, Merton highlighted the importance of being peace before trying to make peace. Merton credited his reading of writings by the Quaker Douglas Steere and observed as follows,

---

61. *Road to Joy*, 319, letter of April 28, 1961.
62. Kingsolver, *Poisonwood Bible*, 532.

... there is a pervasive form of contemporary violence to which the idealist fighting for peace by non-violent methods most easily succumbs: activism and overwork. The rush and pressure of modern life are a form, perhaps the most common form, of its innate violence. To allow oneself to be carried away by a multitude of conflicting concerns, to surrender to too many demands, to commit oneself to too many projects, to want to help everyone in everything is to succumb to violence. More than that, it is cooperation in violence. The frenzy of the activist neutralizes his work for peace. It destroys his own inner capacity for peace. It destroys the fruitfulness of his own work, because it kills the root of inner wisdom which makes work fruitful.[63]

This passage underscores Merton's most significant contribution to understanding the roots of peace. He sought to understand what drove the war system, namely, fear, greed, and misuse of technology. Merton unpacked theoretical Christian, and specifically Catholic social teaching on war and peace by focusing specifically on the nuclear arms race and the Vietnam War.

In a letter to American peace activist Jim Forest, Merton cautioned against being discouraged when the desired results of one's actions do not become reality immediately. "It is important to resist the feelings of resentment and impatience we get over our own failings because this makes us project our faults onto other people, instead of bearing their burdens along with our own."[64]

Merton also wrote European peace activists Jean and Hildegard Goss-Mayr of the International Fellowship of Reconciliation:

It is sometimes discouraging to see how small the Christian peace movement is, and especially here in America where it is most necessary. But we have to remember that this is the usual pattern, and the Bible has led us to expect it. Spiritual work is done with disproportionately small and feeble instruments. And now above all when everything is so utterly complex, and when people collapse under the burden of confusions and cease to think at all, it is natural that few may want to take on the burden of trying to effect something in the moral and spiritual way, in political action. Yet this is precisely what has to be done.[65]

63. *CGB*, 73 (86).

64. *HGL*, 261, letter of January 5, 1962, to Jim Forest.

65. *HGL*, 325.

Merton articulated a new understanding of himself and of the Christian in society. If the Christian is to have any decisive influence upon a disordered world, it could only be with the weapons of the Spirit; namely, love, truth, and non-violence. By his studies of figures such as Gandhi, Martin Luther King Jr., and the French philosopher Simone Weil, and by his encounters with practitioners of non-violence such as the Berrigans, Thich Nhat Hanh, and Tenzin Gyatso, the fourteenth Dalai Lama, Merton concluded that non-violence is a weapon of the weak who are in fact strong. Those who oppose evil with serious and positive resistance by doing good ultimately prove the only effective agents for overcoming the war system.

The death of Dr. Martin Luther King Jr. in Memphis, Tennessee, on April 4, 1968, took place only days before Merton and King were to meet. Merton had visited the Pleasant Hill Village of the Shakers and was returning to the Abbey of Our Lady of Gethsemani. He heard the news of King's death on the car radio. Merton wrote, "I could cry."[66] At the hermitage the next day, Merton said a Mass for King and wrote to King's widow to express his grief, shock, and prayerful concern. He wondered, is the human race self-destructive? Is the Christian message of love but a pitiful delusion? Must one just "love" in such impossible circumstances? What sense could be made that an authoritarian church was coming out a hundred years late with its official pronouncements on war and racism? Many concluded that the tragic death of Dr. King was a sort of post mortem on non-violence, which does not get results.

Merton did not believe this at all. He wrote an article for the September 7, 1968, issue of Ave Maria. It bore the original title: "Non-Violence Does Not . . . Cannot . . . Mean Passivity." Merton concluded that the U.S. had not yet begun to look at nonviolence as an option, or to understand it. Merton saw the then-current rejection of nonviolence as too pragmatic. "But nonviolence," Merton concluded, "is useless if it is merely pragmatic. The whole point of nonviolence is that it rises above pragmatism. Ahimsa is defense of and witness to truth, not efficacy. I admit that may sound odd." Referring to words of Jesus in John 8:32, "and you will know the truth, and the truth will make you free," Merton observed, "It seems to me that this is what really matters."[67]

---

66. Mott, *Seven Mountains*, 520.

67. "Note for *Ave Maria*," *Passion for Peace*, 325.

EIGHT

Twentieth-Century Wisdom for Twenty-First-Century Communities

To discover all the social implications of the Gospel not by studying them but by living them, and to unite myself explicitly with those who foresee and work for a social order—a transformation of the world—according to these principles: primacy of the person—*(hence justice, liberty, against slavery, peace, control of technology etc.).* Primacy of *wisdom and love (hence against materialism, hedonism, pragmatism, etc.).*

—Thomas Merton, *Turning toward the World,* journal entry, June 6, 1960

During the mid-1950s, the numbers in Christian monastic orders grew and subsequently declined. In itself, this was not remarkable. Relatively few persons have ever been inclined to live a cloistered life.

What was noteworthy was the fact that at the very time monasteries began to face some degree of crisis in terms of numbers, ability to sustain the life and work of the community, and finances, this numerically tiny group began to exercise an even more powerful leavening role in the church and in wider society. Over the past few decades, there has been an increase of interest in monasticism of the Western churches and especially in the Roman Catholic Church.

There are many recent signs of interest in monastic life. Often, books about spirituality include a section about Benedictine prayer and some, for example *Wisdom Distilled from the Daily: Living the Rule of St. Benedict Today* by Joan Chittister and *The Cloister Walk* by Kathleen Norris, have become best-sellers in the United States. Recordings of monastic singing have also reached the top of the charts.

Two documentaries released in 2005 have had commercial success and received many awards. *Into Great Silence (Die Große Stille)* allows viewers to experience the everyday lives of monks at the Grand Chartreuse monastery, motherhouse of the Carthusian Order, in the French Alps. Sixteen years after he first requested permission, director Philip Gröning was able to live with the monks for six months and do the film.

The film offers little narration or dialogue. Watching the film for nearly three hours is an occasion for meditation rather than a fact-finding mission or an amazing race. The film ends with a spiritual quotation that conveys the heart of the monastic insight about God: "I am the ONE who is."

The Monastery, a British Broadcasting Corporation production, followed the lives of five men who spent forty days at Worth Abbey in the Benedictine tradition. In response, thousands of viewers contacted Worth Abbey; former Abbot Christopher Jamison wrote two best-selling books; and the network released two more television series: *The Monastery Revisited* (2006) and *The Silence* (2010). The broadcasts introduce ordinary people to Saint Benedict's insights for a balanced life.

A mark of Benedictine spirituality is hospitality. A passage in the *Rule of Saint Benedict* reads, "All guests who present themselves are to be welcomed as Christ" (*Rule*, 53.1).

Growing numbers of people want to experience a monastic retreat. If you want to spend time at the Abbey of Our Lady of Gethsemani in Kentucky, you generally need to make a booking six months in advance.

Many monasteries have opened new guesthouses. For example, on October 22, 2006, the monks of Saint John's Abbey, a Benedictine monastery in Collegeville, Minnesota, dedicated a new facility with thirty guest rooms. As well as attending to guests' housing and meals, staff members assist retreatants with their spiritual needs by providing a meditation chapel, a library, meeting rooms for groups of various sizes, and opportunities for spiritual direction.

Many monasteries have also developed extended monastic life programs. These offer men or women interested in the monastic life opportunities for vocational discernment or for contemplation, prayer, and reflection in the case of those who have already discovered their path in life.

As an example, Our Lady of Guadalupe Abbey, a Trappist monastery in Lafayette, Oregon, offers men an opportunity for an extended stay. Each monastic life retreatant lives within the monastic enclosure and participates in the communal life of the monastery. There is no charge for the program as participants earn their room and board working daily with the professed monks.

Lay vocations outnumber monastic vocations. Many women or men follow the rule of an established order but live in the wider society.

Worldwide, there are over 700,000 third order Franciscans. They come from Catholic, Anglican, Baptist, and other traditions. They seek to live the Franciscan way of life in their ordinary lives.

There are also growing numbers of third order Benedictines and Cistercians. These are people who do not live in monasteries but who follow *The Rule of Saint Benedict* as a way of life in their ordinary lives. A lay associate put it, "We feel it is the gift of a 'way of life' that can be as appropriate for a layperson living in the world as it is for a monk or a nun living in a monastery."[1]

On June 17, 1898, Pope Leo XIII established the first canonical status in the Roman Catholic Church for oblates within the Benedictine order. Until 1962, the statutes and rules of the secular oblates of Saint Benedict allowed only men's monasteries to receive oblates. Since then, women's monasteries have also been able to receive their own oblates.

The word "oblate" means a willingness to offer oneself in service to God and neighbor through a particular monastery without abandoning one's lay vocations. By integrating the rhythm of prayer, study, and work within their chosen ways of life, Benedictine oblates seek to live the teachings of Christ as interpreted by St. Benedict and in association with a specific Benedictine community. Oblates often live in geographic proximity to the monastery. This allows them to participate in the liturgies of the monastery, monthly meetings or an annual retreat of oblates, and other activities that contribute to a widening and deepening of religious commitment.

In the Catholic tradition, other new forms of witness by lay Catholics have developed. For example, the Congregation of the Holy Ghost, or Spiritans, is a Roman Catholic order that began in France almost three hundred years ago. Over three thousand members are involved in di-

---

1. Eleven Lay Associates, "A Lay Response," 235–36.

verse ministries worldwide. They have dedicated themselves to working with the poor and in situations where the church has difficulty in finding ministers.

With the convening of the Second Vatican Council, church groups began to gather to read and study the documents of Vatican II. The laity recognized that the church is comprised of the whole people of God and sought to contribute their talents to building God's realm of love, justice, and peace, on earth as in heaven.

In the early nineteen seventies, Canadian Spiritans created a new form of membership. Lay Spiritans began to explore a ministry of presence. They reached out to others, not primarily to accomplish a task, but rather to be with people, live with them, walk beside them, listen to them, and share their lives with them. Today in Canada, lay Spiritans accept the following vision statement:

> We envision a community, in touch with the signs of the times, refusing to be "stuck in the notions of the past". A community so trusting of the Spirit, that it does not offer the least resistance to where the Spirit's breath may carry it. A community, open and guided by the Holy Spirit in sharing its life, mission and spirituality.
>
> We envision a community, brought together through the prompting of the Spirit, to give options to those who are most poor, vulnerable and excluded from society, enabling them to break out of their cycle of misery.
>
> We envision a community, united in heart and soul. A community of professed and lay Spiritans, whose interior spirit allows for openness, simplicity and gentleness with each other in working together to build God's reign of Love, Justice and Peace. . . .
>
> We dream:
>
> Of religious and Lay working together out of small Christian Communities.
>
> Of clusters of Lay Spiritans in every region where Spiritans live and work.
>
> Of taking Lay and professed Spiritans to places where alone we might not go.[2]

2. These and subsequent reflections are from a presentation to Lay Associates of several Religious Congregations by Joy Warner; email, June 3, 2010. Also, http://www .spiritans.com/layspiritans.htm

For Joy Warner, participation as a lay Spiritan means living in the light of ten principles that she offers as examples of the lived reality of an English-speaking Canadian Lay Spiritan.

1. Availability, taking time versus the frenetic business of modern life. Lay Spiritans value being rather than doing and having more. For Deirdre of Sioux Lookout, Ontario, "the fact that I am an older woman makes it important that I stay. If someone talks, you sit still and listen; if someone holds your hand or weeps on your shoulder, these are silent words. Listen, enter into the pain, and wait."

2. Inclusivity, welcoming the stranger versus erecting barriers, fences, and anti-terrorism legislation. These teach people to be suspicious and fearful of those who are different. From this principle flows compassion for refugees, the outcast, and the poor. For Judith of Winnipeg, Manitoba, Jean Vanier's organization L'Arche is a focus. In Winnipeg, L'Arche has six homes and two apartments for persons living with developmental disabilities.

3. Diversity and interfaith dialogue versus my way or the highway. Gary and Joy of Hamilton, Ontario facilitate the Hamilton Dialogue Group that seeks to address inter-group and intra-group relations through facilitated dialogue, workshops, strengthening awareness of the community's religious and ethno-cultural diversity, and building relationships.

4. Inculturation of the Spiritan Rule of Life in the here and now. This entails resisting pious platitudes and accepting people where they are. For Rose Anne of Laval House, Toronto, this entails helping respond to the spiritual needs of busy people, for example, by offering structured meditation.

5. Valuing women. Lay Spiritans welcome and pay special attention to the gifts and talents that women offer.

6. Commitment to justice and peace. The Rule of Life calls for Lay Spiritans to be advocates, supporters, and defenders of the weak against all who oppress them, especially refugees, prisoners, the poor, and those experiencing racism. Dermot has been instrumental in improving health services for Aboriginal people in northern Canada.

7. Collaboration. Lay Spiritans seek to break down barriers between clergy and laity through mutuality and real cooperation.

8. Celebration and hospitality. Lay Spiritans lift up the importance of good food, music, laughter, jokes, storytelling, an open door and an open heart.

9. Creative liturgy. Lay Spiritans celebrate the mass monthly in homes. People share their worries, celebrate their joys, and reflect together on scripture in a deeper way than is possible in a large parish situation.

10. Community versus the individualism characteristic of wider society.

In April 2010, the Spiritan leadership of North America and the Caribbean gathered in Puerto Rico for a meeting to discuss issues common to the Spiritan mission in that region of the world. These included the need for more vocations, financial strains, issues of justice in a troubled world, and above all, deeper discernment about where the Holy Spirit is calling members to be present. In addition to providing a visible sign and reminder of connectedness and interdependence, the gathering focused on how best to help people in Haiti, devastated by an earthquake on January 12, 2010, and still struggling to begin recovery. At the time of the meeting, the Spiritans were still living in tents and, like much of the rest of the population in Haiti, with uncertainty about the future. Even though the earthquake leveled the *Petit Séminaire College St Martial* in the heart of Port-au-Prince, the Spiritans decided to re-open the school, where students gather on the grounds and use desks that were salvaged from the quake.

Little Portion Community offers another example of lay Christians seeking to balance contemplation and action in community. It is located at Berryville near Eureka Springs in north-west Arkansas. John Michael Talbot describes its beginnings in the 1980s as follows:

> It seemed like we were trying everything and achieving nothing, except with my music and books. . . . We were becoming bogged down, some even began to "fry" emotionally, because we were trying to do so much with so few people who were, at best, novices in this way of life. We were democratic to a fault—we even voted on what dog food to buy! There was no clear direction. Some wanted a more intense expression of religious life. Some wanted less discipline, and yet more freedom to go into town, or

out to dinner, or to a movie even more frequently. Some sisters
wanted a veil, and others did not. Likewise, there were differences
of opinion among the brothers concerning the habit. Dissent began to erode the ranks of our already tiny community. We called
ourselves a "hermitage." But in reality most of our members were
living pretty undisciplined lives . . . I used a very passive form
of leadership, and hesitated to take proper authority as founder.
Frankly, I was still very new to this way of life and simply didn't
know how to lead yet.[3]

The group's lack of a rule was part of the problem, but the members'
varied commitments to celibacy or marriage complicated the creation
of such a rule. During this critical period, Talbot was agonizing over the
community's lack of direction when, like a fresh, spring breeze, Sister
Viola Pratka came to Little Portion Community. An Incarnate Word nun
from Victoria, Texas, she brought twenty-five years of religious life and
training to Little Portion.

Assisted by Sister Viola, Talbot made the decision to grant married
couples and single persons not committed to celibacy the same status
as celibates in Little Portion Community. Subsequently on February 17,
1989, Sister Viola and Brother John Michael married. Though their marriage came as something of a shock to many, this was a logical development whereby the Holy Spirit was leading many Protestants as well as
Catholics to live in the community. For those called to an integrated community of celibate, single, and married lifestyles, Brother John Michael
and Sister Viola offered an exemplary model of radical living in marriage
alongside single people. According to author Dan O'Neill, this integration
and the return of the community to the roots of monastic life have made
the Little Portion Community a source of renewal not only for contemporary monasticism, but also for the wider church.[4]

In 1990, the Catholic Church granted Little Portion Community canonical status as a Public Association of the Faithful under the authority
of the bishop of the Catholic Diocese of Little Rock, Arkansas. Because
the community integrates traditional celibates as well as married couples
and single persons open to marriage, an extensive review process preceded this conferral. The Roman Catholic Church had grave reservations

3. O'Neill, *Signatures*, 175.

4. Ibid., 195. The Little Portion website is http://www.laycontemplative.org/thesites/
little_portion.htm.

about so radical a community wishing to take traditional vows. In the end, the church granted canonical status only to the professed celibates and not to married couples and individuals in the community. However, Little Portion Community regards all professed members as equal in status. The crisis in traditional vocations may contribute to the church ultimately revising its understanding of religious vocations.[5]

Noteworthy developments include the purchase in 1987 of an Episcopalian facility nearby at More Mountain. Now called the Little Portion Retreat and Training Center, it has attracted thousands of persons to conferences, meetings, and retreats led by a wide range of people. Experiencing growth through the 1990s to the present, Little Portion Community has stabilized at around forty members and over five hundred associates. A wider monastic infrastructure has also taken shape, with cell groups around the globe. Members have touched the lives of the poorest of the poor through works of mercy. Locally, members maintain a health clinic for the poor, visit convalescent homes, clean the homes of the elderly and the disabled, and work with supportive agencies such as the St. Vincent de Paul Society. Globally, Little Portion Community operates Mercy Corps International, an agency that works with partners to airlift emergency supplies to devastated areas of the world. Members have served in Honduras, the Philippines, and Palestinian refugee camps.

The vitality of Protestant monasticism is another manifestation of the new monasticism. This development is noteworthy as Luther, Calvin, and other early Protestant reformers rejected the institution. Especially prominent today are the sisters of Grandchamp in French-speaking Switzerland, the brothers of Taizé in France, and the brothers and sisters of Bose in Italy. Those called to communal life draw on older traditions of monasticism and find strength and liberation in a rhythm of contemplation and action. Some offer alternative seminary formation similar to the Confessing Church's "House of the Brethren" described by Dietrich Bonhoeffer in *Life Together*, a book that remains powerful reading today.

Bonhoeffer anticipated the current monastic renewal in a letter to his brother, Karl-Friedrich,

> I think I am right in saying that I would only achieve true inner
> clarity and sincerity by really starting to take the Sermon on the
> Mount seriously. This is the only source of strength that can blow

5. Interviews, Mark Shipler and John Michael Talbot: April 9, 2004.

all this stuff and nonsense sky-high, in a fireworks display that will leave nothing behind but one or two charred remains. The restoration of the church will surely come from a new kind of monasticism, which will have nothing in common with the old but a life of uncompromising adherence to the Sermon on the Mount in imitation of Christ. I believe the time has come to rally people together for this.[6]

Bonhoeffer drafted a proposal for a community house that provided a more detailed analysis of what he understood by "a new kind of monasticism." Those called to communal life would find strength and liberation in service to the community, to those in need, and to the truth. An alternative seminary for leaders of the Confessing Church, the "House of the Brethren" offered a radical witness to a culture in which discipleship was difficult if not impossible. The premature dissolution of the community led to publication of a little booklet entitled *Life Together*, which remains a powerful tract for our time.

New Monastic Communities

Many persons are responding to a call to enter more deeply into the pain of the world through the formation of new monastic communities in North America and around the world. Many members of newer monastic communities think the church in Western society has accommodated itself too easily to the consumerist and imperialist values of the culture. Rather than abandoning formal religion, these Christians come together to pray, simplify their lives, serve the poor, care for the earth, and resist cultures of violence in communities that offer a holistic spirituality that embraces action, contemplation, and conversion of life.

Rutba House in Durham, North Carolina, is one of a number of new monastic communities. In June 2004, Rutba House hosted a gathering of friends from around the country to discern the shape of a radical movement called the new monasticism.

Out of the gathering came a book that offers strategic guidance for the movement characterized by these twelve elements:

1.   Relocation to the abandoned places of Empire.

6. Letter of January 14, 1935, *Gesammelte Schriften* 3, 25, cited by Bethge, *Dietrich Bonhoeffer*, 380.

2. Sharing economic resources with fellow community members and the needy among us.
3. Hospitality to the stranger.
4. Lament for racial divisions within the church and our communities combined with the active pursuit of a just reconciliation.
5. Humble submission to Christ's body, the church.
6. Intentional formation in the way of Christ and the rule of the community along the lines of the old novitiate.
7. Nurturing common life among members of intentional community.
8. Support for celibate singles alongside monogamous married couples and their children.
9. Geographical proximity to community members who share a common rule of life.
10. Care for the plot of God's earth given to us along with support of our local economies.
11. Peacemaking in situations of violence and conflict resolution within communities along the lines of Matt 18.
12. Commitment to a disciplined contemplative life.[7]

The new monastic communities preserve a living tradition that has prospered in Western society for nearly two millennia. Participants honor the wisdom of Western monastic forebears, for example, by committing themselves to conversion of life, to specific practices or a rule of life, and to stability. Many contemporary quasi-monastic communities have some form of enclosure: a collection of houses, perhaps a single dwelling, or even an abbey. The new monastic communities encourage members to have regular contact with the outside world, especially family.

With their monastic forebears, participants share a concern that western society has accommodated itself too easily to the consumerist and imperialist values of the culture. However, the focus of the new monastic communities is very much on the world in which they have established themselves.

Members are generating new forms of communal life discontinuous with older forms of Western monasticism. For example, many new monastic communities have rooted themselves in urban settings. They admit married couples and children into membership. Lacking formal ties to

7. Rutba House, *School(s) for Conversion*, xii–xiii; interview, Leah and Jonathan Wilson-Hartgrove, Durham, June 14, 2008.

traditional orders, members form networks with members of other communities and secular organizations.

Participants in the new monastic movement do not share a common theological tradition or denomination. The new monastic communities draw on the wisdom of a great legacy. As Jonathan Wilson-Hartgrove writes, the movement is "prochurch . . . God only knows if our communities will last or if the practices that have given us life will be of some help to other Christians. . . . We learn who we are in Christ as we find our way together."[8]

In many respects, the lines between monk and non-monk have become indistinct. A new monastic movement is flourishing along with the development of lay vocations in traditional orders, such as the Cistercian Lay Contemplatives, Benedictine Oblates, Third-Order Franciscans, and Lay Spiritans. Thomas Merton anticipated this development and mentored a large and growing number of people who felt called to lives of contemplative prayer and of active service in the world. He encouraged the creation of new forms of monastic and communal life. As he taught students for the priesthood (1951–1955) and novices (1955–1965), he focused increasingly on this question: how can monasteries nurture members in uniting the journey inward and the journey outward, the contemplative and the active as two aspects of one way of life?

In this book, we have been exploring what guidance Thomas Merton offers spiritual seekers. How are we to experience God and shape Christian community in our complex world? What might those who are members of different sorts of communities extrapolate from Merton's writings and experience that might encourage and give direction to this dynamic, unexpected, and new phenomenon? What might Merton praise and what he might find wanting in the new monasticism?

MERTON ON A NEW MONASTICISM

In Biblical narratives of the life of Jesus, there are two accounts of a story that addresses the need to hold together the contemplative and the active. The story concerns two sisters, Martha and Mary, and their brother Lazarus. John 12:1–8 records that Jesus visited the home of Lazarus in

8. Wilson-Hartgrove, *New Monasticism*, 147; for more information about the New Monasticism, see http://www.newmonasticism.com.

Bethany, where his sister Martha served a dinner. When their sister Mary anointed the feet of Jesus with a costly perfume, and Martha complained, Jesus told her to leave Mary alone.

In Luke 10:38–42, Jesus visited a certain village, where a woman named Martha welcomed him into her home. She had a sister named Mary, who sat at the feet of Jesus and listened to what he was saying. According to this account, Martha was annoyed that Jesus seemed to ignore her. Jesus answered her, "Martha, you are worried and distracted by many things; there is need of only one thing. Mary has chosen the better part, which will not be taken from her."

Christians have sometimes associated the three siblings with three vocations: active (Martha); contemplative (Mary); and ascetic (Lazarus). In a foreword to a collection of essays by Merton on the early Cistercian saint, Bernard of Clairvaux, Brother Patrick Hart OCSO addresses a contemporary aspect of these Biblical stories.

> Everywhere one hears the question: how can I lead a deeply contemplative life in the midst of my present activities? How can I combine the activities of Martha, the contemplative leisure of Mary, and the ascetical practices of Lazarus? Is union with God possible?
>
> Thomas Merton struggled with these problems in his own life and finally came to the conclusion that there is a Martha, a Mary and a Lazarus in each of us, and we must learn to live together in peace, ever striving to arrive at a balanced measure in our lives. Likewise, in each community there will be some more closely resembling the contemplative Mary, while others will be more inclined to the activities of Martha (or perhaps through the circumstances of the community needs, find themselves assuming more active roles), and still others the penitent Lazarus. In the final analysis, the most perfect way for each person is the total response in faith and love to one's personal call, to one's God-given vocation.[9]

In his study of "Action and Contemplation in St. Bernard," Merton warned against attributing superiority to any one aspect of the Christian and monastic life and concluded, "every perfect soul combines in itself the vocations of Martha, Mary and Lazarus."[10]

9. *Thomas Merton on Saint Bernard*, 9.
10. Ibid., 79.

In a draft of *The Silent Life*, published in 1957, Merton mentioned Primitive Benedictine communities such as *La Pierre qui Vire* in the Bourgogne region of central France, and the Monastery of the Resurrection, founded by Gregorio Lemercier in Cuernavaca, Mexico. Merton described the latter as follows,

> This small community made up entirely of Mexican Indians (except for the Superior) is one of the most remarkable and courageous experiments in modern monastic history. Struggling against desperate odds, living under very primitive conditions in true poverty and simplicity, depending on the labor of their hands and the Providence of God, the monks of Cuernavaca are perhaps closer to St. Benedict than anyone else on this side of the Atlantic.[11]

Merton returned to the theme of Primitive Benedictinism in an essay entitled "Problems and Prospects," published in *Contemplation in a World of Action*. Merton noted the development in the fifties, more than ten years before the Second Vatican Council, of monastic foundations of a new type, including primitive Benedictine foundations like Mount Saviour Monastery, located between Elmira and Corning in New York State and the Benedictine Monks of Weston Priory in Weston, Vermont, and the Monastery of Christ in the Desert at Abiquiu, New Mexico.

The keynote of the new monasticism was a simple, natural, more or less hard life in contact with nature, nourished by the Bible, the monastic fathers and the liturgy, and faithful to the ancient ideal of prayer, silence, and that "holy leisure" (*otium sanctum*) necessary for a pure and tranquil heart in which God could be experienced, tasted, in the silence and freedom of the monk's inner peace. For Merton, the older monasteries soon began in various ways to imitate them and attempt changes along lines which the Primitive Benedictine experiments had suggested. Thus even before the Council decree *Perfectae Caritatis* all the monks were working more or less at renewal."[12]

Merton's ever deepening journey inward of prayer, contemplation, and union with the Holy One prepared him for a journey outward in relation with others, including persons of other faith traditions. Merton welcomed this remarkable shift during the Second Vatican Council. Merton

11. Mott, 302.

12. *CWA*, 31–32.

was positive about *Lumen Gentium,* the Dogmatic Constitution on the Church. He discerned a shift in understanding of the church, from a static concept of a hierarchical institution to a dynamic, living Body of faithful Christians. He also felt *Perfectae Caritatis,* the decree on the renewal of the religious life, emboldened monks to question the basic institutional structures of the religious life along lines he advocated. He cautioned, however, that merely changing the externals of monastic practice would not in itself guarantee the transformation of consciousness that the contemplative life requires.[13]

Privately, Merton was less circumspect. On November 12, 1963, Merton observed in his journal that some curia officials were "asses . . . parading and gesticulating, proclaiming ten thousand programs."[14]

During the 1960s, Merton wrote several articles on the "renewal of life in the monastic milieu." In "The Identity Crisis," Merton called for recognition of the genuine needs of a new generation and for discovering how God asks the monastic life to meet these needs. Merton mentioned people struggling with the moral disintegration of an affluent society and with broken homes, alcoholism, irresponsibility, delinquency, and other widely prevalent evils; seeking unrestrained pleasure and inevitably getting what they seek; and searching for an outlet in various forms of extremism, fanaticism, nihilism, or mindless conformity. Merton believed these were symptoms of a deep alienation. For those seeking a monastic vocation, Merton saw the need for a "good spiritual father . . . to help in bringing the young monk to face himself."[15]

Merton urged that a new monasticism should neither replicate life in the world, nor provide a refuge from the world. Rather, new communal arrangements could enable monks to claim those basic human values that are so hard to find in the world,

> . . . personal integrity, inner peace, authenticity, identity, inner depth, spiritual joy, the capacity to love, the capacity to enjoy God's creation and give thanks. If the world fails to find these things in the monastery, then there is little value in following the latest in liturgy, having the most efficient machines and operating a profitable business.

13. Ibid., 115. William H. Shannon discusses Merton and Vatican II in *Thomas Merton Encyclopedia.*

14 *DWL,* 34.

15. *CWA,* 80 (98). The essay first appeared in *Spiritual Life* in 1968.

Our first task is to be fully human and to enable the youth of our time to find themselves and develop as men and as sons of God. There is no need for a community of religious robots without minds, without hearts, without ideas and without faces. It is this mindless alienation that characterizes "the world" and life in the world. Monastic spirituality today must be a personalistic and Christian humanism that seeks and saves man's intimate truth, his personal identity, in order to consecrate it entirely to God.[16]

Merton gave increased attention to the growth of new monastic communities. On the eve of his departure for Asia in October 1968, Merton collected several of these articles for a book on renewal of life in the monastic milieu. Published as *Contemplation in a World of Action*, Merton highlighted the need to abandon a triumphal or "holier than thou" attitude sometimes found expression in some monastic communities. He anticipated a new monasticism that would be a "simple, natural, more or less hard life in contact with nature, nourished by the Bible, the monastic fathers and the liturgy, and faithful to the ancient idea of prayer, silence, and . . . inner peace."[17]

Merton envisioned two lines of development. One was the renewal of the existing expressions of monastic life. Monks would enjoy a certain distance from the world in order to concentrate on the quality of life. Those who entered this path would gain a special awareness and perspective, an authentic understanding of God's presence in the world, including the crucial problems of the day such as racism, war, genocide, starvation, injustice, and revolution.

According to Merton, there was a second path. Creative forces were at work, with communities and superiors "fully aware of the real nature of the monastic vocation not simply as a summons to become a cog in an institutional machine, but as a charismatic breakthrough to liberation and love." This path was relevant not only to a Christian, but also to "the unbeliever who is nonetheless concerned with a self-transcending experience, the unpredictable and unexplained illumination that flashes out of the ground of one's own being."[18]

16. Ibid., 82–83 (100).

17. *CWA*, 31.

18. Ibid., 201.

MERTON ON FOUR NEW COMMUNITIES

In 1968, during what proved to be the last year of his life, Merton visited monastic communities in New Mexico, California, Alaska, and Asia. He was looking for places suitable for hermitages. In a talk that he gave at the Monastery of the Precious Blood in Eagle River, Alaska, Merton looked back on the situation of monasticism as it had existed ten years earlier. There was paralysis in the institutional monastic life. It was "static and even a little bit false and liable to breed all sorts of odd things. Instead of deep personal love, you had sentimental attachments."[19]

In the intervening years, monastic life had opened up. Merton saw monks and nuns reaching out to one another, building communities based on God's love, looking beyond their own communities, collaborating in building a new world that would express the fullness of the maturity of people. "We are winning the earth completely for God by experiencing the life of love and working together with his power to transform the world."[20]

During his twenty-seven years as a monk, Merton drew not only on the early Christian forms of monastic life. In the following sections, we briefly explore his engagement with four newer communities. In chronological order of their origins, they are the Shakers; the Hutterian Brethren; Taizé; and the Madonna House Apostolate.

The Shakers

The first example of Merton's wide-ranging familiarity with diverse forms of monastic and communal living was his interest in the Shakers or "The United Society of Believers in Christ's Second Appearing." Merton first wrote about the Shakers in his history of the Cistercian order, *The Waters of Siloe*. He mentioned the origins of the Shakers during the eighteenth century with the teachings of Ann Lee.[21] In the nineteenth century, there were active communities in New England, New York, Ohio, Indiana, and Kentucky. By the middle of the nineteenth century, vocations began to dwindle in part because the Shakers kept the sexes apart. They lived in

19. Merton, in Arnold, *Why We Live in Community*, 38.
20. Ibid., 61–62.
21. *Waters of Siloe*, 67.

community. As people of peace, they saw wars as resulting from lust for land and sexual partners.

On June 7, 1959, Merton and James Laughlin visited Shakertown, now Pleasant Hill, Kentucky, near Lexington about an hour and a half east of the Abbey of Our Lady of Gethsemani. Subsequently, Merton explained that the name Shakers was an expression of their ecstatic experiences, which marked their common worship, and especially their belief that when the Holy Spirit was present, "He made Himself known by 'shaking' the whole community in a kind of prophetic earthquake. The eschatological charity of the order produced an inward power which, they believed, would 'shake' the world and prepare it for the millennial renewal."[22]

The Shaker community in Kentucky had once thrived, but when Merton visited, the buildings were in private hands. Still, Merton found "something young about the old buildings, as if their pioneer hopefulness was still in them." Struggling with the busy-ness and business aspects of life at Gethsemani, Merton mused, "The two contemporary communities . . . were born of the same Spirit. If Shakertown had survived it would probably have evolved much as we have evolved. The prim ladies in their bonnets would have been driving tractors, and the sour gents would have advertised their bread and cheese. And all would have struggled mightily with guilt."[23]

In his journal, Merton reflected on his experience at Shakertown. He observed that for the most part, monastics are no longer puritans but "fall all over ourselves to be non-puritans . . . guilt remains . . . We have become so much puritans in reverse that many of us are frantic . . . This idiotic dilemma is the very heart of Gethsemani. And though it is idiotic, it is not to be despised."[24]

Merton's first visit to Shakertown coincided with his struggle to redefine his vocation. He considered moving to another monastic order, living as a hermit near or on an Indian reservation in New Mexico or Arizona and working a little with the Indians, or undertaking a hermit-mission like that of Charles de Foucauld. Merton returned to Shakertown at least five times: December 22, 1959; January 12, 1962; May and June 1965; and April 4, 1968. The commitment of Shakers to simplicity and the mystical

22. Merton, "Pleasant Hill," in *Mystics and Zen Masters, 194.*

23. *SS*, 286–87, entry for June 7, 1959.

24. Ibid. After 1960, Merton followed plans to develop Shakertown as a heritage site.

path that led adherents to the highest levels of religious or metaphysical awareness continued to excite Merton. The capacity of Shakers to find God in oneself rather than through clergy or rituals, and to see God in everything, even furniture, spoke to Merton of a spiritual grace that was "deeply significant."[25]

The Hutterian Brethren

In his Alaska conferences, Merton drew from an essay entitled "Why We Live in Community" by Eberhard Arnold (1883–1935). Arnold was a German Christian who, in 1920, moved with his wife and children to the village of Sannerz in central Germany. With seven adult members and five children, they founded a community that attempted to put into practice what Arnold believed the Holy Spirit had revealed to him. The community sought to live in accord with Jesus' Sermon on the Mount (Matthew 5–7; Luke 6:17–49). The community experienced growth and, in 1926, moved to the Fulda district where the group established the *Rhön Bruderhof* modeled on Hutterite communities that had begun during the sixteenth century.

Arnold contacted several communities of Hutterian Brethren in North America. In 1930, he visited several of them. That December, they commissioned him as a missionary to Europe. In November 1933, the Gestapo searched the *Bruderhof* for arms or anti-Nazi literature and closed their school. The *Bruderhof* sent their schoolchildren to Switzerland and finally acquired property in Liechtenstein. In March 1934, Arnold founded the *Alm Bruderhof* and spent the last year of his life shepherding his flock in the face of the Nazi threat.

Despite the life-or-death context within which Arnold wrote, Merton noted his basic optimism. For Merton, Arnold stressed the fact that God, not people, builds community. Merton told a story to demonstrate that the basis of community is not sociability but faith, hope, love, and detachment from things.

The story concerned two of the desert saints who had been living together as hermit monks for many years and had never gotten into a fight.

---

25. Letter to Edward Deming Andrews, August 22, 1961, *Seeking Paradise*, 113. In his essay on Merton and the Shakers, Paul M. Pearson highlights two foci of Merton's interest in the Shakers: their embrace of monasticism and their paradise consciousness. *Seeking Paradise*, 17.

One monk said to the other. "Why don't we do like everybody else in the world and get into a fight?" The other monk said, "O.K., how do you do it?" The first said, "Well, fights start over possessions, owning something exclusively so that the other fellow can't have it. Let's look around and get ourselves a possession and then have a fight over it." So he found a brick and claimed it as his own. The other said, "Well, brother if it is your brick, take it." For Merton, the crux of the story was that in community, one is to be free from things so that members might be free to love God and others, not just those formally professed members of the community, but to all those touched by the community.[26]

Merton concluded one of his Alaska conferences by citing Arnold to the effect that communities have but one weapon of the Spirit. This is constructive work carried out in the fellowship of love. Merton recalled Saint Paul who understood the power of the risen Christ, "far above all rule and authority and power and dominion, not only in this age but also in the age to come" (Eph 1:21). Prayer and contemplation are essential for community members to claim such power and to realize who God is in their lives, that we belong to God, and God has given us all we need to work together to transform the world.

In another talk given to the sisters in Alaska, Merton drew on Jewish and Sufi Muslim sources to highlight that monastic communities, with their practices of obedience, poverty, the *Rule* [of Saint Benedict], and prayer, offer a setting in which professed brothers or sisters say yes to God. The contemplative life goes even deeper. It is an "inner 'yes' . . . an unconditional 'yes' to God's love . . . it is simply the Christian way of life."[27]

Taizé

Monastic life has never been entirely absent within the Anglican, Lutheran, and Orthodox traditions. Generally, however, Protestants have been suspicious of monasticism. Nevertheless, since the period of World War II, there has been a remarkable revival of Protestant monasticism. The best known of all the new monastic communities is Taizé in central France. According to the vision of its founder, Brother Roger (1915–2005; baptized Roger Louis Schütz-Marsauche) the community of Taizé began

26. Ibid., 41–42, 65–66.

27. "The Life that Unifies," in Bochen, *Thomas Merton, Essential Writings*, 164.

in 1940 as a place of refuge, notably for Jews. After the war, several men joined Brother Roger's ministry of reconciliation, and on Easter Day, 1949, seven brothers committed themselves to a life following Christ in simplicity, celibacy, and community. During the so-called Cold War, Taizé provided space in which large numbers of young people from around Europe gathered. Taizé has consistently served as a center of liturgical renewal.

In an article on Taizé, Merton noted a crucially important shift in the perspective of many Protestants. No longer did Protestants universally reject monasticism as an invention of people superimposed upon the Gospel of Christ and diverting their attention from the true message of salvation. No longer did all Protestants reject vows as useless constraints. For Merton, Protestant monastic practices such as those of the brothers of Taizé in France signified the recovery of a balance between active works of charity and the contemplative life characteristic of traditional Catholic orders and of the new monasticism.

Merton noted that Protestant monasticism was growing in a general context of Protestant, Catholic, and Orthodox theological awakening. He welcomed renewal manifest in the liturgical, Biblical, and ecumenical movements of the day. For Merton, Taizé offered "a model of simplicity, spontaneity, openness, and vitality which can be profitably considered by the Catholic orders that have, perhaps in the course of centuries, become a little rigid." Above all, such Protestant communities could help Catholic monasticism "to preserve its own authentic sense of values."[28]

Madonna House Apostolate

Through an ongoing relationship with Catherine de Hueck Doherty, Merton followed the experience of another new quasi-monastic community. In 1930, having felt the force of the verse, "If you wish to be perfect, go, sell your possessions, and give the money to the poor, and you will have treasure in heaven; then come, follow me" (Matt 19:21 and parallels), Catherine gave up her worldly goods. She moved into an apartment in a poor area of Toronto, Ontario, where she was committed to living "the gospel without compromise." With the support of the archbishop, she established Friendship House, a storefront center for the works of mercy.

---

28. Merton, "Protestant Monasticism," in *Mystics and Zen Masters*, 191.

In 1938, with encouragement from Dorothy Day, whose Catholic Worker house operated on similar principles in New York City, Catherine moved to Harlem where she created a Friendship House as a place of hospitality, interracial justice, and reconciliation. She provided spiritual direction for people in the community and volunteers.

In 1943, Catherine married a journalist, Eddie Doherty (1890—1975). In 1947, Catherine and Eddie moved to Combermere, two hundred miles northeast of Toronto in rural Ontario. They established Madonna House Apostolate, a community of men, women, and priests dedicated to loving and serving Jesus Christ in everyday life. The spirituality of the community was Eastern Christian. In 1969, Eddie Doherty was ordained in the Eastern rite of the Catholic Church. The Eastern Christian tradition blends Catholic and Orthodox elements and permits married priests.

Catherine Doherty expressed the spirit of the Madonna House Apostolate in a prayer, "Lord, give bread to the hungry, and hunger for you to those who have bread." She also wrote a distillation of the Gospel called the Little Mandate, which came to her throughout the years as a response to prayer from Jesus:

> Arise—go! Sell all you possess . . . give it directly, personally to the poor. Take up My cross (their cross) and follow Me—going to the poor—being poor—being one with them—one with Me.

> Little—be always little!—simple—poor—childlike.

> Preach the Gospel *with your life—without compromise*—listen to the Spirit—He will lead you. Do little things exceedingly well for love of Me.

> Love—love—love, never counting the cost.

> Go into the marketplace and stay with Me . . . pray . . . fast . . . pray always . . . fast.

> Be hidden—be a light to your neighbor's feet. Go without fears into the depth of men's hearts . . . I shall be with you.

> Pray always. *I will be your rest.*[29]

Madonna House Apostolate has developed the leadership gifts of many in the community. This has enabled the community not only to sur-

---

29. Doherty, *People of the Towel and the Water*, 8–9, emphasis in original. Doherty, *Fragments of My Life*; visits, 1980 and 1981. The Madonna House website is www.madonna house.org/.

vive the passing of the founders, but also to grow. Today, it remains a place of prayer, retreat, and service for the rural poor. Under the authority of the bishop of the Catholic Diocese of Pembroke, Madonna House Apostolate is a "Public Association of the Christian Faithful" with more than two hundred members. They are men and women who are dedicated to loving and serving Christ. Living in community, they make the traditional monastic vows of obedience, stability, and conversion of life. In addition to a few staff priests, there are more than a hundred and twenty-five priests, bishops, and permanent deacons who identify with Madonna House and try to live its commitments wherever they serve.

In 1957, Eddie Doherty visited with Merton at the Abbey of Gethsemani. In addition, Catherine Doherty and Thomas Merton corresponded sporadically over the years. During the 1960s, Catherine encouraged Merton as he explored the relevance of silence, solitude, and prayer for lay contemplatives. On December 11, 1968, having learned of Merton's death by telegram from Abbot Flavian Burns, Catherine gave a talk, or spiritual reading, to her community in which she observed, "So, a great friend is home at last! He has given up everything, and he has received everything, so let us rejoice."[30]

MERTON AS MENTOR OF NEW MONASTICS

Merton wrote many letters to young people wrestling with the same issues the new monastics are addressing early in the twenty-first century. For example, in the late 1940s and early 1950s, Marialein Lorenz, a Sinsinawa Dominican sister, was a teacher in Mobile, Alabama. She encouraged her students to write to Merton, who responded to one of the letters that included sample essays they had written about Trappist life. Merton indicated that one of the main reasons he was so glad to hear from them is that they all had the same problems that he once had. Merton believed that God had given him the gift of writing, that he might show others, like these students, a way forward.

> . . . God is a consuming fire. The Holy Ghost gets into your heart and burns you clean and makes you strong. Christ . . . [fills] us with faith and with love, and giving us the strength to resist all

30. In Wild, 95.

the appeals of what is below us and unworthy of men made in the image of God.

It is terribly hard for people to find happiness in our time. Everything is mixed up. All the wrong ideas and all the wrong values are on top. Everywhere you go you find the papers and the movies and the radios telling you that happiness consists in stuffing yourself with food and drink, and dancing and making love. All these things are good and necessary, but they are not the whole reason for existing. They are given us as means to an end. The way to be happy is not to love these things for their own sakes, but to use them wisely for the glory of God. . . .

Merton concluded his long letter by observing, "I believe sometimes that God is sick of the rich people and the powerful and wise men of the world and that He is going to look elsewhere and find the underprivileged, those who are poor and have things very hard . . . and raise them up and make them the greatest saints. . . .[31]

In a letter to Cecilia Corsanego, Merton expressed his sense of having integrated his many selves.

It seems to me that the particular configuration of my own life, with all its shortcomings, demands some sort of synthesis of poetry and prayer. I fully realize that I might perhaps aspire to a technically "higher" kind of life if I would try to refuse to be a poet. But I have reason to think that if I made this refusal it would in fact be an act of pride and disobedience. Others will assume, on the other hand, that it is pride for me to continue to be a poet, especially when I am not a very good one. . . . I owe to the Lord my feeble efforts to synthesize, in my own life, the disparate elements that have been given to me. Hence I am to some extent monk, to some extent poet, and so on, and trying to reduce all this to unity.[32]

In this passage, Merton identified three main spheres of his activity: writing, monasticism, and prayer. Each provided an entrance into Merton's life. Taken in itself, none painted a complete portrait of the man.

One may recall the Jain story of the blind persons who touch a part of an elephant, whether the trunk, a leg, or the torso. None of the blind per-

31. *RJ*, 315, letter of June 2, 1949.

32. Cecelia Corsanego was a student at the *Pro Civitate Christiana*. She asked for Merton's help for a thesis on his poetry. David D. Cooper cites Merton's letter of January 31, 1964, in *Thomas Merton and James Laughlin*, vii.

sons experiences the whole. People enter Merton's world through many windows. One aspect of Merton's genius is his ability to engage people in such a manner that he can be heard from many perspectives. Very different individuals find in Merton a companion who genuinely is present and concerned about him or her.

Merton was by temperament *simpatico*, an Italian word from the Latin, which suggests that Merton had a temperament that led him to be interested in everybody and everything. In some sense, withdrawal from the world made his engagement with the world stronger. He was never disinterested in the world. For Merton, detachment meant knowing that no good action is ever wasted. The ultimate consequences of his becoming a monk were almost certainly different from those he initially hoped to achieve.

REFLECTIONS

Thomas Merton offers wisdom for people seeking to strengthen core values, to adapt, and to become self-aware individually and as part of a distracted society given to gimmicks and gizmos. Peoples' lives are mired in detachment, fragmentation, and diffusion.[33] Pulitzer Prize-winning author Geraldine Brooks comments with respect to a recent book by James Freeman, *The Tyranny of E-mail*, "I'm feeling the same way about my laptop. . . . this so-called boon to communication and productivity has become a distracting, privacy-sapping, alienating, addicting time-suck. He has convinced me that the new mantra for our times ought to be Tune out, Turn off, Unplug."[34]

The new monastic communities offer ways by which persons grounded in the messianic lifestyle of Jesus and of his early followers may address the challenges of post-modern living and become living signs of God's presence in prophetic action. Merton consistently affirmed that the root of happiness is not to be found in externals. He also lamented that many persons are driven to "the private accumulation of rubbish."[35] "Unable to

---

33. Jackson, 25
34. Back cover endorsement to Freeman, *Tyranny of E-mail*.
35. *No Man Is an Island*, 248.

rest in anything we achieve, we determine to forget our discontent in a ceaseless quest for new satisfactions."[36]

Merton taught that people might live in hope knowing only that God loves each and every person irrespective of her or his merits. What is good in a person comes from God's love and neither from our doings, nor from what is external to our true self. By creating communities grounded in love, we are able to center our lives through prayer and meditation, and live more humanly.

Thomas Merton believed that everyone can and should share a rhythm of contemplation and action. In *Conjectures of a Guilty Bystander*, Merton wrote, "We are human, and the only thing stopping us from living humanly is our own deeply ingrained habit of delusion, a habit which some of us stubbornly continue to associate with original sin."[37] Merton also called for living in "obedience to God, who *is* Supreme Life. To believe: to obey Him Who is Life, and consequently to live. To live by submission to the Supreme Authority of Life—self-commitment and submission to God's Truth precisely in its power to give life, *to command to live*. . . . We cannot live in the truth if we automatically suspect all desires and all pleasures. It is humility to accept our humanity, pride to reject it."[38]

Merton's call remains as pertinent today as ever. We need balance in our lives. The contemporary new monastics offer one path to living more humanly.

36. *Ascent to Truth*, 17.

37. *CGB*, 233–34 (256).

38. Ibid., 10–11 (18, 20), Merton's emphasis.

NINE

Building Communities of Love

Do not be afraid.
O my people
Do not be afraid
Says the Lord:

I have called you
By your name
I am your Redeemer
You belong to me.

When you cross the river
I am there
I am with you
When your street's on fire
Do not be afraid . . . .
   —Thomas Merton, "I Have Called You," *Collected Poems*

In December 1967, Thomas Merton gave a retreat for a group of sisters of Loretto. Merton addressed the place of the contemplative life in a world that looks to contemplatives not just for some marginal concern but as central and essential. To preserve the identity of monasticism, Merton advised keeping a certain distance from the world. At the same time, Merton urged that monastics foster compassion in their lives, feel more for those who are suffering, and help people develop new ways of living.

Merton stressed the need for contemplatives to be open spontaneously to the reality of God, to become fully developed persons, and to commit themselves equally to contemplation and identification with the struggles of people in the world. Merton said monasteries should house people fully involved in shedding light on God's will for today.

> This is what we have to do: avoid lining up on the side of a revolution as well as on the side of a counter-revolution. We need to line up on the side of the people. Wherever there is human presence, we have to be present to it. And wherever there is a person, there has to be personal communication. There Christ can work. Where there is presence, there is God. A Christian is one who continues to communicate across all the boundaries, a sign of hope for a convergence back to a kind of unity.[1]

Merton then explored the importance of being what he called a "community of love." He cited Christ's words, "Love one another" (John 13:34), and continued:

> Live in community, have community of love, let God dwell right here among you. God is experientially present, and we are aware that God is with us. This is contemplation, isn't it, the experience of the nearness . . . of God? Therefore, if we love, the love which makes us love one another in community is that which makes us contemplatives. Because we love, God is present. Contemplation is presence. The presence of love to one another goes with the presence of God to oneself. It is in community that this Presence realizes itself through our love . . . . The thing to do is to create a community in which the source of contemplation is this kind of love.[2]

What for Merton was the prophetic vocation of a community of love? Merton explained, "We become prophetic when we live in such a way that our life is an experience of the infallible fidelity of God." For Merton, the kind of prophecy that communities of love should exhibit was not that of some Christians who see prophecy as predicting the future or of some business people who anticipate the latest fashion ten years be-

1. *Springs of Contemplation*, 35.
2. Ibid., 51.

fore it happens. Prophecy does not entail using some technique or telling someone else what to do. For Merton, our lives are prophetic when we are completely open to God's love, to the Holy Spirit, and to being led where God wants us to go.[3]

For Merton, one finds true happiness through unselfish love that increases as one gives it away. This was the theme of "Love Can Be Kept Only by Being Given Away," the first chapter of *No Man Is an Island* (1955). Throughout his writings, Merton emphasized this idea of selfless love as an essential mark of the Christian and of monastic spirituality. "You came to the monastery to learn, or rather to relearn, the love whose seeds were implanted in your very nature. And the best way to do this was to open the eyes of faith and gaze upon the perfect embodiment of God's love . . . Christ on the Cross."[4]

For Merton, the active aspect of love began with silence. Merton developed this theme in a succession of books including *Seeds of Contemplation* (1949), *New Seeds of Contemplation* (1961), and essays collected after his death. Merton criticized "infantile" and "narcissistic" approaches to love characteristic of popular culture. Merton dismissed the images projected by advertising agencies of beautiful and fulfilled lovers or "beatified couples," for whom the years of early middle age are an unending ball, as unconvincing. The mission of the poet, the artist, and the prophet was to explore the reality of love. "Unfortunately," commented Merton, "the confusion of our world has made the message of our poets obscure and our prophets seem to be altogether silent—unless they are devoting their talents to the praise of toothpaste."[5]

> In silence we face and admit the gap between the depth of our being, which we consistently ignore, and the surface which is untrue to our own reality. We recognize the need to be at home with ourselves in order that we may go out to meet others, not just with a mask of affability, but with real commitment and authentic love.[6]

Offering an approach to love that was practical and prophetic, Merton called for the creation of new communities of love. Alive to God's presence in their lives, community members should be open to the Holy

3. Ibid., 64.
4. *Waters of Siloe*, 291.
5. *Love and Living*, 37.
6. Ibid., 41.

Spirit, willing to let the Spirit lead them, and signs of hope in a world that cries out for empathy on behalf of the outcast, release to the captives, recovery of sight to the blind, and liberty for the oppressed (Luke 4:19).

THE NEED FOR COMMUNITIES OF LOVE

In our present circumstances in North America and around the world, there is significant evidence that several trends threaten the quality of human life. To a considerable extent, humankind has failed to create the foundations of a vigorous international system to regulate human behaviors harmful to the planet. It is difficult to mobilize compassion for people who already suffer due to this failure and to sustain social change. In part, this is because a few people exploit and oppress the vast majority of the world's population in the service of their own pleasure, power, or profit. Only a small minority of people have access to institutions, resources, and tools for this purpose. Often, they have succeeded in violation of ethical norms and legal systems that have as their intent promoting the common good.

Several studies explore the consequences of these worrisome trends. In an article that I wrote over thirty years ago, "The Party Goes On: God's People in the Age of Scarcity," I reflected on findings of a think-tank known as the Club of Rome. Their first publication, *The Limits to Growth*, reported that the world would ultimately run out of many resources; that people could alter this trend; and that the sooner this effort started, the greater the chance would be of achieving a condition of ecological sustainability far into the future.

The authors cited a French riddle of the lily pond, according to which a pond has a potentially virulent lily that doubles in size each day. If the lily grows unchecked, it will cover the entire pond in thirty days, choking off all other forms of life in the water by the time it covers the entire pond. The authors asked this question: if a skeptic waited until lilies covered 50 percent of the pond before taking any remedial action, when would she or he act? The answer was, "On the twenty-ninth day, of course. You have one day to save your pond."[7]

The Limits to Growth appeared when people sat with motors idling in long lines waiting for gas. Planet earth was approaching the twenty-ninth

---

7. Dekar, "Party Goes On," 11; *Limits to Growth*, 37.

day. Humanity had little time left to address the challenges of war, energy crisis, environmental crisis, world hunger, and potentially the collapse of our industrial, urban society.

At the time, several paths of action seemed available for humanity. On an individual basis, persons could take responsibility for their part in the human condition by withdrawing from the achievement-neurosis of our high-pressure materialistic society. They could share with others more of what had been given them. They could use their purchasing power to redirect production towards goods and services that meet genuine social needs.

In response to the crisis identified in *The Limits to Growth*, people could have developed a sense of human interdependence and coopera-tion, an attitude toward nature and toward one another based on harmo-ny rather than conquest, and an identification with future generations. Instead, like the proverbial three "wise" monkeys, too many have failed to see the crisis, to hear of it, or to address the authors' warnings in terms of dangerous trends in the interactions of five global economic subsys-tems: population, food production, industrial production, pollution, and consumption of non-renewable resources. In terms of North America, an era of unprecedented but largely unregulated growth has compounded resource shortages and created catastrophic public-health disasters.[8]

Decades ago, C. S. Lewis (1898–1963) cautioned about one of these disasters, the gross disparity of wealth between the rich and the poor. Like Merton, C. S. Lewis achieved fame as a writer of autobiographical and academic works as well as popular science fiction and children's novels. In 1943, Lewis gave the Riddell Memorial Lectures at the University of Durham. He said, "What we call Man's power is, in reality, a power pos-sessed by some men which they may, or may not, allow other men to profit by . . . what we call Man's power over Nature turns out to be a power exercised by some men over other men with Nature as its instrument." Lewis warned of "the rule of a few hundreds of men over billions upon billions of men."[9]

In a recent commentary on I and II Kings, Daniel Berrigan, poet and activist, observes, "To speak of Christians, can our God incarnate in Jesus be one with this Yahweh, a deity of kings and their wars, enthroned in a

8. Jones, *Green Collar Economy*, 4.
9. Lewis, *Abolition of Man*, 34–36.

cloud of moral ambiguity, implicated in wickedness trumpeted as virtue? . . . . Behold the ancestry from which we spring, we children of primal catastrophe. Let us ponder our forebears, and weep." Berrigan is unrelenting in his criticism of political leaders. "They are hardly different at all [from the rulers of old]. Today they create an economic divide of riches and rags, systems of stigma and exclusion, of racism and sexism. And endless wars, incursions, bombings, sanctions."[10]

Like Lewis and Merton, Berrigan insists that the prophets and Jesus and the early church honor Yahweh with a piercing and passionate "no" to the powers that be. He unmasks and condemns the worldly power misused by the rich against the poor.

A cycle of overwork and overspending has ensnared many persons. According to Harvard University sociologist Juliet B. Schor, for many North Americans, "making as much money as possible has become the reigning religion." Schor called for trying to find another way by creating "a model of a decently functioning economy coexisting with a decent cultural and daily life experience."[11] More recently in *Plenitude: The True Economics of Real Wealth* (2010), Schor has welcomed a shift to new sources of wealth, green technologies, and different ways of living.

One problem associated with consumerism and materialism has been the erosion of a sense of the common good. In a book entitled *Bowling Alone*, Harvard sociologist Robert D. Putnam chronicled the extent to which individualism has replaced community. As early as Alex de Tocqueville's report on *Democracy in America* in the 1830s, it was noted that the qualities of compassion, care, and concern for the least and the lost have constituted the heart of civic culture in North America. These marks of a commitment to the commonwealth have since eroded.

As a symbol of the decline of a sense of connection and of a willingness to associate with others, Putnam examined the phenomenon of people bowling alone. He compiled statistics to show that more people are bowling than ever before, but league bowling has plummeted in the last ten to fifteen years. From 1980 to 1993, the total number of bowlers in the United States increased by 10 percent while league bowling decreased by 40 percent. This trend was not trivial. In the United States, eighty million persons went bowling at least once in 1993, nearly a third more than

10. Berrigan, *Kings and Their Gods*, 2–3

11. Schor, *Overspent American*, 172–73.

voted in the 1994 congressional elections and roughly the same number as those who claimed to attend church regularly. Calling for people to become reconnected, Putnam closed with advice by Henry Ward Beecher a century earlier to "'multiply picnics' . . . not because it will be good for America—though it will be—but because it will be good for us."[12]

In North America, we are people in crisis in a system that is in crisis. We have quickened the pace of life only to become less patient. We have structured life in ways that are more organized, but people are less spontaneous and joyful with little or no time to enjoy the beauty of a sunset, the delight of a child taking her or his first steps, or the pleasure of spending an evening with loved ones, a friend, or a new acquaintance. We have made it possible to create a better future for our children, but our children are less able to enjoy the present than in the past. With ever-growing urgency, humankind needs a new degree of spiritual maturity.

As a partial response to this need, I believe Thomas Merton was prescient in calling for the creation of communities of love. What might such community look like?

COMMUNITIES OF LOVE

According to Acts 2:43–47 and 4:32–37, many of the earliest followers of Jesus formed communities of love. They held in common everything they owned. There was no needy person among them. Those who owned lands or houses sold these assets and gave them to the community to be used in service of any who had need. Trying to live in accord with Jesus' teachings, the first Christians clothed the naked, fed the hungry, comforted the sorrowful, sheltered the destitute, bound up the wounded, and witnessed to the risen Christ. Those in the Antioch community modeled Christlikeness and were accordingly called Christians (Acts 11:26).

About a century later, The *Epistle of Mathetes to Diognetus* described another Christian community. The author and recipient were Greek. In defending Christianity from its opponents, the author wrote:

> For the Christians are distinguished from other men neither by
> country, nor language, nor the customs which they observe. For
> they neither inhabit cities of their own, nor employ a peculiar form
> of speech, nor lead a life which is marked out by any singularity.

12. Putnam, *Bowling Alone*, 414.

The course of conduct which they follow has not been devised by any speculation or deliberation of inquisitive men; nor do they, like some, proclaim themselves the advocates of any merely human doctrines. But, inhabiting Greek as well as barbarian cities, according as the lot of each of them has determined, and following the customs of the natives in respect to clothing, food, and the rest of their ordinary conduct, they display to us their wonderful and confessedly striking method of life. They dwell in their own countries, but simply as sojourners. As citizens, they share in all things with others, and yet endure all things as if foreigners. Every foreign land is to them as their native country, and every land of their birth as a land of strangers. They marry, as do all [others]; they beget children; but they do not destroy their offspring. They have a common table, but not a common bed. They are in the flesh, but they do not live after the flesh. (2 Cor 10:3).

They pass their days on earth, but they are citizens of heaven. (Phil 3:20) They obey the prescribed laws, and at the same time surpass the laws by their lives. They love all men, and are persecuted by all. They are unknown and condemned; they are put to death, and restored to life. (2 Cor 6:9) They are poor, yet make many rich (2 Cor 6:10) they are in lack of all things, and yet abound in all; they are dishonored, and yet in their very dishonor are glorified. They are evil spoken of, and yet are justified; they are reviled, and bless; (2 Cor 4:12) they are insulted, and repay the insult with honor; they do good, yet are punished as evil-doers. When punished, they rejoice as if quickened into life; they are assailed by the Jews as foreigners, and are persecuted by the Greeks; yet those who hate them are unable to assign any reason for their hatred.

To sum up all in one word—what the soul is in the body, Christians are in the world. The soul is dispersed through all the members of the body, and Christians are scattered through all the cities of the world. The soul dwells in the body, yet is not of the body; and Christians dwell in the world, yet are not of the world.[13]

Love is a theme running throughout the history of Christian spiritual writing. To cite but one classic written in the seventeenth century, Carmelite lay Brother Lawrence of the Resurrection characterized the practice of the presence of God as "doing all for the love of God." The more one acts in a spirit of loving care and wisdom, the more one is united

13. Online: http://www.newadvent.org/fathers/0101.htm

to God in love. Continual "mindfulness of God" is a source of freedom from "self-love" and motivation to love God in others.[14]

Now, early in the twenty-first century, many Christians are fashioning a way of living in the world through love. Seeking to live humanly and to share their stories, they are signs of hope and midwives to change. Briefly let me share three examples: one from the new monastic movement; one from an ordinary congregation in a typical North American city; and one from an experimental group.

A new monasticism that is gathering momentum takes many forms. In the early 1970s, the Holy Transfiguration Monastery emerged from the youth group of Norlane Baptist Church near Geelong, Victoria, Australia. By November 1976, six youth were gathering for contemplative prayer. They asked if, amidst a culture of materialism, they might model church as a reflection of the Trinity. Wanting a more radical way of life, including celibacy, the group became part of Breakwater Baptist Church and began to receive members from the Anglican, Baptist, Catholic, Pentecostal, and Uniting Church communions in Australia as well as some members from overseas. The community now consists of sketes not only in Victoria, Australia, but also in Canada, the UK, and the U.S.

The skete is a form of monastic life characteristic of the Carthusians, Camaldolese, and Carmelites of the Western Christian churches and of hermitages in Eastern Christian monasticism. In the case of Holy Transfiguration Monastery, sketes offer dispersed members of the community a way of connection and mutual practical encouragement.

Members of the community commit themselves to live as a paradigm for human fulfillment and service in our world. They articulate their commitments in a document known as the *Resolve*. Distilled and refined over a thirty-year period, the *Resolve* is not a legal document but rather is an instrument for growing into Christ-likeness. It reads as follows:

> In honour of the non-violent God, assured of life eternal, with your whole being proclaim your gratitude.
> Reject nothing, consecrate everything.
> Be the good of love, for God, for neighbor, for all creation.
> Judge no one, not even yourself.
> Love beauty.
> Maintain inner-silence in all things.
> Show hospitality; err only on the side of generosity.

14. Lawrence, *Practice of the Presence of God*, 88.

Speak truth to power, especially power without love.
Let your only experience of evil be in suffering, not its creation.
To breathe peace into the world, first disarm your own heart.
For us there is only the trying, the rest is none of our business.

Members have written prayers and liturgies informed by ancient wording in dynamic, meditative, and socially attuned language. Singing is central to all the liturgies. The community has benefited from the gifts of master craftspersons, artists, and architects to create a new complex marked by simplicity, beauty, and holiness.

Community members have created a community of love. They are present to, and see themselves as channels of, God's love in all of life. Members offer a prophetic witness not by being overtly religious, or by preaching, but by being open to making God's presence tangible in the world by transparency and service.

Throughout North America, congregations of faithful people share God's love with one another and the world. As but one example, First Congregational Church in Memphis, Tennessee, affirms its mission in the following way:

We will be together.
We will stand as brothers and sisters given life by one God.
We will be together.
We will watch out for one another.
We will listen to what needs to be said in a spirit of compassion.
We will respect the power of silence.
We will wait for the slowest. We will sooner or later catch up
with the fastest.
We will dry the tears of those who are weeping
and know that they will dry ours when the time comes.
We will let ourselves begin to feel at least a little of the pain of
those we have considered our enemies.
We will entrust our stories to each other.
We will not be skeptical that peace can come.
We will not forget to be grateful.
We will do our best to stir in each other hope, courage and
faith.[15]

15. In an email dated May 29, 2010, pastor Cheryl Cornish explained that around 2002, First Congregational Church adapted words of Mary Farrell Bednarowski, professor emerita at United Theological Seminary of Minnesota, as a blessing that appeared in *Of Rolling Waters and Roaring Wind,* World Council of Churches publication. The

Affirming these words in community life, members describe themselves as a "just peace" congregation. In addition to worship and educational programs, congregation members seek in ordinary ways to make tangible God's love for all. They provide guests from around the world the services of a retreat center and hostel. They support a conference center. They run a Global Goods Fair Trade store in support of farmers and craftspeople from around the world. They assist neighbors and folk from the community who need food and clothing.

In the late 1990s, the congregation promoted (successful) efforts to implement a living wage for city and county workers. Subsequently, members have remained active in providing needed services to the poor, for example, by offering facilities for the repair and recycling of bicycles, professional counseling services, and space for twenty-nine organizations, all of which bring people together in an environment of healing, justice, and reconciliation.

In 1982, a collective in Syracuse, New York, formed an experimental corporation with the intent of being midwife to a culture that honors diversity, celebrates community, respects earth and all its beings, and encourages and supports all forms of creativity. Among the collective's "tools for change" is a poster that reminds me that around the world, people are birthing and nurturing communities of love by the following actions:

> Turn off your TV. Leave your house
> Know your neighbors
> Look up when you are walking
> Greet people. Sit on your stoop
> Plant Flowers
> Use your library. Play together
> Buy from local merchants
> Share what you have
> Help a lost dog
> Take children to the park
> Garden Together
> Support Neighborhood Schools
> Fix it even if you didn't break it
> Have Pot Lucks. Honor Elders
> Pick Up Litter. Read Stories Aloud
> Dance in the Street

Presbyterian Church USA holds copyright and first published the piece in "The Spirit of Reimagining: Setting the Stage," *Church and Society*, May/June, 1994.

Talk to the Mail Carrier
Listen to the Birds. Put up a Swing
Help Carry Something Heavy
Barter For Your Goods
Start A Tradition. Ask A Question
Hire Young People for Odd Jobs
Organize a Block Party
Bake Extra and Share
Ask For Help When You Need It
Open Your Shades. Sing Together
Share Your Skills
Take Back the Night
Turn Up The Music
Turn Down The Music
Listen Before You react To Anger
Mediate A Conflict
Seek To Understand
Learn From New And
Uncomfortable Angles
Know That No One is Silent
Though Many Are Not Heard
Work To Change This[16]

A New Benedictine Charter, the source of which is unknown, expresses the spirit of many new monastic and other experimental communities. Paul M. Pearson, director of The Thomas Merton Center housed at Bellarmine University in Louisville, Kentucky, provides the text, as follows:

We live in a complex and consumer society. We can live simply and respect the material things in our lives and the environment.

We live in a highly competitive and individualistic society that is constantly mobile and changing. We can be stable not only in our inmost selves but in our relations with those around us, above all in our constant and unchanging search for God.

We live in a world of injustice and exploitation, in a class-ridden society where people are denied the right to live with honor and dignity. We can refuse those values since we are people who can accept each other and everyone as Christ.

16. Online: http://syracuseculturalworkers.com/poster-how-build-community.

We live in a world of baffling noise and endless media demands for attention. We can become a listening people, listening to our neighbor and above all to God.

We live in a world that is angry, fear-ridden and distracted. We can with practice carry a heart of stillness in the midst of all this.

We can have an awareness of God's gaze upon us. We can in fact become contemplatives in the most ordinary and demanding events of daily life.

Members of the new monastic and other experimental congregations and communities are slowing down, scaling back, and finding more time to be with each other. This can be something as commonplace as the daily routine of preparing and cooking good meals and then sitting down to enjoy them unrushed with family, community members, or friends. Even cleaning up after dinner can offer a lesson in the pleasures of the ordinary, good things in life.

As they experience change in their own lives, the new monastics are free to mobilize the resources of human ingenuity, love, and wisdom in service of people otherwise disadvantaged. They are creating a deep sense of caring and bridging the gap that often exists between those who have something to share and those who have little or nothing.

In contemporary language, poet Judy Chicago describes communities of love as bringing together all that otherwise divides people. When that happens, compassion can transform a world that has become harsh and unkind. Both men and women will be strong and gentle, and no one will subject another to her or his will. All will be rich and free and varied. Chicago continues,

> And then the greed of some
>   will give way to the needs of many
> And then all will share equally
>   in the earth's abundance
> And then all will care
>   for the sick and the weak and the old
> And then all will cherish life's creatures
> And then all will live
>   in harmony with one another and the Earth
> And then everywhere
>   will be called Eden once again.[17]

17. Roberts and Amidon, *Prayers*, 265.

A union organizing song written by Ralph Chaplin in 1915, "Solidarity Together" asks, "what force on earth is weaker than the feeble strength of one?" My response is this: God has placed power in our hands that is greater than the hoarded gold of people whose greed and lack of mindfulness of the cost of their quest for a certain kind of power have brought on the global economic and environmental crisis. Our power, spiritual power, is greater than the might of armies, magnified a thousand-fold. Members of the new monastic and other experimental communities are bringing to birth a new world from the ashes of the old.

A popular folk song written at a junior high school dance around 1949 by Nancy Schimmel, the daughter of Malvina and William Reynolds, offers a unifying vision of all these communities. The song, "Magic penny," expresses the simple idea that we are to give love away. Like a magic penny, if you hold love tight, you will not have any. However, if you give it away, you end up having more.

MERTON FOR THE NEXT GENERATION

In this book, I have sought to amplify Merton's voice in relation to several values essential to the future of life on earth. As I have reflected on Merton as a prophet for the next generation, two books by a developmental psychologist, Erik H. Erickson, come to mind: *Young Man Luther* and *Gandhi's Truth*. Erickson chose to illustrate aspects of his understanding of the human life cycle by examining Martin Luther, a sixteenth-century monk and theologian, and Gandhi, the twentieth-century architect of the theory and practice of non-violent resistance, as representatives of the journey by which all go through life.

In Erickson's telling, the youthful Luther and aging Gandhi successfully navigated critical life passages. Each was able successfully to communicate to an entire generation something of the personal impact of the wider societal transformations to which they gave leadership. Each was able, through the telling of their stories, to become for others a soul friend, in Gaelic *anam cara*, the person to whom you reveal the deepest intimacies of your life.

Advances in technology were allies for Luther and Gandhi. Advent of the printing press facilitated the wide distribution of Luther's writings. Radios and movies enabled journalists to transmit images of Gandhi's campaigns throughout the world. Similar advances in communications have enhanced the possibility that new readers will find wisdom for the living of our days in Merton's writings.

Thomas Merton followed a creative path. Just as current English language usage cheapens words such as community, love, and peace, Merton criticized misuse of the word "creativity." He believed the secular caricature of the word is a futile and demonic attempt by humans to divinize themselves. Rather, God made it possible for people to share fully the likeness and image of God. Through God's divine power, we have become participants in the divine nature (2 Pet 1:3–4). According to this text, three disciples—Peter, James, and John—came to understand that they were witnesses to the glory of a human being fully alive, the first of their own kind, which the *shekinah* (glory) of God validated and accepted at the time of the transfiguration of Jesus (Matt 17:1–9 and parallels; 2 Pet 1:16–19).

For Merton, there is no genuine creativity apart from God. All persons who attempt to be a creator outside of God or independent of God are bound to forge a graven image designed to elevate simply human creation into the realm of the sacred. Yet God has made it possible for humankind to participate as co-creators with God in the work of restoration of all things to harmony in Christ.[18]

By this understanding, Merton truly walked a creative path that has had an enormous impact. People from all lifestyles read Merton. In Folsom Prison, Eldridge Cleaver is unable to keep Merton out of his cell. Cleaver recalls Merton's description of Harlem as especially haunting: "whenever I felt myself softening, relaxing, I had only to read that passage to become once more a rigid flame of indignation."[19] At Tinker Creek, flowing towards Roanoke River in Virginia, Annie Dillard reads Merton.[20] Charles Clement, a young Quaker medical doctor, carries a Merton title in his pack in rebel-held territory of El Salvador.[21] William Least Heat Moon, the translation of his mixed-blood tribal name, is touring the country after he lost his job at a college in Missouri. Reading *The Seven Storey*

18. "Theology of Creativity," *LE*, 355–70.

19. *Soul on Ice*, 35.

20. Inchausti, *Thomas Merton's American Prophecy*, 75, cites a letter he received from Annie Dillard.

21. Pennington, *Thomas Merton. Brother Monk*, xiv.

Mountain, he has a sensation at the Trappist abbey of the Holy Spirit in Conyers, Georgia, that mirrors Merton's at Gethsemani:

> There was nothing but song and silences. No sermon, no prom-
> ise of salvation, no threat of damnation, no exhortation to better
> conduct. I'm not an authority, God knows, but if there is a way
> to talk into the Great Primal Ears—if Ears there be—music and
> silence must be the best way.[22]

In Michael Ford's book *Spiritual Masters for all Seasons*, the Anglican Archbishop of Canterbury, Rowan Williams, reflects on Merton:

> Every time I read Merton, I have a renewed sense that this is the
> world I want to inhabit. I think Merton has given me a sense of
> the largeness of the classical Christian world—that world of the
> monastic fathers, to some extent the medieval world at its best,
> and that openness to other traditions East and West. I think it is
> the feeling that the classical Christian world of doctrinal vision
> is big enough for far more than a lot of people think. It is hugely
> deep and resilient, capable of engaging intelligently and compas-
> sionately with political reality and other faiths.[23]

Especially through his autobiographical writing, Merton offered his life and the lives of monks and nuns more generally as a counter-cultural model that grows from the monastic lifestyle. Merton had an incredible gift of reaching out to others in friendship and mentorship. Among friends who influenced Merton's interest in Islam, Louis Massignon was a French scholar who published on a ninth- and tenth-century Muslim named Mansur al-Hallāj. Massignon characterized his relation to al-Hallāj as one of "a friendship, a love, a rescue." Massignon did not mean that he had rescued al-Hallāj from historical obscurity but rather that al-Hallāj had somehow reached out across time to rescue him.[24]

Merton reaches out in friendship, love, and rescue to people who, troubled about life, are seeking a new path. He offers an antidote to the labyrinth of propaganda to which people are exposed. Merton cautions about violence exerted when, by means of a cascade of news and informa-tion, people are predetermined to certain conclusions and therefore to a loss of freedom.

22. Least Heat Moon, *Blue Highways*, 83.
23. Ford, *Spiritual Masters for all Seasons*, 56.
24. Palmer, "Contemplation Reconsidered," *Merton Annual* 8 (1995) 22.

During the retreat that Merton led in December 1967 for the Sisters of Loretto, someone asked if nuns should read *Time Magazine*. Merton responded: "if you're asking if nuns should be informed, yes but if it implies that by reading *Time* you are informed, no."[25]

Merton once offered Mass for what he called "the next generation," the new poets, the fighters for peace and for civil rights, and for his novices. He prayed that God would preserve himself and the next generation from becoming "right-thinking men"—that is, "men who agree perfectly with their own police."[26]

During my thirty-three years as a teacher, I sought to live in such a way that I manifested the Divine Nature as one who bears God's image and likeness, restored by Christ (2 Pet 1:4). In Memphis, I communicated with transparency my vision for a better world with students enrolled in the Merton classes. Together, we learned from one another, prayed, and shared burdens similar to those that led me to engage Merton's writings in the first place. Resisting some of the pressures of contemporary life, we felt freedom in serving and transforming our respective congregations into communities of love.

Many of my former students serve small and, in some cases, dying congregations. Renewed by the course, and especially by time at the Abbey of our Lady of Gethsemani, many have introduced monastic wisdom in their own settings. Some have resonated with a story told in *The Different Drum: Community Making and Peace* by the psychiatrist M. Scott Peck (1936–2005). The story concerned a rabbi—not Jesus, certainly not Merton—who gave a special gift—a surprising gift—to another dying community of five old monks, the abbot and four others, all over seventy. The monastery had fallen on hard times and was clearly dying.

In Peck's narrative, in the woods surrounding the monastery, there was a little hermitage occasionally used by a rabbi from a nearby town. Through their many years of prayer and contemplation, the old monks could always sense when the rabbi was in his hut. As he agonized over the imminent death of his monastery, the abbot thought to visit the rabbi and ask, if by some possible chance, he could offer any advice that might save the monastery.

25. *Springs of Contemplation*, 27–28.
26. *CGB*, 225, 247.

When the abbot arrived at the hut, the rabbi welcomed him. However, when the abbot explained the purpose of his visit, the rabbi could only commiserate with him. "I know how it is," he exclaimed. "The spirit has gone out of the people. It is the same in my town. Almost no one comes to the synagogue anymore."

Quietly, the old abbot and the old rabbi wept together. They read parts of Scripture and quietly spoke of deep things. Then the time came when the abbot had to leave. The two old men embraced each other. "It has been a wonderful thing that we should meet after all these years," the abbot said, "but I have still failed in my purpose for coming here. Is there nothing you can tell me, no piece of advice you can give me that would help me save my dying monastery?" "No, I am sorry," responded the rabbi. "I have no advice to give. The only thing I can tell you is that the Messiah is one of you."

When the abbot returned to his monastery, his fellow monks gathered around him and asked, "What did the rabbi say?"

"He couldn't help," the abbot answered. "We just wept and read Scripture together. Just as I was leaving, he did say that the Messiah is one of us. I don't know what he meant."

In the days, weeks, and months that followed, the old monks wondered whether there was any possible significance to the rabbi's words. One pondered, Could one of them really be the Messiah? Had the Christ come again? Which one of them could it possibly be? Did the rabbi mean the abbot? He had been a faithful leader for many years. Or did he mean Brother Thomas? Brother Thomas was an exemplary holy man. It could not be Brother Elrod, could it? Elrod gets so cross at times. And yet Brother Elrod usually turns out to be right about things—about important things—matters of faith. Brother Phillip was certainly out of the question—too passive—a real nobody. But who was there whenever anyone needed somebody? Maybe Brother Phillip is the Messiah. Surely, I am not the Messiah, he thought, I am too ordinary—too old—too worn out—but who knows?

Though it was too wonderful to believe that one of them was truly the Messiah, the old monks began to treat each other with extraordinary respect. Without being consciously aware of it, visitors sensed something different about the monastery, a spirit of extraordinary respect among the monks. On Sundays, people came to pray in the chapel or for a picnic. More and more often, people brought their friends, and their friends brought their friends. Some of the young men who visited talked more and more to the old monks. Some of them decided to stay. Before long, the monastery had become a vibrant center of faith and prayer. Before the oldest monk died, his last words were a prayer of thanks for the rabbi's gift. How thankful he was that the rabbi had taught them to respect one another once again and thereby to manifest the Spirit who had in turn led people to return.[27]

Seeking Wisdom on the Journey

Early—5:00AM early!—on a Monday morning in June 1997, I gathered with a group of students in the parking lot of Memphis Theological Seminary. Six hours later, we arrived for a five-day retreat at the Abbey of Gethsemani where I ceased to be course facilitator; I was simply another person on retreat.

Each morning and afternoon, I walked along a path that meanders through the woods. I looked, listened, prayed, journaled, and paused at two places associated with Merton, including a plot that preserves the outlines of Merton's Zen garden and a shed nearby. Many retreatants visit the shed. Many leave notes that deal with such life situations as illness, decisions about vocation, or life choices facing loved ones. In my own contribution to the notebook, I wrote, "the peace of Christ and place envelops me. The silence is wonderful. Thanks be to God. *Deo gratias.*"

Once after breakfast, a monk escorted me and a few others to the hermitage where Merton spent his last years. Over the door to the hermitage was one word, "Shalom," peace. A small sign adorned an empty chair on the porch with the words, "Bench of Dreams." Nearby were the wheel and cross often associated with the hermitage thanks to an iconic photograph taken by Merton.

On this and other retreats at Gethsemani, I took refuge in a favorite place for meditation, a garden with two large statues created by Walter Hancock in memory of Jonathan M. Daniels. An Episcopalian seminarian and civil rights worker, Daniels was martyred in Alabama, August 20, 1965, when he stepped into a bullet intended for Ruby Sales. William Coolidge of Boston, Massachusetts, donated the statues to the monastery. A memorial plaque called on viewers always to remember that, while the

27. Peck, *Different Drum*, 13–14.

church exists to lead people to Christ in many ways, it is always the same Christ.

With few exceptions, I had little direct contact with the ten students from Memphis. Through the week, we maintained silence on the monastery grounds, including the dining area and the oratory. Only on our journey back to Memphis did students relate their experience. Sharing fresh insights about monasticism and new understandings about their lives, students bubbled over with excitement.

At one point, large hailstones pounded the van. So intense was the storm, we could not continue. The van stopped under an overpass. We climbed out of the crowded van for a stretch. Conversation continued. Like the tsunami-like storm we were in, students wanted to share their experience of an overflow of God's all-powerful presence.

Having moved only recently to Memphis, I was still struggling to accept my new situation. I asked, "Has God called me to Memphis to be a catalyst for this process?" I recognized in a flash that there were no past battles to fight. God had purpose for me in my new teaching milieu. Through this course, I had provided a small group an opportunity to be quiet, to rest, and to grow.

This particular outcome of this, my first Merton class, was crucial for me. No longer dwelling on the past, I was journeying into the future. Another transformation was palpable. The course had tapped into an implicit discontent with church as widely constituted and experienced by most of the students. For me this was a simple lesson about living in the moment. There were no past battles to fight. I could be present fully to the changed circumstances of my life. Savoring the full measure of my new-felt liberty, I experienced enormous gratitude and freedom. I was at peace. With Thomas Merton and members of his community as companions, I had found a way of living more deeply and humanely.

At the end of his early autobiography, *The Seven Storey Mountain*, Merton shared that he felt God urging, "that you may become the brother of God and learn to know the Christ of the burnt men." Merton, Trappist brother and my brother in the journey, then offered in Latin a few closing words. They are equally apt for this book. SIT FINIS LIBRI, NON FINIS QUAERENDI.[28] This may be the end of the book, but it is not the end of the searching.

28. *SSM*, 423.

The Christian in a Technological World

INTRODUCTION

Especially during the last ten years of his life, Merton commented frequently on the impact of new technologies in cybernetics, weaponry, and tools used in every aspect of the Western way of life. Merton gave the talk that follows on June 5, 1966. He observed that a crucial point emerging from Vatican II in documents like the Dogmatic Constitution in the Modern World (*Lumen Gentium*) was that technology must serve humankind and the real interests of real people. Merton also called for dialogue between Christians and Marxists. This theme was the focus of the second appendix.

Merton opened with comments about Dom Vital Klinski. During Merton's novitiate, Dom Vital was novice master and Merton's confessor. In a journal entry for April 11, 1966, Merton mentioned Dom Vital's dementia.[1] Merton also discussed Vital Lehodey (1857–1948), a monk of Notre Dame de Grâce, a Trappist abbey in Bricquebec in Normandy, France, abbot from 1895 to 1929, and Abbot Emeritus at the time of his death. In teaching younger monks, Vital drew from the writings of Bernard of Clairvaux, Teresa of Avila, John of the Cross, Francis of Sales, and others. Merton also discussed Jean-Baptiste Chautard (1858–1935), abbot of another French Trappist abbey, Sept-Fons. Dom Chautard wrote on the interior life. I have not included this discussion in the transcription that follows.

1. *DWL*, 39. Gethsemani tape 161, Track 3, is labeled "Dom Vital. Technological Society."

"The Christian in a Technological World"[2]

I'm talking about the church in the world. And I'm going to talk today about something that is intimately connected with Marxism, and it is without which there could be no Marxism, and that is technology. You have to see that Marxism would not have been possible in the late Roman Empire, for example, it couldn't fit. You've got to have an industrial, or technological society before you can have Marxism. You could not have had Marxism in the age of St. Bernard—it just would not have been possible. It's not comprehensible. Marxism does not become comprehensible until you have got technology. And when you have got technology, then Marxism comes into the picture. Marxism and technology have grown together.

One of the things I might as well say is that I'm no expert in this. I'm talking about things that are not my field. I'm a poet. What do I know about technology? I get into the steel building, and I'm lost [laughter]. This isn't my field. However, I know something about it. And I've read some authors about it, and most of the people I have read are controversial. A lot of the stuff that I am going to be saying is going to be unacceptable. However, it is good to know these things are said. And it is good to take a critical view.

The first thing we have to make quite clear is that there is absolutely no point whatever in monks or anyone standing back and saying we're not going to have technology [Merton laughs]. That's just absolutely stupid. We've got it. We are living in a technological world. You can't get away from technology. You go live on top of a pillar and you are going to have technology up there somewhere. Technology probably put the pillar there in the first place [laughter].

There is no escaping technology. And furthermore, we have to be very, very clear, that we are living in what is strictly a technological revolution. It isn't just that we have got a lot of machines. But that the entire life of man is being totally revolutionized by technology. This has to be made very clear. We are not at all living just in an age when we have more tools, more complicated tools, and things are a little more efficient, and that

---

2. This continues the talk given by Merton on this topic on June 5, 1966, transcribed with permission from the Merton Legacy Trust and the Thomas Merton Center at Bellarmine University. The re-mastered version includes both parts. Merton used notes entitled, "Technology," *Collected Essays* 6, Bellarmine Archives, 53–59.

sort of thing. It's a totally new kind of society that we're living in, dating back about two or three hundred years. I'm not sure when you can say the technological revolution began, but certainly not very long ago. You push it back more than two or three hundred years, and you're pushing it back too far.

If you want to find something on this, who is a good man to read on the history of technology and the relationship of technology and civilization? Who is *the* [his emphasis] man on this? Lewis Mumford. He is an excellent person to read. We should have actually his set. His first book was *Technics and Civilization*.[3] I'm not sure what we have. I think we have his *City in History* in the library.[4] It gives a good picture. The thing about Mumford, he is not only an expert, he is critical. He doesn't just simply accept everything that happens and say this is the way things should be. He suggests ways in which technology is not being properly applied and in which it could be applied better. Don't just take this stuff for granted—think in terms of how it should be used.

Just think, technology is revolutionizing the monastic life. And when I say that, I'm not screaming, or yelling, or anything. I'm just stating a fact. It is revolutionizing the monastic life. And you have to take into account the fact that the monastic life is now deeply influenced by technology. And any concept about *aggiornamento* in the monastic life that does not take into account technology is off the beam. However, most of the shouting about *aggiornamento* pays no attention to technology. The things that we are still saying about how to get the monastic life up to date you could do if you had a water mill down there.

The Rule of St Benedict has principles that can be applied to an age and any kind of culture. But it is not written for a technological culture. Consequently, *The Rule of St Benedict* must be translated into the terms of a technological culture before you can make sense of it. If we do not take account of the fact that the monastery is deeply revolutionized by technology, we're going to be running a museum, with a lot of air conditioning and fans and technology on the side. But it is going to be a museum with people sitting around in funny costumes in air-conditioned rooms and kidding themselves that they haven't got anything to do with technology, which is absurd. So what we have to do, we have to face this fact.

3. *Technics and Civilization*. New York: Harcourt, Brace & World, [1963].

4. *City in History: Its Origins, Its Transformations, and Its Prospects*. New York: Harcourt, Brace & World, 1961.

Now what is technology? Let's define it. Brother Alberic, Brother Bartholomew, who wants to volunteer? It is the idea that man has at his disposition scientific knowledge, and research, and collective research, team research, and all this stuff. And you apply this to practical problems and the practical problems you apply it to are problems about changing the natural environment into an artificial environment. That's what it amounts to, the creation of a completely artificial environment to replace a natural environment. That's not an essential part of the definition, but that is what happens. That's what technology does.

Now an author says this. He defines technology like this. "It is the translation into action of man's concern"—technology is about action, it's not speculative; technology is not sitting around and theorizing. Technology does not bother itself with theories that have nothing to do with immediate application.

Technology goes to work on this and does it. Man works by reason, does it, and finds the best way to do it. Man's concern to master things by means of reason, by means of science—the man is tendentious, but this gives you something of the slant of what you have in a technological society, and what a technological culture can do. It shows what a technological culture is going to do. "To account for what is subconscious, to make quantitative what is qualitative, and make clear and precise the outlines of nature." It's poetry in a way, but it is useful.

Technology has nothing to do with what can't be organized, what has to be left in its own original shape, and so forth. Technology changes what you got in front of you, and makes it manageable. What technology does is, it takes a lot of indiscriminate junk lying around and manages it, gets it into some kind of form where you can do something with it. And since technology is interested with anything it touches then an awful lot starts to get done.

You have examples of this here all over the place. Give me an example of something around Gethsemani that makes it clear and precise over the last couple years. [Someone cites cutting the lawn.] Yes, but cutting the lawn is just one thing. Over the past four or five years, there has been more and more lawn cutting. It's a good thing, it's fine, there is nothing wrong with this, monastic life allows us to do the lawns, to have closely cropped lawns. This is excellent, but this is technology. Technological society around a place like this requires cutting a lot of grass.

The example I was thinking about is that we used to have many creeks around here, and now we have one creek. When it rains, then you have plenty of creeks where the old ones used to be. But this is a problem that technology doesn't solve. Instead of five fields, you have one; you can go down the creek and clean it up in one operation. But that's exactly how technology operates. You can simplify everything and get at it faster.

The ancient monastic outlook on such things is suspicious of this point of the world. I'm not saying at all that we should keep the ancient monastic outlook on this point. I'm just saying, "Is it practical?" I don't know.

A Russian monk of the nineteenth century, Theophan the Recluse, says that this whole instinct of man to gain mastery over his environment, to be constantly expressing his mastery over more and more things, is an effort of man to be god enthroned over the world and to impose his will on everything. And this desire roots him in the world and makes it impossible for him to be a monk. You are going to have a lot of people around the monastery that still feel this way. But if you are going to take this attitude, then you have got to turn the monastery into a kind of museum, or a kind of camp, or something like that. These are some of the issues that you have to think about.

Now on the contrary, Marx is saying just the opposite. Marx envisions a society that is completely technological, in which man replaces nature by technology, so that nature is made a clean sweep of, insofar as it possibly can, and everything is technology. And when the whole world is transformed completely into technology, then it is humanized, then man really becomes himself, then man really attains his true being and vocation in the world. And consequently you have in Marxism an attitude that is intensely active, intensely technological, intensely devoted to changing everything, and organizing everything on a huge scale, and doing it with efficiency.

So technology is changing everything on a large scale. So you have this other view of life which is oriented toward a completely technological world. This is the way that a lot of Catholic thinkers are going to be going. You have some new monastic experiments oriented in this way, like Charles Foucauld's Little Brothers and things like that,[5] they are oriented

---

5. Charles Eugène de Foucauld (1858–1916) was a Catholic priest and writer. He lived among the Tuareg in Algeria. The Little Brothers of Jesus formed after his assassination in 1916. He was beatified by Pope Benedict XVI November 13, 2005.

in this way. The trouble is that, if you get monastic experiments that are only half oriented in this direction, they are ambiguous, and you don't know what you are getting. The trouble with this is that monks do not know what they are talking about when they envision this kind of development. They don't know what they are doing. They get half into it, they put one foot in, but don't realize what they are getting.

Suppose I get the idea that we've got to form a little group. OK, we have got ten monks who will get jobs and drive in to General Electric every morning or every evening or work all night, then go back to the monastery. OK, so let's get ten of us to go work in GE. So what am I doing? What do I think I am working in that place for? Am I just doing it because these other guys are doing it? You may think you are making a good impression on the neighbors. But what is it about, monks working at GE? Why do I have to work at GE? But if I don't know what GE is about, what GE stands for in society, and I don't know what I am trying to do as a monk, this is a problem. But it seems to me that is what some of these experiments are doing, especially the kind where they get a cushy job working half a day. Really interesting. Let's imagine ten of us working half a day at General Electric. GE doesn't fool with that sort of thing. That doesn't fit into a technological society. You have a bunch of kooks coming in for half a day—monks coming in and contemplating half a day—it's hard enough to do that around here. We've got it organized here, we can do it.

Now, what does technology do? It is not just the use of tools, but it involves a systematic application of science not just to getting things done, but to constantly improving and developing the way in which things get done. Technology is not content to develop a good way of doing a thing, and then staying with that, even for ten minutes. If a better way suddenly appears, you take it and it doesn't matter how fast it happens.

And one of the things about the technological revolution is that there is happening faster and faster and faster—someone discovers a better way to keep a jet plane from melting when it's going at supersonic speeds, then the next thing you know they've found an even better way before they've built the new plane. Things are obsolete before they are off the assembly line. So that's what is meant by technological revolution. This systematic application of science and research to the development of new ways of doing things, finding new machines and solutions for practical problems, making progress, and increasing the efficiency with which things are done, and accelerating the rate of progress. This is a problem. This is what you are getting, and this is what the technological revolution is about.

I'm not interested in what this does, but in the effects on people, on life, and on outlook. This profoundly changes one's whole outlook on life. And for us, the huge problem is this: What do you mean by "a contemplative view of life" in this intensely active concern with moving ahead as fast as possible?

If you take an ancient platonic, static view of life, you've got problems. You are in all kinds of difficulties right away. You've got the guy trying to be in the prayer of quiet while he is operating a complicated machine, noisy. Then he may discover by sheer cussedness that he can operate in this racket without being distracted, and he thinks he is contemplating. He may think he is achieving something. This isn't it, a matter of maintaining by hook or by crook a platonic view of contemplation in the middle of a whole lot of technology, a question of developing a whole new view of life in which these things fit and do not bug you. You have to become a person who is not bugged by all this jazz. And how to do that, don't ask me, I have not got that figured out. I gave up on that one a long time ago. My formula is to get the blazes out of the way and live in the woods [laughter] so you only hear it at a distance, you hear that constant hum, it sounds like the world war going on. It's alright, it's fine, it's technology. I'm much better at it than I used to be ten years ago.

Therefore what are the questions that are asked in a technological society? And what are the questions that used to be asked in the old kind of society? What is the big question about technology, what is the question that technological man asks himself at every moment? What is the characteristic question when he approaches something? Not, is it beautiful? But is it practical? Will this work? This is the prime question. What are some of the other questions which he could ask but he doesn't ask because he is asking "will this work?" What will be another question that becomes irrelevant when all you think about is "will this work?" What's another question? "What is it?"

Technology doesn't give a hoot what this is. Only what does it do? How does it run? "What is this?" takes you back to a totally different outlook on things, considering the essences of things. What does it mean? And then that gets you to the question of values. What does this mean for the salvation of my soul? You can save your soul in a technological environment, but there is no machine for saving your soul.

Another thing technology doesn't ask is, "Is this right?" The individual engaged in dealing with technology may ask this question too, but technology as such doesn't.

Where do you find this coming up? You find it coming up in a place where technology is now most at work, namely in war. When you got certain kinds of hardware, that you want to use on lots of people, people who are going to use it do not ask, Are people going to like this? Is it going to hurt people? Is it right to do this? They are going to ask, "Is this going to work?"

This is what is happening in Vietnam; people are asking, If we do this to these guys, is it going to work? Only as an afterthought, you have generals asking themselves not if it is right, but only if the people back home are going to kick about this. The problem of right or wrong is irrelevant. Sometimes these fools back home kick about because they are sentimental, because they are not practical, they are not concerned with how things are going to work. Actually, this is not always the most practical way of looking at these things, because things are not always practical. But they aren't asking this sort of question. Only, how to get things done.

Questions of principle are not necessarily the most cogent thing when you're dealing with technology. They may come in by accident. This is because the person concerned may be a person of principle. But sometimes he is not a person of principle and may only be concerned with how to get this thing done.

Now this technological revolution is mixed up with other things that go with it. And one of the big things, because technology has gotten into medicine, and it is one of the biggest problems in the world today, is population. Because babies don't die so much, then you have this population explosion. Technology can save people's lives easier, and feed people better. All of a sudden, you have this proliferation of people all over the place. This is part and parcel of the whole question of technology. And right away you begin to see one of the problems that arises out of this. Because you have more and more people, but less and less for them to do. Quite apart from how to feed them, "What are they going to do?" because the machines are doing more and more of the work. This is one of the things you have to face that nobody has an answer for.

So what do they do, well they fight. They raise Cain. They run around throwing things. You have trouble. One of the things that follows from this is that you have teenagers running around the streets killing each other with knives. They haven't got anything else to do, and they have no hope of ever having anything else to do. This is part and parcel of the same thing.

Another thing is social mobility. People are all over the lot. In the old days, a person would be born in, say, Bardstown, and live his whole life in Bardstown, maybe three or four times in his life went to Louisville—big deal. But nowadays, people go all over the place, you don't even have to change your job, you're just working for the same corporation, you're over here, over there, living here, living there. Where you live makes no difference; you live in exactly the same kind of house. You have exactly the same sorts of people next door. You move, but you haven't changed a bit. The effect this has is that you are no longer a part of any little group and you lose your roots in small groups, and you become part of a mobile population.

Marxism and Technology

INTRODUCTION

Merton gave this conference on June 26, 1966. During the last years of his life, Merton gave increasing attention to Christian perspectives on Marxism. This talk anticipated themes in Merton's last talk, which he delivered at Bangkok on December 10, 1968. Here, and in his talk two and a half years later, Merton explored the position of the monk in a world of revolution and offered an alternative to a strictly anti-Communist and negative attitude toward Marxism.

Merton differentiated Marxist thought and the experience of specific Communist regimes. In this talk, Merton addressed the possibility of members of the community moving to Chile. Merton highlighted the importance of reaching out to Marxists due to their possible role in fomenting liberation struggles in Latin America.

Among Merton's correspondents was a former novice Ernesto Cardenal Martínez (b. 1925). From 1979 to 1987, he served in Nicaragua's left-leaning Sandinista government as minister of culture.

Merton was prescient in anticipating that Latin America would be the stage on which competition and conflict would play out between three superpowers, two of which already possessed nuclear weapons, and another that would surely follow. Merton not only rightly called for accommodation, but he also correctly anticipated that *détente* between the U.S. and Soviet Union would not necessarily eliminate the threat posed by the clash of highly militarized regimes.

"COMPUTERS–MARXISM. THE 'NO-DIALOGUE' KIND"[1]

I don't know what's on the grapevine about when the Chile foundation is going to be started. But anybody who is going to go to Chile needs to know about Marxism. You really need to know what it is all about because in South America, Marxism is serious—not like cancer is serious; I mean the people take it seriously, intelligent people take it seriously, and most of the smartest people you will meet in South America will be Marxists. And they are not just guys that have bombs in their pockets. There are lots of different approaches to Marxism.

But before you go, I want to clean up one or two points left on technology. You often hear that we have machines that can think, and machines that can create. Back in 1957, some guy was announcing that within the visible future, machines will be able to handle all the problems to which the human mind could be applied. Well, I'd just as soon not turn some of mine over to a machine [laughter]. You put the problem through a sausage grinder.

About ten years ago, somebody said that a computer would win the chess championship of the world, would discover new mathematical theorems, and write music. Recently, a man from MIT [Massachusetts Institute of Technology] said this is not true. He said that computers are not very good at chess. "Computers can play a good game of checkers. Chess, however, where there are so many variations, is more complex. A chess player has a kind of sixth sense, there is more going on than just simple calculation. A group at Los Alamos developed a program that played an inferior though legal game on a reduced board. Ever since that program beat one weak opponent, the forecasts of impending master play have grown increasingly emphatic. But no computer program developed in recent years has failed to play a stupid game. The highly publicized computer was defeated in thirty-five moves by a ten-year novice" [laughter]. So they are not absolutely infallible.

In New York, there's a place called the Lincoln Center, which is a great place for concerts. There are all sorts of things that go on there. You have to have reservations. So they have a computer to process reservations. "During a recent stride towards modernization, an IBM computer made such a botch of handling ticket requests that extra human help re-

1. Gethsemani tape 161, Track 4. Transcribed with permission from the Merton Legacy Trust and the Thomas Merton Center at Bellarmine University.

quired forty-five days working twelve hours a day to straighten things out. Now people are using their hands for the manual process in use now. So now that people do the job, and the computer is fired, we don't care what the machine is going to do."

Now I'm going to read some correspondence in a recent issue of *Scientific American*. They are trying to figure out what is out there. A big question arises. What is going to come from outer space? A scientist who is writing in response to another scientist thinks that this other scientist is naïve. This other scientist expects fabulous intelligence coming from these places. One says, "I would like to advance that there is a distinction between technology and intelligence." This is kind of a bombshell because everybody assumes that if it is technological, it is intelligent. And here is a scientist saying not necessarily so. I'll just read what he says. "I cannot personally accept so and so's view that interstellar communication will necessarily be the perfect deliberate philosophical discourse." See, they are expecting Plato's out there someplace. "Intelligence may indeed be a benign influence creating isolated groups of philosopher kings far apart in the heavens and enabling them to share at leisure their accumulated wisdom; or intelligence may be a cancer, a purposeless technological exploitation sweeping across a galaxy."

Now here is a scientist assuming, which many people do not assume, that there is such a thing as purposeless, technological exploitation that just mushrooms on its own without getting anywhere. It is useless, he is saying, it's not intelligent. The fact that it works does not mean that it makes sense. This is a scientist; this is not a poet saying this stuff.

Poets can get off this kind of stuff all the time; if it comes from a poet, you don't know whether he knows what he is talking about. This man evidently does. "In this connection it is of importance that even at the slow rate of interstellar travel that is unquestionably feasible that the technological cancer can spread over a whole galaxy in a few million years, a time very short compared with the life of a planet." In other words, the whole thing may be taken over by this unintelligence. And that is what we're going to get, if we've got our instruments going, that what we're going to hear, a bunch of kooks like ourselves out there giving off the same sort of stuff. "All of us who think seriously about the detection of extraterrestrial intelligence know that we suffer from one basic limitation, our imagined detectors detect technology rather than intelligence. And we have no idea whether or not a truly intelligent society would retain over millions of years an interest or a need in the advancement of technology."

I'm not going to discuss the Council, but the big point that the Vatican Council makes about technology is that it must serve man. And it must be in the interest of the whole person. And this is what you would expect. There is no point in my discussing this. Read the Constitution on the Church in the Modern World [*Lumen Gentium*]. No sense in my going into this, because what it says is obvious. It is for man.

Now if technology is for man, there are perhaps problems arising from a certain dehumanization in life, as a result of a too Faustian concept of man. I'm not just talking about machines, but this completely technological view of life where the important thing is efficiency. One of the important things, one of the places where this comes up, is the conflict between technology and ethics. Ethics are likely to lose out. For example, you've got a man working on out a nuclear submarine. And his boss wants him to try out this new sort of a thing that is supposed to protect the people from radiation. Someone asks, "What about radiation?" Well, this isn't going to protect anyone. But someone says anyway, "Try it out anyway, see what happens." After a people a few people are knocked off, it is seen not to work.

There is a tendency to take things too lightly. As a matter of fact, I haven't seen the book, but there is a new book out, *Unsafe at Any Speed* [by Ralph Nadar]. I haven't read it, but we ought to have it around here. This is a book in which a brave man attacked the auto industry for putting out unsafe cars. There has been a real war, the industry has smeared the guy—his wife, they have just splattered him all over the place—it would be worth knowing about. But he is hanging in there telling us that they are making unsafe cars. For industry, it doesn't matter if it is safe, what matters is to sell it, get as many of them out on the road moving around all the time and make some money out of it.

This is another aspect of this. Morality comes to be regarded as irrelevant; it only matters whether something works. Morality is regarded as sentimental. Then there is also the psychological aspect of the thing. The great problem that people talk about.

We're getting into a depersonalization of man. What's all this talk about the depersonalization of man in a technological society? What does this mean? How does a person become depersonalized? Are these just words? Does it make any sense? What is depersonalization? [Someone: he doesn't have to decide anything.]

Well, yes and no, that's one approach to the thing, a lot of things are simply decided for him beforehand. Now we're getting into Dan Walsh's specialty. The way I conceive it, it's the idea of a person being cut off from his internal resources, his creative self, spontaneity, direct contact with life. In my language, a depersonalized is person when he has no direct contact with anything. Suppose we talk about a depersonalized approach to food, I don't know, as I have lost appetite since my operation [laughter]. Suppose someone is eating something not because he likes it, but because someone else told him to. He has reactions that are dictated for him by everyone else. Or you may be wearing something because everyone is wearing it. This is not the result of a real, personal reaction to the thing. [Someone: This reminds me of something you said before, advertising serves to create certain needs.]

Yes, he doesn't know. He reacts through this thing. He is pushed this way. He is pushed to want this. You function much better when you go direct to a thing, when you have a real response. A society that leaves a person bereft of a direct approach to life is putting him in bad shape. It doesn't have to be a technological society; any kind of over organized society can do it, a Trappist monastery for example. This is a great place for depersonalized functioning. If you want to really function nicely without having any trouble just get totally depersonalized and work like a machine and you'll have less troubles. If you want to be a little bit individual about things, well life takes on some risks. This devalues the person. This is depersonalization. Any organized place can do this.

[Someone suggests a title, *The Making of a Moron* by Niall Brennan.] It's a very good book. It *is* not a bad book. It is a good book. *The Making of a Moron.* Those who have not yet become morons should read this book; learn how to do it in a week, you'll be all set. It doesn't have to be a technological society, it could be an organized society. The book offers a humane approach along the lines of Eric Gill,[2] Chesterton,[3] and others. It's a good approach, a bit old fashioned. But it's good.

2. Arthur Eric Rowton Gill (1882–1940) was a British sculptor, typeface designer, stonecutter, and printmaker who wrote on the relationship of religion and the arts.

3. Gilbert Keith Chesterton (1874–1936) was an English Catholic writer of biography, Christian apologetics, fiction, philosophy, poetry, and plays.

So let's get on with dialogue between Christianity and Marxism. One of the things that you run into with Marxism is that Marxism has a superstitious reverence for technology. One of the things you get in Marxism is an intense depersonalization. The depersonalization of technological society, the Marxist political totalitarianism, especially in Russia, this is a sensitive area. Another sensitive area is the area of the intellectuals in Iron Curtain countries like Poland and Czechoslovakia; that is an area of sensitive dialogue because these people are reacting, they're fighting back against this bureaucratic Marxism. This is what you are going to run into in Chile.

I know a Marxist in Chile, one of the most important poets in South America. He was here a while back, a very nice civilized person, a quiet man, very monastic, great appreciation for monasticism, appreciation for simplicity. He is reacting strongly against bureaucracy in Marxism, and against this totalitarian stuff, this business of the big machines and the like.

The Russians less, Chinese least of all. So there is a spectrum, different levels of acceptance of the bureaucratic machine. Chinese Marxism is the most organized. In the middle you have the Russians who are half and half. Russians can be extremely obsessive. You've got a compulsive Russian Marxism on a large scale, the old Stalin machine type stuff.

This is the big struggle in Russian today. Actually, the future of Marxism may be decided by the struggle between the rigid organizational types in Russia, and the freewheeling types, the freewheeling revisionist types. This is one of the most important areas in the world today. It's the same everywhere, it's the same in this country from another point of view. In this country you've got a rebellion on the part of a lot of extremely freewheeling kids and so forth who are very smart and they're going places against the generation above them, the organizational business types. People want to loosen things up, get more free. Of course, this doesn't solve all the problems. These are tendencies everywhere, and you have to be sensitive to this.

So, when you run into a Marxist who is looking around for a more free-wheeling approach, there is a possibility for dialogue. I am going to take three approaches to this question of the dialogue with Marxism.

First of all, there is the no-dialogue approach, which is prevalent on both sides, saying no dialogue is possible, these guys are devils. It doesn't matter which side you say it, it's exactly the same argument either way. Just change a few of the words. You can take the propaganda of either side and just leave blanks at certain strategic points and just put slightly different words in the blanks and you'd have exactly the same message, except with slightly different details. There is a certain line of thought that no dialogue is possible. Dialogue equals betrayal. To talk to a Marxist is to be a traitor; you are betraying the Christian cause because these guys are devils and they are fiendish, fiendishly clever devils in everything and if you talk to them, you are selling your soul to the devil by talking to these characters. So you just stay away from them. And of course the Marxist view is exactly the same; you horse around with the capitalists or an American or something like that then you've had it, these guys are devils. Americans are devils. This is the first article of faith in China. If you go to China if you want to get along, you've got to believe at the fundamental starting point of all your actions that Americans are devils. Then you can function, you can fit into the Chinese context. Then the rest of life makes sense. If you don't have that particular dogma straightened out, then you'll have a lot of trouble adjusting to all these other things because everything else presupposes that.

Then there is the non-dialogue approach, which we will go through very fast because it is not very interesting. You run across this approach everywhere, for example in the Catholic press. There is no point in emphasizing it.

Then there are the revisionist Marxists in Iron Curtain countries and in Italy and France. There is a fellow named Garaudy[4] who is very important in this Marxist–Christian dialogue. He is sort of a professional dialoguer with Christians; he's written books on the subject. You're going to hear more of him. He is always talking with Rahner, Küng, Teilhard—they are a sort of club, they are all real buddy buddies. This is the stuff that is selling. Wherever you get Rahner and Küng and Teilhard, you're going to get Garaudy in the middle of it. Herder and Herder publishers will publish something by Garaudy with a commentary by someone. There is a good fellow up in Toronto named Leslie Dewart. There is going to be book dialogues between these people. This is selling. If I write a book, obviously I've got to include Garaudy [laughter].

4. Roger Garaudy (b. 1913–) wrote on Marxist-Christian dialogue, including *Perspectives de l'homme, existentialisme, pensée catholique, marxisme* (1962) and *From anathema to dialogue; a Marxist challenge to the Christian churches*, translated by Luke O'Neill (1966). For more information, *Asian Journal*, 328, note 2.

Much better is a Czech Protestant called Ramanka, who ten years ago was already saying from the Christian point of view that Christians in Iron Curtain countries should talk with the Marxists. Christians, get out of the ghetto.

This idea that Christians should get out of the ghetto was a new message ten years ago. Great deal of screaming about this. When this got through to the Protestants in this country, there was a great deal of fuss. Why is this Christian in an Iron Curtain country talking about getting along with an atheist government?

This is the hard Chinese line and also the basis of the American policy in Vietnam. Robert McNamara (the Secretary of Defense) spelled this out in the paper. This speech by this Chinese minister of Defense and McNamara said, "My God, this is what they're saying these awful devils, so this is what we've got to base ourselves on." It is completely dogmatic. How do they interpret the situation? How do they see the world? They go back to something that happened, something they did that proved to their mind that this is the way reality was.

At one time, they were cooperating with the Kuomintang, with Chiang Kai-shek.[5] They were supposed to be collaborating and these guys threw them out. And then they moved on, like the Jews crossing the Red Sea. What is the sacred history, the great Red Sea experience for the Chinese? [Someone: The bomb.] No, before that, before Korea. [Someone: The Long March.] Yes, the Long March was like the Jews in the desert. This was a legendary event that took place in the 1930s, when they were getting a lot of support from the villages. But then they were able to consolidate their position. This great salvation event proved that Mao was right. Mao did a great thing with rifles and clubs. They ate off the land. The Long March was a kind of salvation event, like Moses. They picked up supporters as they went along. "Who are you?" They were saying, "We are your friends." They ended up with lots of success, like a salvation event. By the time the Japanese war began, most of China was red. This was the basic line.

So this was the salvation event, this was the approach. If you follow the correct Marxist-Leninist-Maoist line you will realize that salvation

5. Chiang Kai-shek (1887–1975) chaired the National Military Council of the Republic of China from 1928 to 1948. He led China in the Second Sino-Japanese War, during which Mao's power and prominence grew. In 1948, Chiang Kai-shek fled to Taiwan where he served as President and Director-general of the Kuomintang.

comes from the outlying countries, from the peasants and the guerillas, who are the most numerous, and have nothing but rifles and pistols, and there are the imperialist nations representing the cities who have the equipment but who don't have the motive to fight as they don't know what they're fighting for like the GIs in Vietnam who have no idea what it is all about. Whereas you have these peasants and guerillas who must win because they say that they are the majority, they are the eschatological class, they say we are the "people of God."

This is religious thought. Consequently, applying this salvation event, what do you get? You get the cities and you get the hinterland. What are the cities? The advanced countries. According to the Chinese, the Soviets have sold out to the West, Russia has become an imperialist lackey. The cities then are these advanced countries, and Maoist dogma is that you surround the city with the hinterland, and what's the hinterland? It's Asia, Africa, and Latin America, by far the majority of the people of the world. There's your starting point.

The second dogmatic premise is that there can be no accommodation between the two. No coexistence is possible. It's a dogma. You don't look for coexistence. It is either/or. We are going to bury the capitalists—Khrushchev was saying this. You bury the capitalists, or the capitalists bury you. It's capitalist or communist. You cannot make a deal.

Now the Russians, on the contrary, are saying, things have changed. You have these bombs and must accommodate, or else the capitalists are going to let go of the bomb. The Chinese say no, if you push them, you don't need to worry about the bomb. Just go in there.

In a sense, this works. Vietnam is an example of this sort of strategy. You have this war going on but no one has used any bomb in Vietnam. They are fighting the war on their terms. The guerillas are doing good. So the Chinese come along and say, this proves we have the right line.

They transfer this to the whole world. What this man came up and said was do not follow this line: the Russians are crazy trying to have peaceful existence with capitalists. They are selling out the masses. Surround the cities. Don't dialogue with anyone. Start brush fire revolutions all over the world, keep the Americans occupied and you will destroy them in ten years. This is the Chinese approach.

So as a result of this, the Marxist approach in Latin America is this: you have revolutions all over the place. As soon as possible. How many countries in South America have guerilla wars going on as of now? Peru has one; Colombia—several; Brazil is trying on a nonviolent basis. Chile hasn't yet. Ecuador just had a revolution. Venezuela has a guerilla war going. Argentina hasn't but it is in an awful mess. Bolivia is always in a mess. What is left? Panama? Something like that.

So you can expect guerilla warfare all over the place. It is not always clear who is on the side of the angels and the devils. Don't assume the guerillas are the bad guys. In Colombia, a very fine priest was just killed fighting with the guerillas. I don't remember his name. He had a radio station. Was educating the people. Don't assume the church is always on the side of the government. [Someone shouted out a name.][6] Merton: might have been I don't know. I forgot what his name was. But he really was cutting a lot of ice. The thing is, if in these countries, the church simply lines up with the dictator with tanks, this is the suicidal position for the church. And the church is realizing this. Some are saying, we can't just line up with people like Trujillo.[7] We don't just line up with people like this. That is the great mistake. If you take the position that it is right for the church to be automatically on the side of the people with money, that is a problem. The Chinese line goes on with the dogmatic statement that war inevitable. That the U.S. will start World War III. This is an article of faith with them.

6. The name is inaudible. Most likely, it is Father Camilo Torres Restrepo (1929–1966), member of a guerilla movement who tried to reconcile Marxism and Catholicism.

7. Rafael Leonidas Trujillo Molina (1891–1961) ruled the Dominican Republic from 1930 until his assassination in 1961.

BIBLIOGRAPHY

Thomas Merton wrote a substantial body of prose and poetry, as have many friends who knew him personally. For those of us who have not had the privilege of a first-hand encounter with him, we may nonetheless hear Merton's voice on tapes, compact discs, and three outstanding films: *Merton: A Film Biography; Soul Searching, the Journey of Thomas Merton;* and *Original Child Bomb: Meditations on the Origin of the Atomic Age.*

The Merton Seasonal appears quarterly with articles, book reviews, and information of interest to ITMS members. Two issues a year include a newsletter. The year 2010 marks the thirty-fifth anniversary of the *Seasonal.* Currently, the *Seasonal* has over 1,000 subscribers.

The Merton Annual publishes articles about Thomas Merton and related topics arising from his life and work. The purpose of the journal is to enhance Merton's reputation as a writer and monk, to continue to develop his message for our times, and to provide a regular outlet for substantial Merton-related scholarship. Regular features of the *Annual* include first appearances of previously unpublished Merton materials, obscurely published articles by Merton, book reviews and review-essays, a bibliographic survey, interviews, photographs, and art. Currently, there are over 400 subscribers. Booksellers, the Internet, and Fons Vitae also market the *Annual.*

Similar periodicals appear in Britain and Holland. Because of the diversity of material and contributors, these journals reach out to a wider audience than typical scholarly publications.

The Merton Institute for Contemplative Living is located in Louisville, Kentucky. Its mission is to develop interest in contemplative living through the writings of Thomas Merton. With a mailing list of 16,000 individuals from around the world, the Merton Institute sends periodic mailings about publications in North America or other countries such as Brazil, Russia, and Poland. It also distributes weekly reflections by Merton by email to over 9,000 persons and publishes a Bridges to Contemplative Living series. Some of the Institute's work focuses directly on providing ways for people to understand and experience contemplation through retreats near the Abbey of Our Lady of Gethsemani.

Around the world, colleges, universities, and seminaries cultivate interest in Merton by offering courses. These have helped engender broad and lasting interest in prayer and other enduring concerns of Merton.

Merton died in 1968. Since then, friends, companions, scholars, and critics have added to Merton's considerable productivity with a vast outpouring of art, music, writing, and, sometimes, controversy. Five volumes of Merton's letters have appeared, along with correspondence with Catherine Doherty, Wilbur H. (Ping) Ferry, James Laughlin, Robert Lax, Jean Leclercq OSB, Czeslaw Milosz, and Rosemary Radford Ruether. Publication of seven volumes of Merton's private journals, closed to researchers for twenty-five years after his death, have fueled an ever-growing list of publications, dissertations, conferences, concerts, and exhibits. These attest to an ongoing fascination in Merton. Bibliographic sources include the following books:

Breit, Marquita E. and Robert E. Daggy. *Thomas Merton: A Comprehensive Bibliography.* New York: Garland, 1986.
Burton, Patricia A. *Merton Vade Mecum.* Louisville: Thomas Merton Center Foundation, 2001.
———. *More Than Silence: A Bibliography of Thomas Merton,* foreword by Paul M. Pearson. ATLA Bibliography Series 55. Lanham: Scarecrow, 2008.
Dell'Isola, Frank. *Thomas Merton: A Bibliography.* 1956; Kent: Kent State, 1975.

MERTON TITLES BY CATEGORY, DATE OF PUBLICATION

Poetry

Thirty Poems. Norfolk: New Directions, 1944.
A Man in the Divided Sea. New York: New Directions, 1946.
Figures for an Apocalypse. Norfolk: New Directions, 1948.
The Tears of the Blind Lions. New York: New Directions, 1949.
The Strange Islands. New York: New Directions, 1957.
Selected Poems of Thomas Merton. 1959; New York: New Directions, 1967.

Original Child Bomb: Points for Meditation to the Scratched on the Walls of a Cave. New York: New Directions, 1962.

Emblems of a Season of Fury. New York: New Directions, 1963.

Monk's Pond: Thomas Merton's Little Magazine. Edited with an introduction by Robert E. Daggy. Afterword by Patrick Hart. 1968. Reprint, Lexington: University Press of Kentucky, 1989.

Cables to the Ace, or Familiar Liturgies of Misunderstanding. New York: New Directions, 1968.

The Geography of Lograire. New York: New Directions, 1969.

Early Poems 1940–42. Lexington: Anvil, 1971.

Collected Poems of Thomas Merton. New York: New Directions, 1977.

Eighteen Poems. New York: New Directions, 1985.

In the Dark before Dawn: New Selected Poems of Thomas Merton. Edited by Lynn R. Szabo. New York: New Directions, 2005.

Fiction

My Argument with the Gestapo: A Macaronic Journal. Garden City, NY: Doubleday, 1969.

Autobiographical Books and Journals

The Seven Storey Mountain. New York: Harcourt Brace, 1948; also published under the title *Elected Silence*. London: Hollis & Carter, 1949.

The Sign of Jonas. New York: Harcourt Brace, 1953.

The Secular Journal. New York: Farrar Straus & Cudahy, 1959.

Conjectures of a Guilty Bystander. Garden City, NY: Doubleday, 1966.

The Asian Journal. Edited by Naomi Burton, Patrick Hart, and James Laughlin. New York: New Directions, 1973.

A Vow of Conversation: Journals 1964–1965. Edited by Naomi Burton Stone. New York: Farrar Straus & Giroux, 1988.

Day of a Stranger. Introduction by Robert E. Daggy. Salt Lake City: Gibbs M. Smith, 1981.

Woods, Shore, Desert: A Notebook. Santa Fe: Museum of New Mexico, 1982.

Thomas Merton in Alaska. Introduction by Robert E. Daggy. New York: New Directions, 1989.

Run to the Mountain: The Journals of Thomas Merton vol. 1, 1939–1941. Edited by Patrick Hart. San Francisco: HarperSanFrancisco, 1995.

Entering the Silence: The Journals of Thomas Merton vol. 2, 1941–1952. Edited by Jonathan Montaldo. San Francisco: HarperSanFrancisco, 1996.

A Search for Solitude: The Journals of Thomas Merton vol. 3, 1952–1960. Edited by Lawrence S. Cunningham. San Francisco: HarperSanFrancisco, 1996.

Turning toward the World: The Journals of Thomas Merton vol. 4, 1960–1963. Edited by Victor A. Kramer. San Francisco: Harper HarperSanFrancisco, 1996.

Dancing in the Water of Life: The Journals of Thomas Merton vol. 5, 1963–1965. Edited by Robert E. Daggy. San Francisco: Harper HarperSanFrancisco, 1997.

Learning to Love: The Journals of Thomas Merton vol. 6, 1965–1967. Edited by Christine M. Bochen. San Francisco: HarperSanFrancisco, 1997.

The Other Side of the Mountain: The Journals of Thomas Merton vol. 7, 1967–1968. Edited by Patrick Hart. San Francisco: HarperSanFrancisco, 1998.

The Intimate Merton: His Life from His Journals. Edited by Patrick Hart and Jonathan Montaldo. San Francisco: HarperSanFrancisco, 1999.

Essays on Monasticism

Cistercian Contemplatives. Trappist: Abbey of Our Lady of Gethsemani, 1948.

Gethsemani Magnificat. Trappist: Abbey of Our Lady of Gethsemani, 1949.

The Waters of Siloe. New York: Harcourt Brace, 1949.

"Your Will and Your Vocation." *Merton Seasonal* 34 ([November 1955] Summer 2009) 3–11.

Silence in Heaven: A Book on the Monastic Life. New York: Thomas Y. Crowell, 1956.

The Silent Life. New York: Farrar Straus & Cudahy, 1957.

Monastic Peace. Trappist, KY: Abbey of Our Lady of Gethsemani, 1958.

God Is My Life: The Story of Our Lady of Gethsemani. Trappist: Abbey of Our Lady of Gethsemani, 1960.

The Wisdom of the Desert: Sayings from the Desert Fathers of the Fourth Century. New York: New Directions, 1960.

Come to the Mountain: New Ways and Living Traditions in the Monastic Life. Snowmass: St. Benedict's Monastery, 1964.

Monastic Life at Gethsemani. Trappist, KY: Abbey of Our Lady of Gethsemani, 1966.

Gethsemani: A Life of Praise. Trappist, KY: Abbey of Our Lady of Gethsemani, 1966.

"A Memorandum on Monastic Theology." *Cistercian Studies Quarterly* 26, 1 ([1967] 1991) 91–94.

The Monastic Journey. Edited by Patrick Hart. Kansas City: Sheed Andrews & McMeel, 1977.

Cassian and the Fathers: Initiation into the Monastic Tradition. Vol. 1. Edited by Patrick F. O'Connell. Kalamazoo, MI: Cistercian, 2005.

Pre-Benedictine Monasticism: Initiation into the Monastic Tradition. Vol. 2. Edited by Patrick F. O'Connell. Kalamazoo, MI: Cistercian, 2006.

An Introduction to Christian Mysticism: Initiation into the Monastic Tradition. Vol. 3. Edited by Patrick F. O'Connell. Kalamazoo, MI: Cistercian, 2008.

The Rule of Saint Benedict: Initiation into the Monastic Tradition. Vol. 4. Edited by Patrick F. O'Connell. Kalamazoo, MI: Cistercian, 2009.

Monastic Observances: Initiation into the Monastic Tradition. Vol. 5, edited by Patrick F. O'Connell. Kalamazoo, MI: Cistercian, 2010.

Essays on History and Doctrinal Theology

A Cistercian Monk of Our Lady of Gethsemani. *The Spirit of Simplicity: Characteristics of the Cistercian Order.* Trappist, KY: Abbey of Our Lady of Gethsemani, 1948.

Exile Ends in Glory: The Life of a Trappistine, Mother M. Berchmans O. C. S.O. Milwaukee: Bruce, 1948.

What Are These Wounds? The Life of a Cistercian Mystic, Saint Lutgarde of Aywieres. Milwaukee: Bruce, 1950.

The Ascent to Truth. New York: Harcourt Brace, 1951.

The Last of the Fathers: Saint Bernard of Clairvaux and the Encyclical Letter, "Doctor Mellifluus." New York: Harcourt Brace, 1954.

Thomas Merton on Saint Bernard. Cistercian Studies 9. 1970. Reprint, Kalamazoo, MI: Cistercian, 1980.

Seeking Paradise: The Spirit of the Shakers. Edited with an introduction by Paul R. Pearson. Maryknoll: Orbis, 2003.

Essays on Biblical and Liturgical Themes

Bread in the Wilderness. New York: New Directions, 1953.

Praying the Psalms. Collegeville, MN: Liturgical, 1956.

The Living Bread. New York: Farrar Straus & Cudahy, 1956.

Nativity Kerygma. Trappist: Gethsemani, 1958.

Seasons of Celebration. New York: Farrar Straus & Giroux, 1965.

Opening the Bible. Collegeville, MN: Liturgical, 1970.

Essays on Spiritual Direction, Prayer, and Contemplation

What Is Contemplation? Notre Dame: Saint Mary's College, 1948.

Seeds of Contemplation. New York: New Directions, 1949. Rev. ed., London: Hollis & Carter, 1950.

No Man Is an Island. New York: Harcourt Brace, 1955.

Thoughts in Solitude. New York: Farrar Straus & Cudahy, 1958.

Spiritual Direction and Meditation. Collegeville, MN: Liturgical, 1960.

The New Man. New York: Farrar Straus & Giroux, 1961.

New Seeds of Contemplation. New York: New Directions, 1961.

Life and Holiness. New York: Herder & Herder, 1963; introduction to the 1996 edition by Henri J. M. Nouwen.

The Climate of Monastic Prayer. Spencer: Cistercian, 1969; also published as *Contemplative Prayer.* Foreword by Douglas V. Steere. New York: Herder & Herder, 1969; introduction to the 1995 edition by Thich Nhat Hanh.

Contemplation in a World of Action. Introduction by Jean Leclercq. New York: Doubleday, 1971; foreword to the 1998 edition by Robert Coles. Notre Dame: University of Notre Dame Press, 1998.

The Springs of Contemplation. Edited by Jane Marie Richardson. New York: Farrar Straus & Giroux, 1992.

The Inner Experience: Notes on Contemplation. Edited with an introduction by William H. Shannon. San Francisco: HarperSanFrancisco, 2003.

Essays on Literary Themes and Contemporary Issues

Disputed Questions. New York: Farrar Straus & Cudahy, 1960.

The Behavior of Titans. New York: New Directions, 1961.

Breakthrough to Peace: Twelve Views on the Threat of Thermonuclear Extermination, edited with an introduction by Thomas Merton. New York: New Directions, 1962.

Seeds of Destruction. New York: Farrar Straus & Giroux, 1964.

Raids on the Unspeakable. New York: New Directions, 1966.

Faith and Violence: Christian Teaching and Christian Practice. Notre Dame: University of Notre Dame Press, 1968.

"Symbolism: Communication or Communion." *Mountain Path* 3 (1966) 339–48. Reprinted in *New Directions in Prose and Poetry.* Edited by James Laughlin. New York: New Directions, 1968.

"The Wild Places." *The Center Magazine* (1968) 40–44.

"Learning to Live." In *University on the Heights,* edited by Wesley First. Garden City, NY: Doubleday, 1969. Also in *Love and Living,* edited by Naomi Burton Stone and Patrick Hart. New York: Farrar Straus & Giroux, 1979.

Peace in the Post-Christian Era. Edited with an introduction by Patricia A. Burton. Foreword by Jim Forest. Maryknoll, NY: Orbis, 2004.

Essays on Asian and Native American Religion

Gandhi on Non-Violence: Selected Texts from Mohandas K. Gandhi's Non-Violence in Peace and War. New York: New Directions, 1965.

The Way of Chuang Tzu. New York: New Directions, 1965.

Mystics and Zen Masters. New York: Farrar Straus & Giroux, 1967.

Zen and the Birds of Appetite. New York: New Directions, 1968.

Ishi Means Man: Essays on Native Americans. Foreword by Dorothy Day. Greensboro: Unicorn, 1976.

Letters

The Hidden Ground of Love: Letters on Religious Experience and Social Concerns. Edited by William H. Shannon. New York: Farrar Straus & Giroux, 1985.

The Road to Joy: Letters to New and Old Friends. Edited by Robert E. Daggy. New York: Farrar Straus & Giroux, 1989.

The School of Charity: Letters on Religious Renewal and Spiritual Direction. Edited by Patrick Hart. New York: Farrar Straus & Giroux, 1990.

The Courage for Truth: Letters to Writers. Edited by Christine M. Bochen. New York: Farrar Straus & Giroux, 1993.

Witness to Freedom: Letters in Times of Crisis. Edited by William H. Shannon. New York: Farrar Straus & Giroux, 1994.

At Home in the World: The Letters of Thomas Merton and Rosemary Radford Ruether. Edited by Mary Tardiff. Maryknoll: Orbis, 1995.

Striving towards Being: The Letters of Thomas Merton and Czeslaw Milosz. Edited by Robert Faggen. New York: Farrar Straus & Giroux, 1997.

Thomas Merton and James Laughlin, Selected Letters. Edited by David D. Cooper. New York: Norton, 1997.

When Prophecy Still Had a Voice: The Letters of Thomas Merton and Robert Lax. Edited by Arthur W. Biddle. Lexington: University Press of Kentucky, 2001.

Survival or Prophecy? An Exchange of Letters, Thomas Merton and Jean Leclercq. Edited by Patrick Hart. New York: Farrar Straus & Giroux, 2002.

Cold War Letters. Edited by Christine M. Bochen and William H. Shannon. Maryknoll: Orbis, 2006.

Compassionate Fire: The Letters of Thomas Merton and Catherine de Hueck Doherty. Edited by Robert A. Wild. Notre Dame: Ave Maria, 2009.

Anthologies

Merton, Thomas, John Howard Griffin, and Monsignor Horrigan. *The Thomas Merton Studies Center.* Santa Barbara: Unicorn Press, 1971.

A Thomas Merton Reader. Edited by Thomas P. McDonnell. 1962 expanded edition. Garden City, NY: Doubleday, 1974.

Thomas Merton on Peace. Edited by Gordon C. Zahn. New York: McCall, 1971. Revised edition published under the title *The Non-violent Alternative.* New York: Farrar Straus & Giroux, 1980.

Love and Living. Edited by Naomi Burton Stone and Patrick Hart. New York: Farrar Straus & Giroux, 1979.

The Literary Essays of Thomas Merton. Edited by Patrick Hart. New York: New Directions, 1981.

Introductions East & West: The Foreign Prefaces of Thomas Merton. Edited by Robert E. Daggy. Foreword by Harry James Cargas. Greensboro: Unicorn, 1981. Expanded and published as *"Honorable Reader." Reflections on My Work.* London: Fount Paperbacks, 1989.

Through the Year with Thomas Merto:. Daily Meditations from His Writings. Selected and edited by Thomas P. McDonnell. Garden City, NY: Image, 1985.

Thomas Merton: A Selection of His Writings. Edited by Aileen Taylor. Springfield: Templegate, 1990.

Thomas Merton, Spiritual Master. Edited by Lawrence S. Cunningham. Foreword by Patrick Hart. Mahwah: Paulist, 1992.

Dialogues with Silence. Prayers and Drawings. Edited by Jonathan Montaldo. San Francisco: HarperSanFrancisco, 2001.

Thomas Merton, Essential Writings. Edited by Christine Bochen. Maryknoll: Orbis, 2002.

Seeds. Edited by Robert Inchausti. Boston: Shambhala, 2002.

When the Trees Say Nothing: Writings on Nature. Edited by Kathleen Deignan. Notre Dame: Sorin, 2003.

A Book of Hours. Edited by Kathleen Deignan. Notre Dame: Sorin, 2007.

Introductions, Talks, Unpublished essays

Arnold, Eberhard. *Why We Live in Community with Two Interpretive Talks by Thomas Merton.* Foreword by Basil Pennington. Farmington, PA: Plough, 1995.

Chautard, Jean-Baptiste. *The Soul of the Apostolate.* Translated with an introduction by Thomas Merton. 1946; Garden City, NY: Image, 1961.

Delp, Alfred. *The Prison Meditations of Father Delp.* Introduction by Thomas Merton. New York: Macmillan, 1963.

Merton, Thomas. "Technology." *Collected Essays* 6, Bellarmine Archives, 53–59 [ca. 1966].

———. "The Christian in a Technological World." June 5, 1966, tape 161, track 3b.

———. "Dom Vital. Technological Society." June 5, 1966, tape 161, track 3a.

———. "Computers-Marxism." June 26, 1966, tape 161, Track 4.

Periodicals

The Merton Annual.
The Merton Journal.
The Merton Seasonal.

Other Sources

Andrews, Edward Deming. *The People Called Shakers.* New York: Dover, 1963.

Andrews, Edward Deming, and Faith Andrews. *Religion in Wood: A Book of Shaker Furniture.* Bloomington: Indiana University Press, 1973.

Apel, William. *Signs of Peace: The Interfaith Letters of Thomas Merton.* Maryknoll, NY: Orbis, 2006.

Assadourian, Erik. "The Rise and Fall of Consumer Cultures." In *State of the World 2010. Transforming Cultures from Consumerism to Sustainability: A Worldwatch Institute Report on Progress toward a Sustainable Society.* New York: Norton, 2010.

Aprile, Dianne. *The Abbey of Gethsemani. Place of Peace and Paradox.* Louisville: Trout Lily, 1998.

Baker, Rob, and Gray Henry, editors. *Merton and Sufism, The Untold Story: A Complete Compendium.* Louisville: Fons Vitae, 1999.

Bamberger, John Eudes. *Thomas Merton: Prophet of Renewal.* Kalamazoo: Cistercian, 2005.

Bass, Diana Butler. *The Practicing Congregation: Imagining a New Old Church.* Herndon: Alban Institute, 2004.

Benedict. *The Rule of St. Benedict in English.* Edited by Timothy Fry. Collegeville, MN: Liturgical, 1982.

Berrigan, Daniel. *The Kings and Their Gods: The Pathology of Power.* Grand Rapids: Eerdmans, 2008.

Bethge, Eberhard. *Dietrich Bonhoeffer: Theologian. Christian. Contemporary.* Translated by Edwin Robertson. London: Collins, 1970.

Bonhoeffer, Dietrich. *Life Together*. Translated with an introduction by John W. Doberstein. New York: Harper & Row, 1954.

Brennan. Niall. *The Making of a Moron*. New York: Sheed & Ward, 1953.

Byassee, Jason. "The New Monastics: Alternate Christian Communities." *Christian Century* 122 (October 18, 2005) 38–47.

Campbell, Will. *Brother to a Dragonfly*. New York: Seabury, 1977.

Campolo, Tony. *Red Letter Christians: A Citizen's Guide to Faith and Politics*. Ventura: Regal, 2008.

Canham, Elizabeth J. *Heart Whispers: Benedictine Wisdom for Today*. Nashville: Upper Room Books, 1999.

Capps, Walter. *The Monastic Impulse*. New York: Crossroad, 1983.

Carmichael, Stokely, and Charles V. Hamilton. *Black Power: The Politics of Liberation in America*. New York: Vintage, 1967.

Carson, Clayborne, and Peter Holloron, editors. *A Knock at Midnight: Inspiration from the Great Sermons of Reverend Martin Luther King, Jr.* New York: Time Warner Audio, 1998.

Carson, Rachel. *Silent Spring*. Boston: Houghton Mifflin Company, 1962.

Cashen, Richard Anthony. *Solitude in the Thought of Thomas Merton*. Kalamazoo, MI: Cistercian, 1981.

Charters, Ann, editor. *The Portable Sixties Reader*. New York: Penguin, 2003.

Chenu, M.-D. *Nature, Man and Society in the Twelfth Century: Essays on New Theological Perspectives in the Latin West*. Selected, edited, and translated by Jerome Taylor and Lester K. Little. Chicago: University of Chicago, 1968.

Chittister, Joan. *The Rule of Benedict: Insights for the Ages*. New York: Crossroad, 1996.

———. *Wisdom Distilled from the Daily: Living the Rule of St. Benedict Today*. San Francisco: HarperCollins 1991.

Claiborne, Shane. *The Irresistible Revolution: Living as an Ordinary Radical*. Grand Rapids: Zondervan, 2006.

Cleaver, Eldridge. *Soul on Ice*. New York: McGraw-Hill, 1968.

Clooney, Francis X. "In Memoriam: Mahanambrata Brahmachari (25 December 1904–18 October 1999)." *Merton Annual* 13 (2000) 123–26.

Collins, John P. "Thomas Merton and the PAX Peace Prize." *Merton Seasonal* 33 (Spring 2008) 3–14.

Conrad, Jack. *Living before Dying: Reflections of a Hospice Chaplain*. Mustang: Tate, 2008.

Cooper, David D. *Thomas Merton's Art of Denial: The Evolution of a Radical Humanist*. Athens: University of Georgia Press, 1989.

Cunningham, Lawrence S. *Thomas Merton and the Monastic Vision*. Grand Rapids: Eerdmans, 1999.

Dart, Ron. "In the Footsteps of Thomas Merton: Alaska." *Merton Seasonal* 33:44 (Winter 2008) 14–19.

———. "Thomas Merton, Leslie Dewart, George Grant and the 1963 Federal Election in Canada." *Merton Seasonal* 32:4 (Winter 2007) 19–23.

Dear, John. "'Blessed are the Meek': The Non-violence of Thomas Merton." *Merton Annual* 5 (1992) 205–13.

Dekar, Paul R. "Asking Questions about Technology, with Specific Reference to Computers." *Evangelical Review of Theology* 26 (July 2002) 208–22.

———. *Community of the Transfiguration. Journey of a New Monastic Community*. Foreword by Phyllis Tickle. Eugene: Cascade, 2008.

———. "Gandhi, Thomas Merton and the 'Uprising' of Youth in the 60s." *Merton Seasonal* 31 (Winter 2006) 16–23.

———. "The Party Goes On. God's People in the Age of Scarcity." *Canadian Baptist* (February 1981) 11–15 and (March 1981) 12–17.

———. "The Spirit of Simplicity: Thomas Merton on Simplification of Life." *Merton Annual* 19 (2006) 267–82.

———. "Spiritual Resources for Ministry." *McMaster Divinity College Theological Bulletin* 5:2 (1979) 17–29.

———. "Teaching Evangelism in a Community of Learning." *Journal of the Academy for Evangelism in Theological Education* 22 (2006–2007) 62–80.

———. "Thomas Merton, Prophet of the New Monasticism." *Canadian Society of Church Historical Papers* (2008) 121–32.

———. "What the Machine Produces and What the Machine Destroys: Merton on Technology." *Merton Annual* 17 (2004) 216–34.

Del Prete, Thomas. "'Teaching is Candy': Merton as Teacher at Columbia and Bonaventure." *Merton Annual* 9 (1996) 152–69.

Deschamps, Gaston. "Interview." *Maclean's*, April 6, 2009, 16–17.

Diamond, Jared. *Guns, Germs, and Steel: The Fates of Human Societies*. New York: Norton, 1997.

Doherty, Catherine De Hueck. *Essential Writings*. Introduction by David Merconi. Maryknoll, NY: Orbis, 2009.

———. *Fragments of My Life*. Notre Dame, IN: Ave Maria, 1979.

———. *The People of the Towel and the Water: The Spirituality of Madonna House*. Denville, NJ: Dimension, 1978.

Douglass, James W. *Lightning East to West: Jesus, Gandhi, and the Nuclear Age*. New York: Crossroad, 1984.

———. *The Non-Violent Cross: A Theology of Revolution and Peace*. New York: Macmillan, 1968.

Dozier, Verna. *The Dream of God: A Call to Return*. Boston: Cowley, 1991.

Draper, Hal. *Berkeley: The New Student Revolt*. Introduction by Mario Savio. New York: Grove, 1965.

Eagles, Charles W. *Outside Agitator: Jon Daniels and the Civil Rights Movement in Alabama*. Chapel Hill: University of North Carolina Press, 1993.

Eleven Lay Associates. "A Lay Response to the Reflections of Dom Bernardo Olivera on Charismatic Associations." *Cistercian Studies Quarterly* 32 (1997) 235–44.

Ellsberg, Robert. *All Saints: Daily Reflections on Saints, Prophets, and Witnesses for Our Time*. New York: Crossroad, 1997.

Erickson, Erik H. *Gandhi's Truth: On the Origins of Militant Non-violence*. New York: Norton, 1969.

———. *Young Man Luther: A Study in Psychoanalysis and History*. New York: Norton, 1958.

Farnham, Suzanne G., et al. *Listening Hearts: Discerning Call in Community*. Harrisburg: Morehouse, 1991.

Ferguson, Ron. *Chasing the Wild Goose: The Iona Community*. London: Collins, 1988.

Fischer, Louis. *The Life of Mahatma Gandhi*. 1950; New York: Harper & Row, 1983.

Flannery, Austin P. *The Documents of Vatican II*. Grand Rapids: Eerdmans, 1975.

Ford, Michael. *Spiritual Masters for all Seasons*. New York: HiddenSpring, 2009.

Forest, Jim. "A Great Lake of Beer," in *Apostle of Peace. Essays in Honor of Daniel Berrigan.* Edited by John Dear. Maryknoll: Orbis, 1996.

———. *Living with Wisdom: A Life of Thomas Merton.* Rev. ed. Maryknoll: Orbis, 2008.

Fox, Matthew. *Sheer Joy: Conversations with Thomas Aquinas on Creation Spirituality.* San Francisco: HarperSanFrancisco, 1992.

Freeman, Jo, and Victoria Johnson, editors, *Waves of Protest: Social Movements since the Sixties.* Lanham, MD: Rowman & Littlefield, 1999.

Freeman, John. *The Tyranny of E-mail: The Four-Thousand-Year Journey to Your Inbox.* New York: Scribner, 2009.

Freeman, Laurence. *Jesus, the Teacher Within.* New York: Continuum, 2002.

Furlong, Monica. *Merton: A Biography.* London: Collins, 1980.

Garaudy, Roger. *From Anathema to Dialogue: A Marxist Challenge to the Christian Churches.* Translated by Luke O'Neill. St. Louis: Herder & Herder, 1966.

———. *Perspectives de l'homme, existentialisme, pensée catholique, marxisme.* Paris: Presses universitaires de France, 1962.

Gathje, Peter R., editor. *A Work of Hospitality: The Open Door Reader 1982–2002.* Atlanta: Open Door, 2002.

Grayston, Donald, and Michael W. Higgins, editors. *Thomas Merton: Pilgrim in Process.* Toronto: Griffin House, 1983.

Griffin, John Howard. *A Hidden Wholeness: The Visual World of Thomas Merton.* Boston: Houghton Mifflin, 1970.

Guenther, Margaret. *At Home in the World: A Rule of Life for the Rest of Us.* New York: Seabury, 2006.

Gyatso, Tenzin. "Many Faiths, One Truth." *New York Times,* May 25, 2010.

Hahn, Thich Nhat. *Being Peace.* Edited by Arnold Kotler. Berkeley, CA: Parallax, 1987.

Hart, Patrick, editor. *The Legacy of Thomas Merton.* Kalamazoo, MI: Cistercian, 1986.

———, editor. *A Monastic Vision for the 21st Century: Where Do We Go from Here?* Kalamazoo, MI: Cistercian, 2006.

———, editor. *Thomas Merton, Monk. A Monastic Tribute.* Garden City, NY: Image, 1976. Expanded ed. Kalamazoo, MI: Cistercian, 1983.

Hawken, Paul. *Blessed Unrest: How the Largest Social Movement in History Is Restoring Grace, Justice, and Beauty to the World.* New York: Penguin, 2007.

Herron, Fred. *No Abiding Place: Thomas Merton and the Search for God.* Lanham, MD: University Press of America, 2005.

Higgins, John J. *Thomas Merton on Prayer.* Garden City, NY: Image, 1975. Originally published as volume 18 of the Cistercian Studies Series under the title *Merton's Theology of Prayer.*

Higgins, Michael W. *Heretic Blood: The Spiritual Geography of Thomas Merton.* Toronto: Stoddart, 1998.

Hobday, José. *Simple Living: The Path to Joy and Freedom.* New York: Continuum, 1998.

Hyde, Lewis. *The Gift: Creativity and the Artist in the Modern World.* New York: Vintage, 2007.

Inchausti, Robert. *Thomas Merton's American Prophecy.* Albany: State University of New York Press, 1998.

Irving, Mark. "Simplicity of the Cloister." *Tablet,* September 11, 2004.

Jacobs, Jane. *Dark Age Ahead.* New York: Random House, 2004.

Jack, Homer A. *The Gandhi Reader: A Source Book of His Life and Writings.* New York: Grove, 1956.

Jackson, Maggie. *Distracted: The Erosion of Attention and the Coming Dark Age.* Foreword by Bill McKibben. Amherst, NY: Prometheus, 2008.

Jamison, Christopher. *Finding Sanctuary: Monastic Steps for Everyday Life.* London: Weidenfeld & Nicolson, 2006.

———. *Finding Happiness.* London: Weidenfeld & Nicolson, 2008.

Jones, Van, with Ariane Conrad. *The Green Collar Economy: How One Solution Can Fix Our Two Biggest Problems.* New York: HarperCollins, 2009.

Katsuno-Ishii, Lynda, and Edna J. Orteza, editors. *Of Rolling Waters and Roaring Wind: A Celebration of the Woman Song.* Geneva: WCC, 2000.

King, Robert H. *Thomas Merton and Thich Nhat Hanh: Engaged Spirituality in an Age of Globalization.* New York: Continuum, 2001.

King, Ursula. *The Search for Spirituality: Our Global Quest for a Spiritual Life.* New York: BlueBridge, 2008.

Kingsolver, Barbara. *The Poisonwood Bible.* New York: HarperCollins, 1999.

Knowles, David. *Christian Monasticism.* New York: World University Library, 1969.

———. *Cistercians and Cluniacs: The Controversy between St. Bernard and Peter the Venerable.* London: Oxford University Press, 1955.

Koehlinger, Amy L. *The New Nuns: Racial Justice and Religious Reform in the 1960s.* Harvard: Harvard University, 2007.

Kulzer, Linda. "Monasticism beyond the Walls." In *Benedict in the World,* edited by Linda Kulzer and Roberta Bondi. Collegeville: Liturgical, 2002.

Kurzweil, Ray. *The Age of Spiritual Machines: When Computers Exceed Human Intelligence.* New York: Penguin, 1999.

Labrie, Ross. *Thomas Merton and the Inclusive Imagination.* Columbia: University of Missouri, 2001.

Lasch, Christopher. *The Culture of Narcissism: American Life in an Age of Diminishing Expectations.* New York: Norton, 1979.

Laughlin, James. *Random Essays: Recollections of a Publisher.* Mt. Kisco: Moyer Bell, 1989.

Lawrence, Brother, *The Practice of the Presence of God.* Translated by John J. Delaney, foreword Henri J. M. Nouwen. New York: Doubleday, 1977.

Least Heat Moon, William. *Blue Highways: A Journey into America.* Boston: Little, Brown, 1982.

Leclercq, Jean. *The Love of Learning and the Desire for God: A Study of Monastic Culture.* Translated by Catharine Misrahi. New York: Fordham University Press, 1961.

Lederer, William J. and Eugene Burdick. *The Ugly American.* New York: Fawcett Crest, 1958.

Lehodey, Vital. *Holy Abandonment.* Translated by Ailbe J. Luddy, O.Cist, with an introduction by Dom Herman-Joseph Smets. Dublin: Gil,: 1934; reprint, Charlotte, NC: Tan, 2004.

Leonard, Annie. *The Story of Stuff: How Our Obsession with Stuff Is Trashing the Planet, Our Communities, and Our Health-and a Vision for Change.* New York: Simon & Schuster, 2010.

Leopold, Aldo. *A Sand County Almanac with Essays on Conservation from Round River.* 1949; San Francisco: Sierra Club, 1970.

Lewis, C. S. *The Abolition of Man.* 1943; Glasgow: Collins, 1978.

Lewis, Gloria Kitto. "Learning to Live: Merton's Students Remember His Teaching." *Merton Annual* 8 (1995) 88–104.

MacIntyre, Alasdair. *After Virtue: A Study in Moral Theory.* Notre Dame: University of Notre Dame, 1981.

MacQueen, Graeme, editor. *Unarmed Forces.* Toronto: Science for Peace, 1992.

Maitland, Sara. *A Book of Silence.* London: Granta, 2008.

Martínez, Sonia Petisco. "La Poesía de Thomas Merton: Creación, Crítica y Contemplación." Ph.D. Dissertation, Universidad Complutense de Madrid, 2003.

Marty, Martin E. *Pilgrims in Their Own Land. 500 Years of Religion in America.* Boston: Little, Brown, 1984.

Massignon, Louis. *The Passion of al-Hallāj: Mystic and Martyr of Islam,* translated from the French by Herbert Mason. Princeton, NJ: Princeton University Press, 1982.

McDonald, Joan C. *Tom Merton: A Personal Biography.* Milwaukee: Marquette University Press, 2006.

McDonnell, Killian. *Nothing but Christ: A Benedictine Approach to Lay Spirituality.* St. Meinrad, IN: Grail, 1953.

McFague, Sallie. *Super, Natural Christians: How We Should Love Nature.* Minneapolis: Fortress, 1997.

McLaren, Brian D. *Everything Must Change: Jesus, Global Crises, and a Revolution of Hope.* Nashville: Thomas Nelson, 2007.

Meadows, Donella H., et al. *Beyond the Limits: Confronting Global Collapse. Envisioning a Sustainable Future.* White River Junction: Chelsea Green, 1992.

———. *The Limits to Growth: A Report for the Club of Rome's Project on the Predicament of Mankind.* New York: New American Library, 1972.

Merritt, Joyce. *Naked before God: A Journey into Light and Life.* Mustang: Tate, 2008.

Miller, Donald. *Blue Like Jazz: Nonreligious Thoughts on Christian Spirituality.* Nashville: Thomas Nelson, 2003.

Moll, Rob. "The New Monasticism." *Christianity Today* 49 (September 2005) 38–46.

Monks of New Skete. *In the Spirit of Happiness: Spiritual Wisdom for Living.* Boston: Little, Brown, 1999.

Montaldo, Jonathan. "A Gallery of Women's Faces and Dreams of Women from the Drawings of Thomas Merton." *Thomas Merton Annual* 14 (2001) 155–72.

———, editor. *Merton and Hesychasm.* Louisville: Fons Vitae, 2003.

Morris, Colin. *The Discovery of the Individual: 1050–1200.* New York: Harper & Row, 1972.

Mott, Michael. *The Seven Mountains of Thomas Merton.* Boston: Houghton Mifflin, 1984.

Mumford, Lewis. *City in History: Its Origins, Its Transformations, and Its Prospects.* New York: Harcourt Brace, 1961.

———. *Technics and Civilization.* New York: Harcourt Brace & World, [1963].

Nadar, Ralph. *Unsafe at Any Speed: The Designed-in Dangers of the American Automobile.* New York: Pocket, 1966.

Nash, Roderick. *Wilderness and the American Mind.* New Haven: Yale University Press, 1967.

Neufeld, Doreen and Hugo Neufeld, *Affluenza Interrupted: Stories of Hope from the Suburbs.* Calgary: Millrise, 2009.

Northbourne, Lord. *Religion in the Modern World.* Rev. ed. Hillsdale, NY: Sophia Perennis, 2002.

Norris, Kathleen. *The Cloister Walk.* New York: Riverhead, 1996.

O'Connell, Patrick F., editor. *The Vision of Thomas Merton.* Notre Dame: Ave Maria, 2003.

O'Connor, Elizabeth. *Servant Leaders, Servant Structures*. Washington, DC: Servant Leadership School, 1991.

O'Donohue, John. *Anam Cara: A Book of Celtic Wisdom*. Toronto: HarperCollins, 1997.

O'Neill, Dan. *Signatures: The Story of John Michael Talbot*. Berryville, AR: Troubadour for the Lord, 2003.

Orbinski, James. *Imperfect Offering, Humanitarian Action in the Twenty-First Century*. Toronto: Doubleday, 2008.

Pahl, Jon. *Empire of Sacrifice: The Religious Origins of American Violence*. New York: New York University Press, 2010.

———. *Shopping Malls and Other Sacred Spaces*. Eugene, OR: Wipf & Stock, 2009.

Palmer, Parker J. *A Hidden Wholeness: The Journey toward an Undivided Life*. San Francisco: Jossey-Bass, 2004.

———. "Contemplation Reconsidered." *Merton Annual* 8 (1995) 22.

Patnaik, Deba Prasad. *Geography of Holiness: The Photography of Thomas Merton*. New York: Pilgrim, 1980.

Peck, M. Scott. *The Different Drum: Community Making and Peace*. New York: Simon & Schuster, 1987.

Pennington, M. Basil. "Father Louis' First Book: *The Spirit of Simplicity*." In *Studiosorum Speculum. Studies in Honor of Louis J. Lekai, O.Cist*, edited by Francis R. Swietek and John R. Sommerfeldt. Cistercian Studies #141. Kalamazoo: Cistercian, 1993.

———. *Thomas Merton, Brother Monk: The Quest for Freedom*. Toronto: HarperCollins Canada, 1990.

———, editor. *Toward an Integrated Humanity: Thomas Merton's Journey*. Cistercian Studies #103. Kalamazoo: Cistercian, 1993.

———, editor. *The Works of Bernard of Clairvaux*. Cistercian Fathers 1. Spencer: Cistercian, 1970.

Perrucci, Robert, and Marc Pilisuk. *The Triple Revolution Emerging: Social Problems in Depth*. Boston: Little, Brown, 1971.

The Philokalia. The Complete Text Compiled by St. Nikodimos of the Holy Mountain and St. Makarios of Corinth. Translated and edited by G. E. H. Palmer, Philip Sherrard, and Kallistos Ware. London: Faber & Faber, 1979.

Plank, Karl A. "The Eclipse of Difference: Merton's Encounter with Judaism." *Cistercian Studies Quarterly* 28:2 (1993) 179–91.

Polner, Murray and Jim O'Grady, *Disarmed and Dangerous: The Radical Lives and Times of Daniel and Philip Berrigan*. New York: Basic, 1997.

Pramuk, Christopher. *Sophia: The Hidden Christ of Thomas Merton*. Collegeville, MN: Liturgical, 2009.

Prevallet, Elaine. *Toward Spirituality for Global Justice: A Call to Kinship*. Louisville: Just Faith, 2005.

Putnam, Robert D. *Bowling Alone: The Collapse and Revival of American Community*. New York: Simon & Schuster, 2000.

Pycior, Julie Leininger. "We Are All Called to Be Saints: Thomas Merton, Dorothy Day and Friendship House." *Merton Annual* 13 (2000) 27–62.

Rice, Edward. *The Man in the Sycamore Tree: The Good Times and Hard Life of Thomas Merton*. Garden City, NY: Image, 1972.

Rich, Adrienne. *The Fact of a Doorframe: Poems Selected and New 1950–1984*. New York: Norton, 1984.

Rickover, Hyman George. "A Humanistic Technology." *Nature* 208 (November 20, 1965). Reprinted in Noel de Nevers, editor. *Technology and Society*. Reading: Addison-Wesley, 1972.

Riddell, Michael. *Threshold of the Future: Reforming the Church in the Post-Christian West*. London: SPCK, 1998.

Rifkin, Jeremy, and Ted Howard. *The Emerging Order: God in the Age of Scarcity*. New York: Putnam, 1979.

———. *The End of Work: The Decline of the Global Labor Force and the Dawn of the Post-Market Era*. New York: Putnam, 1995.

———. *Time Wars*. New York: Simon & Schuster, 1987.

Roberts, Elizabeth, and Elias Amidon, editors. *Prayers for a Thousand Years: Blessings and Expressions of Hope for the New Millennium*. San Francisco: HarperSanFrancisco, 1999.

Romero, Oscar. *Voice of the Voiceless: The Four Pastoral Letters and Other Statements*, translated from the Spanish by Michael J. Walsh. Maryknoll, NY: Orbis, 1985.

Rule for a New Brother. London: Darton Longman & Todd, 1973.

Rutba House, editor. *School(s) for Conversion: 12 Marks of a New Monasticism*. Eugene: Cascade, 2005.

Sacks, Jonathan. *To Heal a Fractured World: The Ethics of Responsibility*. New York: Continuum, 2005.

Said, Edward W. *Orientalism*. New York: Vintage, 1979.

Santos, Jason Brian. *A Community Called Taizé: A Story of Prayer, Worship and Reconciliation*. Downers Grove, IL: InterVarsity, 2008.

Schneider, William J. *American Martyr: The Jon Daniels Story*. Harrisburg: Morehouse, 1993.

Schor, Juliet B. *The Overspent American: Upscaling, Downshifting, and the New Consumer*. New York: HarperPerennial, 1998.

———. *The Overworked American: The Unexpected Decline of Leisure*. New York: Basic, 1991.

———. *Plenitude: The True Economics of Real Wealth*. New York: Penguin, 2010.

Seitz, Ron. *Song for Nobody: A Memory Vision of Thomas Merton*. Liguori, MO: Triumph, 1993.

Shannon, William H. *Thomas Merton's Dark Path. The Inner Experience of a Contemplative*. New York: Farrar Straus & Giroux, 1981.

Shannon, William H. et al., editors. *The Thomas Merton Encyclopedia*. Maryknoll, NY: Orbis, 2002.

Shepard, Mark. *Gandhi Today: A Report on Mahatma Gandhi's Successors*. Foreword by Arun Gandhi. Arcata: Simple, 1987.

Smith, Natalie. *Stand on Your Own Fee:. Finding a Contemplative Spirit in Everyday Life*. Allen: Thomas More, 2002.

St. John, Donald P. "Technological Culture and Contemplative Ecology in Thomas Merton's *Conjectures of a Guilty Bystander*." *Worldviews* 6:2 (2002) 159–82.

Stannard, Martin. *Evelyn Waugh: The Later Years 1939–1966*. New York: Norton, 1992.

Stock, Jon, et al. *Inhabiting the Church: Biblical Wisdom for a New Monasticism*. Eugene, OR: Cascade, 2007.

Süssman, Cornelia and Irving: *Thomas Merton*. Garden City, NY: Image, 1980.

Sutera, Judith. *Work of God: Benedictine Prayer*. Collegeville, MN: Liturgical, 1997.

Tacey, David. *The Spirituality Revolution: The Emergence of Contemporary Spirituality.* Sydney: Harper, 2003.

Taizé. Community of. *The Rule of Taizé.* New York: Seabury, 1968.

Talbot, John Michael. *The Way of the Mystics: Ancient Wisdom for Experiencing God Today.* San Francisco: Jossey-Bass, 2005.

Thompson, E. P. *The Making of the English Working Class.* London: Gollancz, 1964.

Thompson, Phillip M. *Between Science and Religion: The Engagement of Catholic Intellectuals with Science and Technology in the Twentieth Century.* Lanham, MD: Lexington, 2009.

Tickle, Phyllis. *The Great Emergence: How Christianity Is Changing and Why.* Grand Rapids: Baker, 2008.

"The Triple Revolution." *Liberation* (April 1964) 9–15.

Turner, Graham. *A Comparison of the Limits to Growth with Thirty Years of Reality.* CSIRO Working Paper Series, 2008–09.

Twomey, Gerald, editor. *Thomas Merton: Prophet in the Belly of a Paradox.* New York: Paulist, 1978.

Van Doren, Mark. *Autobiography.* New York: Greenwood, 1968.

Voices United. The Hymn and Worship Book of The United Church of Canada. Etobicoke: United Church of Canada Publishing House, 1996.

Waal, Esther de. *Seeking God: The Way of St. Benedict.* Collegeville, MN: Liturgical, 1985.

Wallis, Jill. *Valiant for Peace: A History of the Fellowship of Reconciliation 1914 to 1989.* London: Fellowship of Reconciliation, 1991.

Washington James M., editor. *A Testament of Hope. The Essential Writings of Martin Luther King, Jr.* San Francisco: Harper & Row, 1986.

Weis, Monica. "Kindred Spirits in Revelation and Revolution: Rachel Carson and Thomas Merton." *Merton Annual* 19 (2006) 128–41.

White, Lynn. "The Historical Roots of Our Ecological Crisis." *Science* 155 (10 March 1967) 1203–7.

Whyte, David. *House of Belonging. Langley:* Many Rivers, 1997.

———. *The Three Marriages. Reimaging Work, Self and Relationship.* New York: Riverhead, 2009.

Wilkes, Paul, editor. *Merton, by Those Who Knew Him Best.* San Francisco: Harper & Row, 1984.

Wilson, Jonathan R. *Living Faithfully in a Fragmented World: Lessons for the Church from MacIntyre's After Virtue.* Harrisburg, PA: Trinity Press International, 1997.

Wilson, Paul. *Instant Calm: Over 100 Easy-to-Use Techniques for Relaxing Mind and Body.* New York: Penguin, 1995.

Wilson-Hartgrove, Jonathan. *Free To Be Bound: Church beyond the Color Line.* Colorado Springs: NavPress, 2008.

———. *God's Economy: Redefining the Health and Wealth Gospel.* Grand Rapids: Zondervan, 2009.

———. *New Monasticism: What It Has to Say to Today's Church.* Grand Rapids: Brazos, 2008.

Wink, Walter, editor. *Peace Is the Way: Writings on Non-violence from the Fellowship of Reconciliation.* Maryknoll: Orbis, 2000.

Woodcock, George. *Thomas Merton, Monk and Poet: A Critical Study.* Vancouver: Douglas & McIntyre, 1978.

Wu, John, Jr. "Technological Perspectives: Thomas Merton and the One-Eyed Giant." *Merton Annual* 13 (2000) 80–104.

Zalot, Charlotte. "The Inward, Outward and Upward Vision of Frank Kacmarcik, Obl.S.B., Liturgical Artist and Design Consultant." Ph.D. diss., Drew University, 2004.

Zablocki, Benjamin David. *The Joyful Community: An Account of the Bruderhof, a Communal Movement Now in Its Third Generation.* Harmondsworth, UK: Penguin, 1971.

Zuercher, Suzanne. *Merton: An Enneagram Profile.* Notre Dame: Ave Maria, 1996.

Films

Atkinson, Morgan C. *Soul Searching, the Journey of Thomas Merton.* 2007.

Benaquist, Lawrence, and William Sullivan. *Here Am I, Send Me: The Journey of Jonathan Daniels.* 1999.

Gröning, Philip. *Into Great Silence (Die Große Stille).* 2005.

Merton, Thomas. *Original Child Bomb: Meditations on the Origin of the Atomic Age.* 2004.

Wilkes, Paul. *Merton: A Film Biography.* 1984.

Web Material

Community of Communities. Online: http://communityofcommunities.info/

"Definitor (in Canon Law)." *Catholic Encyclopedia* read on line, November 24, 2009. Online: http://www.newadvent.org/cathen/04676a.htm

Forest, Jim. "Thomas Merton's Advice for Peacemakers." Online: http://www.jimand nancyforest.com/2006/05/02/mertons-advice/

Into Great Silence. Online: http://www.youtube.com/watch?v=ag751MB00AQ&feature= related

John XIII. *Allocuzione del Santo Padre Giovanni XXIII con la Quale Annuncia il Sinodo Romano, Il Concilio Ecumenico e l'Aggiornamento del Codice di Diritto Connonico,* Online: http://www.vatican.va/holy_father/john_xxiii/speeches/1959/documents/ hf_j-xxiii_spe_19590125_annuncio_it.html

Malvina Reynolds: Song Lyrics and Poems. Online: http://people.wku.edu/charles.smith/ MALVINA/mr101.htm

The Monastery. Online: http://www.worthabbey.net/bbc/links-youtube.htm

Leonard, Annie, "The Story of Stuff." Online: http://www.youtube.com/watch ?v=gLBE5QAYXp8

Lotz, Ezekiel. "Thomas Merton and Technology. Paradise Regained Re-lost." Online: http://www.monasticdialog.com/a.php?id=856

Spiritans. *Lay Spiritan Guide.* Province of TransCanada. 2010. Online: www.spiritans. com/

Talbot, John Michael. "Call." Online: http://www.johnmichaeltalbot.com

Winfrey Oprah interview of Thich Nhat Hanh, February 16, 2010. Online: http://www .oprah.com/spirit/Oprah-Talks-to-Thich-Nhat-Hanh

Waters, David. "'God gap' impedes U.S. foreign policy, task force says." *Washington Post,* February 24, 2010. Online: http://www.washingtonpost.com/wp-dyn/content/article/2010/02/23/AR2010022305103_pf.html

Interviews

Connor, James OCSO interviewed at the Abbey of Our Lady of Gethsemani in 2001

Filut, Mark OCSO interviewed at Our Lady of Guadalupe Trappist Abbey in 2005

Forest, James H. interviewed at Aalkmar, Holland in 1991

Garcia, Marcella OCSO interviewed at the Abbey of Our Lady of Gethsemani in 1999

Hart, Patrick OCSO interviewed at the Abbey of Our Lady of Gethsemani in 2001 and 2002

Hays, Bryan Beaumont OSB interviewed at St. John's Abbey in 2003

Henry, Patrick interviewed at the Institute for Ecumenical and Cultural Studies in 2003

Herzfeld, Noreen interviewed at St. John's University in 2003

Hinson, E. Glenn interviewed in Louisville, August 20, 2002

Kacmarcik, Frank OblSB interviewed at St. John's Abbey in 2003

Kasprick, Roger OSB interviewed at St. John's Abbey in 2003

Kelty, Matthew OCSO interviewed at the Abbey of Our Lady of Gethsemani in 1997 and 1999

McDonnell, Killian Perry OSB interviewed at St. John's Abbey in 2003

Marty, Martin E., interviewed in Memphis in 2006

O'Mara, Shaun OSB interviewed at St. Benedict's Monastery in 2003

Pedrizzeti, Ray OSB interviewed at St. John's Abbey in 2003

Shipler, Mark at Little Portion Community in Berryville, Arkansas, April 9, 2004

Talbot, John Michael at Little Portion Community in Berryville, Arkansas, April 9, 2004

Tobin, Mary Luke SL interviewed at the Sisters of Loretto Motherhouse in 2002

Wilson, Jonathan, interviewed in Vancouver, British Colombia, June 3, 2008

Wilson-Hartgrove, Leah and Jonathan interviewed in Durham, June 14, 2008

Other Material

Abbey of Our Lady of Gethsemani Schola. *Compassion: Special Message from His Holiness The Dalai Lama.* 2000.

Holy Transfiguration Monastery. *The Beacons.* Manuscript. Breakwater, Australia: n.d.